Economic Reform in Asia

To my dear parents, Joyce Keller and John Hsu

Economic Reform in Asia

China, India, and Japan

Sara Hsu

Assistant Professor of Economics, State University of New York at New Paltz, USA

Edward Elgar
PUBLISHING

Cheltenham, UK • Northampton, MA, USA

Published by
Edward Elgar Publishing Limited
The Lypiatts
15 Lansdown Road
Cheltenham
Glos GL50 2JA
UK

Edward Elgar Publishing, Inc.
William Pratt House
9 Dewey Court
Northampton
Massachusetts 01060
USA

A catalogue record for this book
is available from the British Library

Library of Congress Control Number: 2015952668

This book is available electronically in the **Elgar**online
Economics subject collection
DOI 10.4337/9781784711542

ISBN 978 1 78471 153 5 (cased)
ISBN 978 1 78471 154 2 (eBook)

Typeset by Servis Filmsetting Ltd, Stockport, Cheshire
Printed and bound in Great Britain by TJ International Ltd, Padstow

Contents

1. Introduction to development in China, India, and Japan

WHAT IS DEVELOPMENT?

Development economics examines the economics of the developing world, or countries with low and middle levels of income. The gap between the developing and developed world is large in terms of both levels of income and various measures of living standards. The concept of development has evolved over time, from one of measuring gross domestic product (GDP) per capita, to one that takes into account a variety of other measures, such as health and education, and institutions.

Societies choose development trajectories based upon political conditions, availability of natural resources, characteristics of the population, geography, and other factors. The outcomes of development policies in different contexts vary wildly, and countries that follow the same policies do not necessarily end up at the same level of development. For example, structural adjustment programs implemented in developing countries to encourage privatization, trade and financial liberalization, and deregulation often resulted not in economic development, but in various stages of economic degradation, including crisis.

A concerted economic development program may include programs to stimulate industrialization, service expansion, trade, infrastructure, education, health, social services, and more. Development occurs as GDP per capita and well-being are raised, access to goods and services is improved, and individuals have more capacity to pursue their life goals. It often includes knowledge transfer, increase in productive efficiency, encouragement of innovation, increase in skilled labor, reduced costs of doing business, increased foreign investment, and improved access to medicine and medical technology. Development may or may not occur under a concerted reform program, under different types of political regimes.

Increasingly, the term "sustainable development" is also used to describe an economic, environmental, and social system that is reproducible. While not synonymous with economic development per se, sustainable development takes a fashionable holistic approach to development, stressing that economic activity must strive to be environmentally and socially friendly.

Changing definitions of development has influenced development theory. Development theory was used in earnest after World War II to better understand how South-Eastern European countries and newly independent colonies could develop. Countries remaining in poverty were said to be caught in a vicious circle of poverty and low productivity that required a clear plan to resolve. Theory seeks to explain how countries grow, and how they can overcome the vicious circle. The "big push" theory and its ilk emphasized that concerted policy focus in several areas, or across several industries, was necessary to end low levels of employment, investment, demand, and skills formation at the center of the vicious circle.

Theory has also explained how policies that are successful in one country may not be successful in another. For example, convergence theories assumed that developing countries would converge to the standard of living that developed countries held, but this has rarely occurred in history. There are several strains of convergent as well as non-convergent economic development theory that reflect the struggle to understand development trajectories and development policy, which I explore in Chapter 3. Convergent theories include those supporting the absolute, conditional, and club convergence hypotheses that predicted convergence under varying conditions. While convergence theories were seriously considered through the 1990s, they were ultimately displaced by theories of non-convergence. In particular, economists such as Pritchard (1997) stress that rather than convergence, divergence occurred between developed and developing countries from 1870 to 1990.

Non-convergence theories include theories that emphasize expectations and multiple equilibria, that society can end up in a variety of development levels depending on what individuals have an incentive to do; theories of aspiration gaps, in which society may end up at a low level of development if individuals do not aspire to more; theories of history dependence, in which low levels of development are perpetuated through history; and theories of institutions, where particular organizations or practices influence economic development (Ray 2008).

Contemporary development economics has favored empirics over theory, examining data and case studies to support proposed development policies, but both empirics and theory have proven central to understanding development trajectories and associated policies. Using theory alone, one can bypass reality and end up with an idea of the way development arises that misses critical aspects of the situation. On the other hand, one can use empirical data to examine relationships between variables, but this does not necessarily present a clear understanding of the big picture (Bardhan 2005). Both are necessary in order to understand how and explain why an economic develops as it does.

Although economists do not agree on the "right" mix of theory and empiricism, most development economists have accepted the once revolutionary idea that economic development is about more than increasing GDP or GDP per capita. The idea that development was more than economic growth is rooted in academic research of the 1970s. Gunnar Myrdal, a Nobel prize-winning economist, emphasized that development embodies the "upward movement of the entire social system," including not only economic factors and particularly production, but also consumption across all levels of society, health, education, all institutions, and the generation of progressive attitudes (Myrdal 1974). Myrdal importantly viewed production and distribution as interrelated, with more equitable distribution improving production, and production boosting the income distributed. Later, economists added to this the notions of improving capabilities of individuals (Amartya Sen) and focused on additional criteria for well-being, such as environmental sustainability and gender equality.

Focus in the 1980s and 1990s upon privatization, liberalization, and deregulation ran contrary to Myrdal's development perspective. Myrdal asserted that equality is an essential aspect of economic development, rather than an afterthought that should be carried out through redistribution of income. But so-called Washington Consensus policies focused on economic growth by country, even if few citizens were enriched, rather than improvements in living standards for the masses. The Washington Consensus period posed a challenge for developing countries that were attempting to combat low levels of living. Washington Consensus policies were aggressively promoted by the International Monetary Fund (IMF) and World Bank, and backed vigorously by the United States. These policies exacerbated adverse economic conditions experienced in developing countries throughout the world. For example, as South Korea experienced high corporate debt-to-equity ratios during the Asian financial crisis, the capital market opening required under the Washington Consensus increased South Korea's external debt to more than one-third of Korean GDP (McCleery and De Paolis 2008).

Later in the Washington Consensus period, in response to poor outcomes resulting from Washington Consensus policies, leading scholars such as Joseph Stiglitz and Amartya Sen reiterated Myrdal's sentiment about human-focused development. Myrdal's view of development, embodied in the work of development experts for some time, had been quashed by financial interests; so much so that in the late 1990s, the revival of human-focused development was as revolutionary as it had been in Myrdal's time. Hoff and Stiglitz (2001) wrote that "market economies do not 'naturally' make the right trade-offs." Sen emphasized that human capabilities matter. He focused on freedom of choice as an essential component of quality of life.

What is more, China's rise to power in the 1990s underscored the fact that sudden liberalization under Washington Consensus policies was not necessary for economic development. China was able to lift more than 500 million people out of poverty (World Bank 2014) while very selectively and slowly opening to the outside world. Because China was more insulated against external financial flows, China also emerged from the Asian financial crisis relatively unscathed. Even today, China remains closed to large financial flows, and state-owned banks and enterprises persist.

In the 1990s and 2000s, the field of development devoted its focus to capabilities and institutions. Economies that possessed institutions such as property rights, rule of law including legal protections for creditors, democratic political institutions, and low levels of corruption appeared to some economists to do better. Institutions could reduce transaction costs. It seemed that progress could be made. Countries such as South Korea, which took up the above institutions, were held up as examples of "getting institutions right." The impact of strong formal and informal institutions on economic development was believed to surmount barriers to development, and provided the backdrop against which policy changes could be effective.

The 2008 financial crisis that stemmed from extensive financial institutions' holdings of new types of mortgage-backed assets began the reversal of development in many countries, including China, India, and Japan. All three countries worked to stem the crisis.

ASIAN DEVELOPMENT

Economists have asked many times whether there is a specific strain of Asian development. During the 1990s, the South-East Asian nations of Thailand, Indonesia, South Korea, Malaysia, Singapore, the Philippines, and Hong Kong experienced a dramatic economic boom that was referred to as the "Asian economic miracle." Lessons drawn from growth of the Asian Tigers before the Asian financial crisis asserted that macroeconomic performance, high savings rates, strong education, and openness to foreign technology were important.

However, the proper combination of growth ingredients remained elusive, even for the Asian miracle countries. Stanley Fischer of the IMF wrote in 1996: "[An] important point on East Asia . . . is that there is almost no generalization that applies to every fast-growing country in East Asia, not even the fact of very high rates of investment and saving, where

Hong Kong is the exception." Growth cannot be merely attributed to high rates of savings. Fischer also notes that the experiences of Malaysia, Indonesia and Thailand are particularly encouraging since they lack previous growth histories.

Despite the fact that no specific recipe for growth could be found for the Asian Tiger, economists have continued to search for one. Other sets of Asian economies have also reinforced the notion of an Asian development model. Kuznets (1994) characterizes East Asian development as shifting workers from agriculture to industry, expanding exports, and providing competitive labor markets due to surplus populations. Drawing on the experiences of Japan, South Korea, and Taiwan, Kuznets describes the industrialization process as being influenced by "developmental" or interventionist governments that intentionally accelerate the growth rate. These economies were unusually successful in raising the growth rate and therefore are of special significance. Park (1990) looks at the experiences of South Korea and Taiwan, which have common structural characteristics and export-led industrialization processes. Park emphasizes the key role of government in bringing growth about, whether under a leading role in Korea or in a supportive role in Taiwan. The ongoing presence of growth in China and India and the history of growth in Japan creates an interesting study, and we examine the concerted reform trajectories or intentional growth periods in each of these countries.

ECONOMIC REFORM

A period of economic reform is a time of accelerated development; one that is intentionally undertaken by policy makers, that is timely in its appearance, and that places emphasis on loci of comparative advantage. Often it is initiated as a response to economic repression or perceived economic weakness. It is defined by a clear break, in one or more ways, from business as usual, and may be led by a strong leader and/or group of economically progressive individuals.

The economic reform process is also timely in its appearance, in the sense that the policies that are implemented are viewed as necessary to further economic development, and also in relation to the external environment. The reform process may require more caution, for example, in an extremely competitive global environment. The process may require more extensive changes in the face of impending crisis.

Economic reform underscores a country's comparative advantage, or production at its lowest opportunity cost. Economic policies have been shown to fail when they hinge upon a development process that is unnatural or external to a nation. When a country's comparative advantage is incorporated into the reform program, economic development stands a better chance of becoming self-sustaining.

A country's reform strategy is unique in what programs are undertaken, and in which order. Stages or tiers of reform can be used to classify different time periods of the unique reform process, with Tier One introducing basic reforms, Tier Two representing more enhanced reforms, and Tier Three displaying advanced reforms. The reason for tiered reform within a successful reform program is that development policies must necessarily change as an economy develops, since various levels of financial, physical, and human investment, as well as institutions at different stages of development, are available. We have seen in practice that "big bang" reforms often lead to financial crisis or incomplete progress. Therefore, although reform "tiers" are rarely so clearly defined at the time of reform, they can be used to generally classify reform policy measures.

While there is no handbook or prescription to reform, Tier One reforms may include agricultural reform, an improved tax system, and a basic health and education system, in order to build basic human capital and reproductive capabilities, and to establish funds for the government to embark on the reform process. Light industry development and some trade may occur to create an economic base for further growth. Tier Two reforms may include development of light industry, a financial system, a more sophisticated trade regime, and a better educational system. Tier Three reforms may implement heavy industry or more technology-infused manufacturing, a services industry, a more complex financial system, and more open trade. This type of progression is reflected to a large degree in the reform trajectories of China and Japan in particular. We now provide a general overview of the reform processes in China, India, and Japan.

PERSPECTIVES ON REFORM IN CHINA, INDIA, AND JAPAN

China, India, and Japan are all strong examples of economic growth. Growth took place as a result of new policies, and institutions were put in place. These were a clear break with the past and instilled purposely, to foment growth.

Economic reform began in China in 1979 at the Third Plenum, where Deng Xiaoping took power. Reform began as a response to the stilted economic progress over the period of Mao Zedong's tyrannical rule. From a closed, command economy, China became an open, dominantly market economy by the year 2000. The transition was gradual but dramatic, affecting every citizen, rural and urban. Leaders first set out to reform the agricultural sector, changing from communal farming to own-plot farming. Some freeing up of township and village enterprises in rural areas from state control allowed them to produce for market demand, turning a profit for some. Marketization took hold more fiercely, and China indeed became the world's factory. China's accession to the World Trade Organization in 2001 and its increasingly dominant position in the global economy sealed its status as one of the most successful growth stories of all time.

In India, economic reform started in due course. State-owned enterprises in urban areas were given market incentives and were allowed to enjoy some autonomy. Reform began in India at independence in 1947, when India became a democracy and a planned economy. India embarked on a path of capital accumulation and industrialization, which succeeded during the earlier years but faltered in the late 1960s and early 1970s, after famines set in. Import substitution industrialization undertaken from independence until the 1990s did not lead to a significant take-off in growth. Growth occurred, but Indian citizens were often untouched by it. India's significant policy reversals in the 1990s, that substantially reduced barriers to trade, led in the late 1990s and early 2000s to the take-off of India's information and communication technology (ICT) service sector.

Japan's reform began in 1868 with the coming of the Meiji Restoration. The Emperor Meiji eliminated the feudal system that had enabled economic stagnation and military weakness. The monetary and fiscal systems were modernized, and the government sought to improve infrastructure and technological knowledge. As Japan's agricultural sector increased in productivity, workers were freed to move to urban areas. Heavy industry expanded in the early twentieth century. After World War I, Japan was provided access to Western technology as an ally of the United States. Trade boomed. Japan's occupation after World War II led to some reversals that were countered by the Allies under the Dodge Plan. Increasing industrialization and export activity, coupled with increasing levels of technological innovation, led to Japan's promotion to developed-country status in the 1970s and 1980s.

How can we put in perspective the comparative development paths of China, India, and Japan? These three countries experienced rapid economic growth, due to changes in economic policy, accumulation of human capital, and improvements in technology. They developed in distinct ways, given their vastly different political systems and economic conditions at the outset of reform. The degree of financial liberalization that the countries allowed has also greatly impacted their level of success.

China, India, and Japan are often used as examples of how development can or should take place. Separating growth success from institutional context, however, it is more difficult to tell which policies or patterns are transferable to other countries. China's gradual approach to development was successful, but government control over the economy and capital controls ensured that other plans would not usurp the slow unfolding of development policies. India's success in information and communication technology originated from a coincidence of yet-untapped supply and new demand, when companies began to prepare for the year 2000 (Y2K) by having their computer software scoured for potential bugs when the year changed back to '00. Japan's success rose out of a long process of growth-oriented policy and planning.

The relationship between institutions and economic development has been studied in the economics literature in order to shed light on what policies and patterns may be transferable to other countries. In some of the latest research, Acemoglu et al. (2006) distinguish between technology adoption-based strategies of development and innovation-based strategies of growth, in terms of the institutions present. Institutions present were achieved as equilibria in the home economy and were not imposed from outside, and these same institutions likely necessarily changed over the course of development. "Getting institutions right" depends on the "right" institutions for the pre-development economy, which can be transmutable over time to fit an economy progressing through development. In other words, the current thinking in development economics is that development is contextual, and that the success of policies and patterns of development depend on local institutions, which in turn depend on current competitive equilibria, if and where they exist.

This provides us with a contemporary framework to analyze the progression of economic development in China, India, and Japan. We may consider the institutions that were consistently present and important throughout the development process, and how they changed. We can compare these institutions between countries and consider their interaction with policy that propelled the economies into various stages of growth.

Institutions that were in place at the outset of economic reform vary. In China, the People's Bank was transformed from a deposit-holding institution to a central bank in 1983, creating an institution with the ability to control money. Special Economic Zones (SEZs) were set up in 1979–80 to open up trade to the outside world in specific cities. Township and village enterprises were, prior to reform, low-technology firms with little competitiveness; after reform, they were transformed into profitable institutions. The household responsibility system allowed farmers to transition from communal farming to farming of private plots, which vastly increased agricultural productivity. State-owned enterprises continued to provide the urban population with employment, housing, and social services.

In Japan, we take the outset of reform to be the Meiji Restoration of 1868, rather than the American Occupation after World War II. The Meiji Restoration set Japan on a path of intentional modernization and economic growth, interrupted only by World War II. The Meiji period is notable for eliminating institutions that had become counterproductive, namely those of the feudal system. With elimination of the feudal system, the country was oriented toward production and industrialization. The institution of private land ownership was an important replacement for tenancy and subjugation, and a critical base for taxation.

In India, the Planning Commission was created at independence to industrialize the economy. As the strategy of capital investment became insufficient for growth, the Planning Commission was itself reformed in the 1990s to accede to market forces.

Some institutions ushered in a new phase of development after reform was already under way. The Green Revolution, institutionalized in various ways in India, improved agricultural production over the 1970s. The Integrated Rural Development Programme, created in the 1980s, set out to address the poorest of the poor households (Laxminarayan 1990). In India, a rejection of the growth ideology of the first decades of reform, including rejection of "heavy industrialization, self-reliance, the socialist pattern, the public sector and the control of monopolies" (Ghose 1990), necessitated a new wave of reform and hence new institutions.

Japan's Ministry of International Trade and Industry (MITI) was created in 1949 and propelled Japan to its modern level of development. In Francks's (1992) analysis of MITI's predecessor, the Ministry of Commerce and Industry (MCI), the institution had a middling impact on the iron and steel industries, while its reincarnation as MITI was much more successful in bringing about industrialization, due in part to its close relationship with industry.

China is notable for sharply changing some institutions after the reform process began. State-owned enterprises laid off vast numbers of workers as the economy was increasingly privatized. The state-owned sector subsequently shrank. Township and village enterprises lost out to competition from private enterprises during the 1990s and played a much less important role in the economy thereafter. The People's Bank of China was reorganized in 1998 along the lines of the US Federal Reserve Board, becoming more powerful (Naughton 2007).

All of these institutions played critical roles in shaping the reform and growth process in China, India, and Japan. They were institutions that existed at the beginning equilibrium and that transformed to meet with successive equilibria. They worked for their home economies; in the case of Japan, innovation was so successful as to push Japan into the realm of a developed country.

INITIAL CONDITIONS AND REFORM

The three countries of study, China, India, and Japan, began their growth processes intentionally, through guided and targeted economic policies. The growth process was first catalyzed in Japan, during the Meiji Restoration and again during extensive restructuring post-World War II; in China, in response to Western intervention in the nineteenth and early twentieth century, Communism, and the death of Mao Zedong in the late 1970s; and in India, after independence from Britain in 1947 and again with the implementation of structural adjustment reforms in the early 1990s.

These three countries began with different initial conditions. Japan began its modernization period in 1868 during the Meiji Restoration, as a reaction to Western demands. This island country with few natural resources turned for its source of comparative advantage to technological prowess. Since modernization began so early, Japan had time to study Western technology and update its level of technological know-how in time to "catch up" to Western innovations and accompanying standards of living. The Western world was in the process of industrializing; the industrial revolution had just ended, and standards of living were on the rise.

China's and India's legacies of economic repression led to widespread support for a wider availability of products and better living circumstances. Chinese citizens were ready to purchase a wider range of products than the usual drab clothing and basic offerings. They were also interested in earning higher incomes. Indian citizens were also ready, in the 1990s, to put their higher education to use and obtain better opportunities in the ICT services industry or in other industries that received the knock-on effects of increased domestic consumption.

China and India began the process of reform much later than Japan, when Western nations had already reached a relatively high standard of living. Hence there were vastly different global economic conditions in each nation: different political economies, different economic institutions, and varying levels of production. During this period, complex financial products were being offered in developed countries and global financial flows became increasingly volatile. Global consumption also increased, creating a need for production of inexpensive goods and services.

China and India began the reform process after Western countries were already industrialized and living in a modern, consumer society. Both countries were able to integrate their growth processes with a globalizing world. China built up its manufacturing sector and generated many types of goods for export to other nations. From 1979, when China was almost entirely closed off to the rest of the world in trade, to 2009, when China was the largest exporter of consumer products in the world, China altered its economic paradigm dramatically to work in concert with the rest of the world.

India did the same; its leading sector in terms of economic transformation, information and communication technology, boomed as global internet and telecommunications technology rapidly developed. India built up its services sector based on the needs of Western businesses. Hence the timing of India's reform process and global conditions were essential to India's growth.

China and India had resources in human capital. First, China and India were both home to vast labor forces, the largest in the world. Second, overseas Chinese and overseas Indians were important in helping nationals establish businesses. Overseas Chinese invested in manufacturing enterprises and helped to establish business connections with corporations from Hong Kong, Taiwan, and the US. Overseas Indians had experience in information technology (IT)-related industries and therefore resident Indians had access to potential clients in the USA and Western Europe, as well as access to high-quality engineers (Arora and Bagde 2010).

Although both China and India attempted economic reform in the 1950s, neither was truly successful until the 1980s or 1990s. Both China and India followed the Soviet model of capital accumulation, which did not make sense in these high-population countries. Promotion of heavy industry, with little attention to manufacturing and light industry, did not foment growth as policy makers desired. It was not until both governments (at different times) opened up to some trade and reduced barriers to entry into labor or human capital industries that reform was truly successful.

All three development trajectories involved selective liberalization in particular industries. Japan's government gave priority to the export of heavy industrial goods, while China's gave priority at first to export of light consumer goods sent out from Special Economic Zones. India embarked on a range of gradual liberalization policies in the areas of licensing reduction, some trade liberalization, and reduced role of the state.

These initial conditions helped to shape the nature of reform policies and their resulting success. Talented reform leaders had to take into account the resources and circumstances of each nation in order to create policies that would function well in each environment. Policy makers built on initial conditions to gain acceptance as well as to ease the transition from low levels of development to industrialization and modernization.

Next, we examine the reform process from a general perspective, in each country in turn. We begin with the case of Japan, then turn to China and India.

Japan

Japan began its growth trajectory during the Meiji era, 1868–85. Western Europe and the United States had, at this time, just completed the industrialization process. Feudal institutions of the previous period (Tokugawa) were eliminated, reducing privileges based on title and increasing privileges based on merit. Monetary and fiscal systems were modernized, and people were educated to use modern technology. The Tokugawa fiscal system had many tax rates (based on the rice tax), so the Meiji government implemented a modern form of taxation on land, which was not subject to harvest. This also made the taxpayer the legal owner of the land (Yoshihara 1994).

The Meiji government also centralized the issue of money, and made uniform measurement units (Yoshihara 1994). The decimal system was implemented and the yen was used as the basic monetary unit (gold and silver coins were previously used). The Meiji government also built up the country's infrastructure. In 1869, the government began constructing railways. Railway mileage increased rapidly, and sea transportation was modernized by importing steamships from the West. The network of communications was built up, with the introduction of postal and telegraphic services.

Joint stock companies were formed in the fields of transportation, finance, and land reclamation (Yoshihara 1994). Machines began to be used widely, as machines were imported from the West and foreign technicians were invited to Japan. The government was able to operate mines and factories in textiles, metals, cement, glass, and shipbuilding. Spinning was given first priority for modernization. The rise of the textile industry increased Japan's exports to China. The Japanese textile industry phased out imports of textiles.

Development also took place in agriculture, with an increase in the production of rice due to the introduction of new strains which were responsive to the application of fertilizer and were resistant to cold (Yoshihara 1994). Silk was also an important good. With development, more and more people moved from the agricultural to the non-agricultural sector. Hence an increasingly large percentage of the population was forced to purchase food. Increased production of tea and raw silk made it possible to earn enough foreign exchange to buy machinery and industrial raw materials from abroad.

Heavy industry increased between 1912 and 1936 (Yoshihara 1994). Over this period, Japan became less dependent on agriculture since the colonies it had acquired during war, Taiwan and Korea, became Japan's food suppliers. There was a rapid increase in cotton fabric production, a light industry, while armaments production, a heavy industry, increased as well. Japan was producing weapons for other countries in World War I.

After World War I (1918), the West had reduced economic capacity, and Japan experienced a severe recession in the 1920s, with many bankruptcies and high unemployment. Concentration on heavy industry and finance increased (Yoshihara 1994). The intensification of output concentration remained for some time, with several *zaibatsu*, or family-controlled conglomerates, exerting large influence on the economy in the latter part of this period (1930s). The relationship between the *zaibatsu* and the government became very close, with the *zaibatsu* evolving into powerful politico-economic organizations.

Japan's economy after World War II was devastated, and the threat of famine was real (Yoshihara 1994). The Allies, who occupied Japan after the war, imposed democratic reform both politically and economically. Land was redistributed and the *zaibatsu*, large business conglomerates, were broken up. The US transferred technology to Japan, giving way to advances in production based on chemistry, physics, and electronics. The post-war economic system promoted free trade, which was beneficial for Japan, an exporting nation. Freer international trade strengthened internationally competitive industries and weakened uncompetitive ones, enhancing the efficiency of the economy (Yoshihara 1994).

Sustained increase in exports required that heavy industrial goods become major exports since their terms of trade were more favorable and their demand elasticity was higher than that of other goods (Yoshihara 1994). Subsidies for industrial expansion and renewal were given to encourage the introduction of more up-to-date machinery and technology in heavy industry. To protect the companies which were producing heavy industrial goods, the government restricted imports of these goods through foreign exchange control.

By 1960, the government's industrialization policy began to show returns (Yoshihara 1994). Heavy industry had become internationally competitive in steel, ships, and radios, and was becoming the propelling force of Japanese exports. By the mid-1960s, motor cars, synthetic fibers, and new electronic products like tape recorders and TV sets had joined the list of major exports. Textile products declined in importance in the face of growth in heavy industry.

By 1972, Japan had become the world's largest producer of synthetic fibers, rubber products, pig iron, and passenger cars, and Japanese industry had become one of the most advanced in the world (Yoshihara 1994). Machinery and equipment replaced industrial materials as Japan's leading industrial sector in the mid-1970s (Yoshihara 1994). The growth of electrical machinery, including electronics, was spectacular. In the early 1980s, integrated circuits, videotape recorders, and computers became the growth points of the industry. The shift overall was toward high-value-added, low-energy-using industries. Cars became Japan's major export item.

China

The Chinese economy, as rational as it may appear after reform was begun, was led not by an external economic theory, but by the ideology of a single man. Transformed into an ideology-centered state by Mao Zedong, a cult of personality surrounded Chinese leadership well into reform. For the lacuna that Mao left when he died in 1976, a leadership such as Deng Xiaoping's, embodied in one man, was arguably necessary.

China's leadership under Mao was effectively a dictatorship. There can be no other explanation for the continuing dedication of civil servants to Mao's changing, sometimes irrational, ideology other than the idea that Communist Party officials swore allegiance to Mao himself. This can be illustrated in multiple ways; the Great Leap Forward and the Cultural Revolution, in which millions of people died, have been viewed by Maoist scholars as demonstrations of a Leftist turn in Mao's ideology which were not in line with the common view of Mao Zedong Thought (Womack 1986). And yet these schemes were carried out by committed government officials who upheld the cult of personality, whether for fear of reprisal if they diverged from doing so, or from a true belief in the system.

By 1978, China was clearly ready for a new direction but hungry for a new, powerful leader. At this time, the rest of the world was about to embark on a period of neoliberalism and high consumption. China wanted to join in. Given the eagerness that the Chinese showed to break with the past and promote growth rather than economic stagnation, Deng Xiaoping, who was previously purged from the party as an opponent of the Cultural Revolution, represented opposition to the anti-capitalist movement of his predecessor, and emerged as a leader during the meeting of the Third Plenum in December 1978. Deng Xiaoping, although far less dictatorial than Mao Zedong, was followed with much of the same exuberance and devotion that Mao had experienced in his cult of personality.

Deng Xiaoping Theory guided the Chinese economy during the first phase of reform. This was entirely separate from economic development theory of the day. The Theory advocated pragmatism and truth-seeking in its objective of joining a market economic system to a socialist political system. It was unrelated to accumulation of capital, which the Maoist economy had focused on, and it broke with rising neoliberal attitudes among Western nations that emphasized rapid liberalization of trade and financial channels.

Deng and other policy makers increased China's competitiveness in incremental five-year plans that carefully accommodated prior policy successes. The Chinese economy was first reformed to continue producing for the planned economy, while beginning to produce for the market, outside of the plan (Naughton 2007). The plan was aimed to decline over time in a process called "growing out of the plan." Market forces were allowed to arise slowly, with market prices increasingly permitted.

Quite notably, significant reform began in the countryside, with the implementation of the household responsibility system, which allowed famers to contract individual plots of land from the collective. The household responsibility system was initiated by farmers in Anhui province, and officially adopted by the Fourth Plenum of the Eleventh Central Committee of the Communist Party in September 1979 (Chow 2007). Traditional production, rather than collective production, re-emerged, and greatly enhanced productivity in the agricultural sector. Farmers were allowed to raise chickens, pigs, and ducks, and to sell on the market food produced in excess of the target. Township and village enterprises, rural industrial enterprises controlled by local governments, were allowed to produce for the market.

State-owned enterprises, formerly fully controlled by the state, underwent a process of incentivization through profit retention and reward for work effort. The process was begun in 1978 with six pilot enterprises in Sichuan province, and was spread to 6600 industrial enterprises by June 1980 (Chow 2007). In 1987, the state-owned enterprises were contracted to pay the government a fixed tax rather than surrendering most of their proceeds. This helped to free the enterprises from direct financial obligation to the central government. During the 1980s, however, policy makers continued to control many aspects of these firms; control was lessened gradually, and more extensive privatization of state-owned enterprises would occur more than a decade later.

Price reform was an essential part of reform that began in October 1984, with the decision of the Central Committee of the Communist Party to begin to decontrol prices gradually. Part of the output produced was sold at controlled prices, while additional output above the target could be sold at prices determined by the market. This was part of the dual track system. Importantly, food prices did not rise even after they were decontrolled due to the large rise in agricultural output as a result of the household responsibility system (Chow 2007). Low and very gradually rising housing prices in urban areas maintained social stability until the end of the 1990s, when urban housing was mainly privatized.

The banking system was entirely altered from a deposit-taking monobank operating as the People's Bank of China, to a central bank with specialized banks underneath it. The People's Bank was given more independence as a central bank in the 1990s, and loans were increasingly extended to businesses outside the state-owned enterprise sector.

Exports through Special Economic Zones were permitted and consumer goods were increasingly produced. The Special Economic Zones were coastal areas in which foreign enterprises were given tax breaks and other incentives to establish factories to produce goods for export. The number of Special Economic Zones expanded through the reform period, and were a key element in attracting foreign capital.

The reform process was increased in the 1990s, as Deng Xiaoping became unable to participate in politics, and focused on some sectors over others. The nature of the reform process turned toward further trade and financial liberalization of the economy. Zhu Rongji became Premier in 1998, but even as Vice-Premier he was heavily involved in the direction of economic reform. Reform in the 1990s included market reunification, producing more extensively for the market (Naughton 2007). Macroeconomic austerity, including tighter fiscal and monetary policy, and banking restructuring were also key elements of reform in the 1990s.

Although during the Maoist era "privatization" was a dirty word, it eventually was necessary to increase economic productivity. The privatization process of the 1990s resulted in mass lay-offs from state-owned enterprises. Privatized state enterprises were then listed on the stock exchanges, although the majority shareholder often continued to be the state. Despite the fact that it was a big step toward reduced direct state intervention in the economy, privatization was unpalatable to former employees and resulted in widespread demonstrations among those let go. Because of large-scale lay-offs, the 1990s have often been referred to as a period of "reform with losers."

Many state-owned enterprises were shut down over this period of "grasping the large and letting the small go." This meant that the central government forced smaller enterprises to change ownership or close down. This was a period of employment churning and a large change in the economic mentality in an embrace of market forces.

China's accession to the World Trade Organization underscored its importance in the global economy. Trade barriers were lowered and competition increased. China's trade cooperation with other nations in the region rose and helped to sustain its status as the "factory of the world." Growth seemed limitless in the early 2000s.

India

India attempted to reform immediately after independence in 1947 under a planned economy with a heavy emphasis on heavy industry but, as in China under Mao, was unsuccessful in this approach. Unlike China, India neglected agriculture until it was faced with famine in the 1960s. The government realized that low productivity in agriculture was a result not of ignorance, but of real constraints, and encouraged the implementation of high-yielding seed varieties and better fertilizer with the Green Revolution (Chai and Roy 2006). Although helpful, the lack of proper irrigation, the third leg of the Green Revolution triad, caused the Indian agriculture sector to continue to suffer. Low growth in the 1970s perpetuated India's stagnation.

In the 1980s, India increased market orientation and implemented some deregulation policies, improving the growth of the economy (Chopra et al. 1995). Partial trade liberalization and loosening of domestic industrial controls were carried out. Expansionary fiscal policies stimulated domestic demand as well. This was successful in bringing about some growth. Growing government expenditures and falling revenues, however, contributed to the economic crisis India experienced in 1991 that began India's current trajectory of reform.

India's reforms accelerated in the 1990s. The reforms were stimulated by a balance-of-payments crisis and a subsequent IMF package that required fiscal tightening (Panagariya 2002). The crisis, coupled with the decline of the Soviet Union, an important trading partner, and with increasing globalization and subsequent availability of portfolio investment and world trade, led to a dramatic opening up of the country (Kohli 2006). The collapse of the Soviet Union, contrasted with the growth of China, set the stage for India's dramatic reforms, as the country turned away from extensive government intervention to a more market-based economy (Singh and Srinivasan 2006). The fast pace of the globalization process in the rest of the world also put pressure on India to change its economic circumstances. The development of a need in the rest of the world for cheap goods and services also influenced India's reform trajectory.

Many of the high-impact reforms were carried out at this time under the New Economic Policy of July 1991, including the abolition of industry licensing, implementation of policies to attract foreign portfolio investment and foreign direct investment (FDI), and reduction of customs duties to improve the export outlook (Acharya 2002). In addition, the role of the public sector was reduced, restrictions on new manufacturing projects were loosened, and industrial location policy was liberalized (S. Mitra 2008).

Heavy industry, heavily monopolized by the state prior to reform, and other industries, subject to industrial licensing or reserved for small enterprises, were decontrolled. The number of government-controlled industries was reduced over time to three: defense aircraft and warships, atomic energy generation, and railway transport (Ahluwahlia 2002). Imports, formerly subject to tariffs as high as 400 percent, became more commonly accessible (Panagariya 2002). In addition, private sector firms were allowed to invest in industries previously reserved for the public sector, and limits on foreign equity holdings were increased from 40 to 51 percent for many industries (Athreye and Kapur 2006).

Later, the number of industries requiring licensing decreased even further, and infrastructure industries such as telecommunications opened up to the private sector, including foreign ownership (Athreye and Kapur 2006). Tariffs were further reduced, and the list of freely importable goods was expanded. The pricing of pharmaceuticals was deregulated. A depreciated exchange rate was maintained to encourage exports, and exporters gained better access to foreign exchange (Wignaraja 2011). The dual exchange rate was unified and the current account became convertible. Impressively, Indian industries responded to the measures with enthusiasm, upgrading technology, improving managerial efficiency, and engaging in increased competition (A. Mitra 2008).

India's banking system was also reformed, removing interest rate controls, introducing capital adequacy requirements, and allowing expansion of private and foreign banks (Ahluwahlia 2002). The government continues to attempt to reduce its ownership stake in the banking system. A new bankruptcy law has also been introduced to allow creditors to enforce their claims.

In 2003, a Special Economic Zones (SEZ) Act was passed to promote exports (Wignaraja 2011). These SEZs offered financial incentives to attract foreign corporations. The US, after Mauritius, is the largest supplier of inward FDI into India. FDI brought with it new technologies, skills, and marketing connections. However, inward FDI in India has been used to produce goods for the domestic economy and has not been used to produce manufactured goods for the world, as it has in China. Indian outward investment increased before the global crisis in the areas of information technology, pharmaceuticals, petroleum and natural gas, consumer goods, and steel (Wignaraja 2011). Most outward FDI was invested in the US and the UK.

Growth increased after 2003 as domestic industry restructured and corporate profits increased. The financial sector expanded and infrastructure was somewhat improved. Education and health programs reached more individuals. India became a star performer in terms of economic growth.

THE POLITICAL ECONOMY OF REFORM

The political economies of reform in China, India, and Japan are vastly different from one another. The development of these economies has changed some views on the role of the state toward a more pluralistic approach. From a perspective in the 1950s and 1960s of viewing state intervention as essential, to a perspective in the 1980s and 1990s of viewing markets as essential to development, economists now generally accept that different combinations of markets and state are possible in development.

How did reform come about politically in China, India, and Japan? The political climates during the creation of the reform period differed in the three nations, but all had the effect of prompting reform, out of political and economic needs. While the histories of all three countries have in a sense defined their current political economies, their histories have greatly diverged in that sense. China has, for the most part, been in control of its destiny through history, while India was only clearly defined under British colonial rule (Desai 2003). Japan itself was a colonial power in recent history. India's economy was left in a weakened state as a result of colonial rule, since the British ruling class set up institutions that allowed those at the top to gain financially from economic activity while neglecting to provide social services for the poor. Society was thus quite stratified, only the elite were educated, and the state was mainly a vehicle for the military, policy, and justice systems, as tax revenues were kept minimal (Maddison 1971). Left to a large degree unmolested by foreign powers at the outset of reform, both China and Japan had a strong sense of shared culture among the citizenry that propelled forward the acceptance of economic reforms.

Economic histories also diverged in that China's and India's pre-reform periods focused on industrialization and capital accumulation, while Japan's pre-reform period failed to focus on either industrialization or other elements of economic growth. China's and India's tendency during the post-World War II period to follow the socialist pattern of physical capital accumulation, however, did not result in growth, such that these economies, like Japan's, lacked sources of growth at the outset of reform.

In Japan, restoration of Meiji rule occurred after the Tokugawa Shogun's forces were defeated. Although the Shogun had resigned the year before, he had remained powerful and had to be physically defeated in order to restore direct imperial control. Young samurai were hostile to the Tokugawa Shogun, as it was felt that Japan was increasingly behind the rest of the world in the industrialization process. The Tokugawa regime's prohibition of trade with Western nations prevented merchants from developing a potentially profitable export sector. Mounting opposition to the government, along with famines that resulted in peasant uprisings, set the stage for the Tokugawa regime to be defeated.

The Tokugawa regime, however, had not been without its successes. During the seventeenth and eighteenth centuries, the Tokugawa regime had seen increased agricultural production, including in staple and cash crops, and in commerce and manufacturing (History Channel 2014). Urbanization increased and peace prevailed. Urban commercial activities brought economic participation from all ranks of individuals, including townspeople themselves and not just the nobility, and increased demand for agricultural products from the countryside.

The Tokugawa Shogun's requirement that the feudal lords, the *daimyo*, reside alternately in Edo (now Tokyo) and in their own home regions resulted in the construction of an extensive road system, which would provide infrastructure necessary for enhanced growth in the Meiji period, and help to unite the country under a sense of shared culture, with socialization at a national level occurring in the capital of Edo (Pyle 1996). Large family enterprises grew during the Tokugawa period and became the precursors to the *zaibatsu*, or large industrial enterprises, during the Meiji period.

It was when the Tokugawa regime became unable to satisfy the economic needs of the peasantry, the merchant class, and the samurai that a strong sense of dissatisfaction emerged, opening the way for the Meiji Restoration to take place. Satsuma and Choshu were the two domains that overthrew the Tokugawa Shogunate, and the Meiji period thus began as an alliance between those two regions. The Charter Oath was laid out on April 6, 1868 to establish that feudal institutions would be dissolved, and that assemblies would create policies based on public discussion. In 1889, Japan's first constitution was introduced and a parliament, or Diet, was established, with the Emperor as the leader.

In China, reform occurred only after Mao Zedong died, and after a short period, Deng Xiaoping took power. Deng Xiaoping was more popular than Mao's chosen successor, Hua Guofeng, and was supported by the Communist leadership, which felt that China was economically lagging behind the rest of the world. As in Japan, his economic policies and attitudes had the support of the leadership. China was also moving out of a period of brutality and particularly weak economic performance, and many people were discontented with their lives.

The Cultural Revolution had taken place between 1966 and 1976. Led by the so-called "Gang of Four," the aim of this revolution was to rout

out capitalist and traditional thinking and to reinforce Maoist doctrine. During this period, millions of Chinese citizens were persecuted and even killed. The psychical damage done to the citizenry during this period was considered a setback for the Communist Party; by the time of Mao's death, ordinary citizens and many party members were hoping for a period of clemency.

This occurred under the leadership of Deng Xiaoping, who had himself experienced life as a target during the Cultural Revolution. Despite that, Deng remained in the political realm and stressed national unity as a precursor to economic growth. After Mao's death, Deng criticized the Cultural Revolution and brought about the "Beijing Spring," allowing open dissent toward the Cultural Revolution (PBS Newshour 2009). The positive energy that Deng carried into the reform period propelled his popularity as a de facto reform leader.

India had begun some reforms through the 1980s, but an economic crisis speeded up the process. In order to avoid defaulting on its debt, India requested financial assistance from the IMF. The IMF extended a $2.2 billion loan, with additional requirements for economic restructuring. The Prime Minister, P.V. Narasimha Rao, who took over in June 1991 at the peak of the crisis, took seriously the task of economic restructuring and reform.

Rao came to office at a time of political chaos; Rajiv Gandhi had just been assassinated by a Sri Lankan terrorist (Aiyar 2011). However, although Prime Minister Rao is not as celebrated as Nehru or other Indian leaders, he had the foresight to induct an economist rather than a politician into his cabinet as Finance Minister (Wadhva 2004). This Finance Minister was Manmohan Singh, who would later himself become Prime Minister. Prompted by IMF conditionality in response to a government bailout, the Rao administration implemented some major changes into India's economy, shifting toward an export-oriented model.

Vested interests were not unanimously approving of the aggressive pace of reforms, so two years into the reform trajectory, the Rao administration slowed down its rate of implementation (Wadhva 2004). At this time, since economic stability had been greatly improved, the Rao government also came out with its own vision for reform. India's economy began to grow at an annual rate of 7.5 percent, and this lasted between 1994 and 1997. The economy had made an impressive turn toward market institutions.

Effects of Reform

As Wignaraja (2011) points out, China was much "swifter, more coordinated, and more credible in its overall reform process than India." China's five-year plans reflected streamlined goals for the outcomes the leadership wanted to see take shape. China introduced an open-door policy in 1978, while India opened up trade after 1991. China was quick to adopt a growth strategy, that of export-oriented manufacturing, while India was slow to find its niche in service exports.

Japan's reform process was arguably more coordinated than that of China; it necessarily had to be so since it covered an entire century. And it is the ultimate success story, transforming a poor, developing country with few natural resources and relatively low population and population growth into a modernized economy with a very high standard of living.

Growth was a focus of reform in all three countries, and the status of social service provision has been wildly divergent as a result. In China, social services such as health insurance, unemployment provisions, and social security benefits have lagged behind since reform began and particularly since the 1990s. Rural Chinese suffered greatly due to the lack of access to medical care. Individuals were unable to pay out of pocket for their health care. The New Cooperative Medical Scheme has sought to cover all individuals for basic medical services, but has been unable to cover services for catastrophic illnesses (Zhang et al. 2010). Unemployment benefits began in 1986 for urban workers if the state-owned enterprise they worked for declared bankruptcy (Duckett 2003). In 1999, unemployment insurance participation became mandatory for all urban firms and their employees. Employees who were laid off from state-owned enterprises were eligible for a living allowance for three years, after which time they could be eligible for unemployment benefits for two years if the employer had contributed to the unemployment fund for that purpose. Currently, workers are eligible for unemployment insurance or one-off redundancy payments alone. Pensions for urban workers were developed, but pensions for rural workers arose only in wealthy rural areas. The National Social Security Fund, created in 2000, strove to provide income where pensions could not. The fund is invested in global capital markets and seeks to alleviate the burden of the aging population which was entirely on the shoulders of the government, by sharing it between the government, employers, and employees (Leckie 2009).

India has fallen behind greatly in social services. Sixty-eight percent of global leprosy cases are in India (Kapila 2008b). India also has an above-average incidence of nutrition-related illnesses. Public expenditure is extremely low, at 0.8 percent of GDP. Although national health care has expanded in quantity, quality has suffered. Social security is in a somewhat better position: the National Social Assistance Programme was introduced in 1995, providing social assistance in the case of old age, widowhood, and maternity (Justino 2003). The support is minimal, particularly for old age assistance (at 75 rupees a month), but it is a step in the right direction.

Japan's social services are much better developed than in India and China. Its national pension program paid out 7.8 percent of monthly wages in 2010. Those who are eligible include individuals age 65 and older with at least 25 years of contributions. An early pension may be available starting at age 60 with at least 25 years of contributions (US Social Security Administration 2012). Disability and survivor benefits are also paid out as part of the pension system. Japan also has a universal health care system that costs patients less and yet comprises a relatively low percentage of GDP.

DATA TRENDS

Next, I look at these countries from a general perspective over time. To start with, one of the most commonly used indicators of economic development and well-being is GDP per capita. Figures 1.1 and 1.2 illustrate the rate of growth in modern times of the three countries. GDP per capita increased from $186 in China and $229 in India in 1980, to $2423 in China and $830 in India in 2010. This is more than a threefold increase for India and an elevenfold increase for China. GDP per capita in Japan increased from $7241 in 1960 to $39 733 in 2010, a fivefold increase. Important to

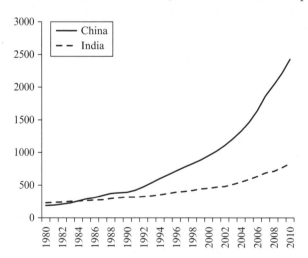

Source: World Development Indicators Database, World Bank.

Figure 1.1 China and India, GDP per capita (2000 US$)

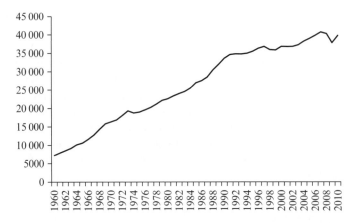

Source: World Development Indicators Database, World Bank.

Figure 1.2   Japan, GDP per capita (2000 US$)

note is that in Japan, even during the "lost decade" and long recession of the 1990s, GDP per capita continued to rise.

The trend in exports of goods and services as a percentage of GDP was on the whole increasing in China and India between 1970 and 2010, but somewhat stagnant in Japan over this period. The Great Contraction of 2008 caused a major decline in exports toward the end of the period in all three countries (Figure 1.3).

Over the years, Japan has become a productive manufacturing nation that specializes in advanced technology for export. Japanese diversification, especially within the manufacturing sector, has produced high-quality goods such as games, computers, and cars, which have been in demand in global markets for decades. The top five export trade partners with Japan – the US, China, the European Union, South Korea, and Taiwan – account for two-thirds of total Japanese exports based on World Trade Organization (WTO) statistics for 2005. Most Japanese trade today comes from its multinational corporations. In 2000, multinational firms accounted for 95.1 and 85.4 percent of its exports and imports, respectively (Kiyota and Urata 2005).

Japan also necessarily imports many goods due to its dearth of natural resources. It is dependent on overseas imported supplies of petroleum, aluminum, nickel, uranium, iron ore, and other resources. Japan imports mainly from China, the United States, Australia, Saudi Arabia, and South Korea.

China is a large exporter of manufactured goods. Most of these goods

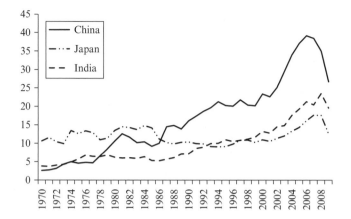

Source: World Development Indicators Database, World Bank.

Figure 1.3 Exports of goods and services (% of GDP)

are labor-intensive, although goods for export are becoming increasingly technology-intensive. China's main trading partners are the US, Hong Kong, and Japan (US Department of State 2011b). China has become, through both exports and imports, a driver of world growth.

India's economy was closed until the 1990s, with extremely high tariffs in place. India has opened since then, with trade increasing to 35 percent of GDP in 2005, although tariffs continue to be high (World Bank 2011). Agricultural tariffs remain at around 30–40 percent, and anti-dumping measures are also used. India's main trading partners are the European Union, the United States, and China (Polaski et al. 2008).

As in many other countries around the world, China, India, and Japan improved in terms of health indicators over the modernization period. Japan's infant mortality rate (deaths per 1000 live births) declined from 30 to 2 between 1960 and 2010 (Figure 1.4); while China's declined from 62 in 1975 to 16 in 2010 (Figure 1.5); and India's declined from 114 in 1975 to 48 in 2010 (Figure 1.5).

Gross fixed capital formation as a percentage of GDP increased in China and India between 1965 and 2010, and declined over the period in Japan (Figure 1.6).

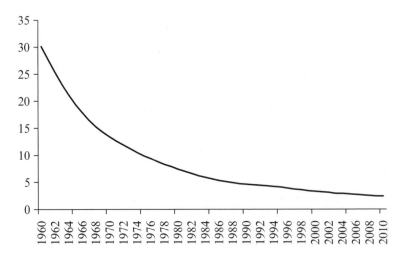

Source: World Development Indicators Database, World Bank.

Figure 1.4   Japan's infant mortality rate (per 1000 live births)

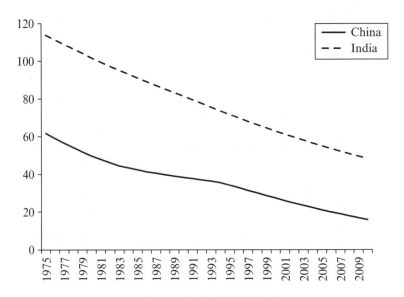

Source: World Development Indicators Database, World Bank.

Figure 1.5   China's and India's infant mortality rate (per 1000 live births)

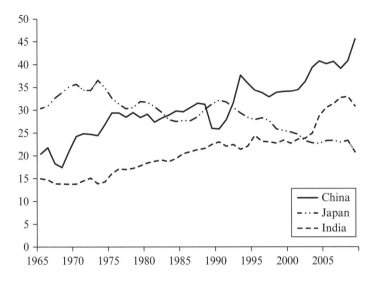

Source: World Development Indicators Database, World Bank.

Figure 1.6   Gross fixed capital formation (% of GDP)

POVERTY LEVELS

Poverty levels declined in China, India, and Japan as economic development came about. Poverty declined as better jobs arose, medical technology
and services progressed, and nutrition improved. Explicit poverty-oriented
social welfare programs also reinforced this trend. China's percentage of
extreme poverty declined to 9.2 percent of the population by 2010, while
India's fell to 32.7 percent by 2010 (Figure 1.7).

In Japan, the poverty rate at under 200 yen was 17.7 percent of all
households in 1930 (Chūbachi and Taira 1976). The poverty rate at
under 100 000 yen in 1968, a comparable level almost 40 years later, was
14.4 percent. Therefore while poverty was not exceedingly high in Japan
in the early stages of its reform period, it did not decline as much as one
might expect, as in the case of China.

BOTTOM LINE

Development and reform unfolded in China, India and Japan at different
times, incorporating distinctive institutions. Unique political systems and

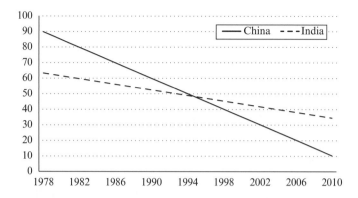

Source: World Development Indicators Database, World Bank.

Figure 1.7   *Poverty headcount ratio trend line at $1.25 per day, China and India (% of population), 1978–2010*

initial economic conditions gave rise to individual reform paths. China, India and Japan grew rapidly after concerted reform efforts under different internal and external circumstances. Their reform trajectories emphasized using their strengths, or comparative advantages, in order to foment growth. All three countries worked to build human capital, financial systems, infrastructure and trade, with varying degrees of progress and success.

In this book, we discuss the evolution of development in China, India, and Japan. Chapter 2 explores development theory and its associated modeling. Chapters 3, 4, and 5 look at the development trajectories of Japan, China, and India, respectively. Chapter 6 analyzes the status of poverty and inequality in these countries. Chapter 7 focuses on urbanization and migration patterns within China, India, and Japan. Population, human capital, and labor are described in Chapter 8; and the impact of reform on the environment in Chapter 9. Chapter 10 examines the trade status of these nations; and Chapter 11 concludes with a discussion of the economic future of China, India, and Japan.

DISCUSSION QUESTIONS

1. What can be said about the time period in which reforms began in China, India, and Japan?
2. Did the external context (global conditions) play a part in the success of reforms and if so, how?

3. How did the reform trajectories of Japan, China, and India differ from one another?
4. In what ways were the reform trajectories of Japan, China, and India similar?
5. What are some necessary initial conditions for reform?

2. Development theory

Development theory seeks to help us understand how countries develop as they do, looking for patterns and explanations of the most essential components of the development process. Questions that economic theorists ask are: "Is this policy essential to the development process?", "What do countries have in common in how they develop?", "Why do some nations fail and some succeed economically?" Some understanding may be found by modeling the proposed answers to these questions and putting forth a theory. In this chapter, we first discuss economic modeling, then development theory. We discuss economic reform theory, and development theory as it applies to China, India, and Japan.

ECONOMIC MODELING

Economic models provide a representation of reality, on any scale. Economic models are generally represented by mathematics and therefore include variables, assumptions that relate the variables, and predictions that explain what the outcome of the model is supposed to be.

Variables can be of a number of different types, including (but not limited to) dichotomous or binary types, meaning that they have one of two values, continuous or interval types, possessing an infinite number of values, discrete types, possessing only integer values, or categorical or nominal types, classifying values into several categories. Some variables are considered endogenous, or determined within the economic model, while some variables are classified as exogenous, or determined outside of the model.

The model takes in exogenous variables and alters endogenous variables, whose values are of interest to the economist. They are related using assumptions; it is an assumption from the outset, for example, to assume that some variables are endogenous and some are exogenous. The model is constructed based on assumptions taken from observation of reality. Hypotheses about how different economic factors relate to one another determine how the model will function and what the outcome may be.

A simple Keynesian macroeconomic model may look like the following set of equations (Sargent 1987):

$$Y = F(K,N) \tag{2.1}$$

$$\frac{w}{p} = F_N \tag{2.2}$$

$$C = C\left(Y - T - \delta K - \frac{M + B}{p}\pi, r - \pi\right) \tag{2.3}$$

$$I = I(q(K,N,r - \pi,\delta) - 1) \tag{2.4}$$

$$C + I + G + \delta K = Y \tag{2.5}$$

$$\frac{M}{p} = m(r,Y) \tag{2.6}$$

The purpose of this model is to show how the macroeconomy functions; full employment is not guaranteed and fiscal and monetary policies do impact employment. This is not an economic growth or development model per se, but is a rather straightforward model that can be used as a basis for explaining how models function.

In this model, the exogenous variables include w, T, G, K, π, M, and δ. Endogenous variables include p, Y, N, r, C, and I. The exogenous variables are defined as follows: w is the money wage rate, T is taxes, G is government spending, K is capital, π is the rate of inflation, M is the quantity of money, and δ is capital depreciation. In turn, the endogenous variables are defined as follows: p is price, Y is output, N is employment, r is nominal interest rate, C is consumption and I is investment.

The first equation states that output is a function of capital and employment. The second can be interpreted as saying that the real wage is equal to the marginal product of labor. The third equation means that consumption is a function of real income after taxes and capital depreciation and real interest rates. The fourth equation says that investment is a function of real returns to capital minus the real rate of depreciation. The fifth states that consumption, investment, government spending, and capital depreciation determine output. The sixth equation asserts that the real quantity of money is a function of interest rates and output. All of the equations are assertions regarding the macroeconomy and how it functions.

WHAT IS DEVELOPMENT THEORY?

Development theory seeks to explain how and why countries develop. The ways in which countries develop may include a series of stages or a product of various combinations of integral factors, such as migration, colonial history, and/or rule of law. Various theories have been prevalent at different times, depending on the real-world examples available and the presence or absence of assumed integral factors.

The study of economic development was begun in earnest after World War II to address economic underdevelopment among South-Eastern European nations and former colonies. Some of the first theories viewed poverty as a product of vicious circles, and stressed the importance of a "big push" in overcoming barriers to growth, discussed below. Other theories viewed economic development as a prescribed set of policies or stages that were similar for each developing country. The stages of growth model was first presented by Walt Whitman Rostow in 1960 and asserted that economic growth occurred in five stages, from a traditional society to a consumer society.

Another development theory originating in the post-war period was based on the idea of convergence, that countries with low levels of capital will have a high rate of return to capital so that they can converge to higher levels of development. This type of theory began with the Solow (1956) model, which found that economies converge to a "steady state" of growth. Convergence theories were popular through the 1990s, and include theories of absolute convergence, which state that per capita incomes converge in the long run no matter the initial conditions of a nation; theories of conditional convergence, which assert that per capita incomes converge when countries have the same structural conditions no matter the initial conditions; and theories of club convergence, which state that per capita incomes converge when countries have the same structural characteristics and the same initial conditions (Galor 1996). Theories of convergence were largely discredited in the late 1990s, as a growing body of empirical research showed that economies trended away from convergence.

There are several general categories of theories based on non-convergence, which states that countries with low development levels do not necessarily "catch up" to rich countries. These include theories that emphasize expectations and multiple equilibria, theories of aspiration gaps, theories of history dependence, and theories of institutions (Ray 2008).

Theories that emphasize expectations and the potential for multiple equilibria to occur are theories in which society fails to coordinate development. These theories include those created by Rosenstein-Rodan (1943) and Hirschman (1958), and rely on the presence of externalities that make particular actions look more attractive, even though other actions would lead to a higher equilibrium. Rosenstein-Rodan (1943) addresses issues of industrialization in Eastern and South-Eastern Europe, referring to the high unemployment rates in this region as a "wastage of labor," and proposing solutions to the region's industrialization problem in terms of coordinating the coexistence of capital and labor. This paper provided four innovations that served as the basis for building the "big push" theory of industrialization, including the idea that there is surplus labor in the agricultural sector, that there are external industries that should be incorporated in the economic planning process, that social services should be provided for the public as private firms would not bring these about, and that technology and skills training could become external to firms when workers were free to leave their jobs (returns on workers were not internalized) (Rosenstein-Rodan 1984). In other words, the "big push" theory focused on simultaneous industrialization of several sectors of the economy so that external industrial profits and technology could be captured.

Theories of aspiration gaps refer to the gap between what one aspires to (given by society's standard of living) and what one has. These theories are laid out in Appadurai (2004) and Ray (2006). Preferences (or aspirations) are viewed as socially shaped and given by one's experience as a member of society. If someone is surrounded by individuals with low aspirations, they may not be driven to enhance their circumstances (Ray 2006). In addition, if they are surrounded by images that represent high aspirations, they may feel that they have failed before even beginning to change their economic circumstances. Therefore it is the situation of both being in poverty and lacking connectedness to individuals who are somewhat better off that causes the poor to attribute their poverty to fate.

Theories of history dependence include those by Dasgupta and Ray (1986) and Banerjee and Newman (1993). These state that inequalities persist because society remains path dependent in terms of income and accumulation. Dasgupta and Ray (1986) explain why some individuals remain undernourished for their lifetimes while others are able to escape the cycle of undernourishment, drawing out a rigorous model. They find that competition increases inequality by providing landowners with a larger wage income than in the case of no competition. Banerjee and Newman (1993) assert that poor workers work for a wage rather than set up their own businesses since they lack sufficient capital, while rich workers start their own businesses and monitor the poor workers. Hence initial income distributions have long-run effects, resulting in either widespread factory employment or self-employment.

Theories of institutions place a primary importance on establishing development-friendly institutions. Examples of these theories include those by Sokoloff and Engerman (2000) and Acemoglu et al. (2001, 2002). Sokoloff and Engerman (2000) stressed the importance of institutions in replicating initial conditions in the development process, noting that strong inequality arose in Latin America as a result of government policies and laws that reinforced elite access to resources. Acemoglu et al. (2001) found that high settler mortality rates in some colonies induced Europeans to set up extractive institutions, which have influenced current institutions and economic performance.

Currently, there is little written about economic reform theory per se. While economic development is closely tied to economic reform, the two concepts diverge in the sense that reform, when successful, distinguishes itself as somehow superior to ongoing economic development. Economic reform theory should postulate why and how this can be so, but this field is vastly underdeveloped. There is not even a sufficient definition for economic reform. We assert that a proper definition for economic reform is the following: "Economic reform is the large scale, intentional shift of an economy away from areas in which there is weak comparative advantage to key areas in which there is strong comparative advantage."

Economic reform theory can encompass elements of economic development and economic growth. The difference should be an emphasis on several factors rather than on particular causes by themselves. Sharma (2011) asserts that reforms are sustainable when several factors become favorable. These factors include changing the dominant view of international intellectuals, providing illustrative country cases, changing executive orientations, gathering political will, heightening the degree and the perceived causes of economic crisis, improving attitudes on the part of donor agencies, and enhancing the perceived outcomes of economic reforms. Once some sort of political–economic–psychological threshold is passed, the reform process may be embarked upon, and Tier One reforms undertaken.

DEVELOPMENT THEORY IN CHINA, INDIA, AND JAPAN

China, India, and Japan utilized theories of marketization and trade liberalization in different ways. Japan, the first to industrialize, was a student of industrialization theory as embodied in the theories of Walt Whitman Rostow and W. Arthur Lewis. Japan was also used as a prime basis for the theory of Ranis and Fei (1961) and as the prime exception for Moulder's (1977) dependency theory.

The first theory to attempt to explain Japanese development was the flying geese theory, originated in the 1930s by Kaname Akamatsu. Akamatsu's (1962) theory holds that economic development takes place on a global scale, and that external relations with developed countries contribute greatly to economic development in a developing country. Akamatsu described Western Europe as a lead goose on a global scale, and Japan as a lead goose on a regional scale, with Japan leading the rest of Asia. The model laid out seven stages of economic development that took place in Asian history:

- In the first period, Asian countries traded Asian products for Western European industrial products.
- The second period occurred when the Asian handicrafts industry was destroyed by increased amounts of Western European manufactured products entering the area, after the industrial revolution in Western Europe.
- In the third period, Western European techniques and capital flowed into Asia to support large-scale production of raw materials for export to Europe, in exchange for consumer goods.
- The fourth period is similar to the third period, in that Western European capital flowed into Asia to support production, this time of processed raw materials.
- In the fifth period, Asian domestic capital was used to generate raw materials. Capital was imported from Western Europe to produce consumer goods in Asian countries. Therefore, imports shifted from trading in consumer goods to trading in capital goods.
- In the sixth period, manufactured goods were produced by domestic Asian industries. Capital goods were imported from Western Europe.
- In the seventh period, Asian countries were able to export manufactured consumer products, and to produce some capital goods themselves.

Akamatsu's theory would later be reformulated by Raymond Vernon in the 1960s, and by Kiyoshi Kojima in the 1970s. Kojima (1978) examined the flying geese model in the context of multinational corporations, incorporating foreign direct investment into the model. Kojima was critical of foreign direct investment, which was not often implemented in a way that was complementary to balanced economic development in the host country. The flying geese theory of development remains an important point of reference in framing Asian development as part of a larger, global structure. The theory is used in both academic and policy circles.

More widely applied is Walt Whitman Rostow's theory of development.

Rostow's theory laid out five stages of development through which each economy must pass: the traditional society, the preconditions for take-off, the take-off, the drive to maturity, and the age of high mass consumption (Rostow 1960). Traditional societies faced limited production and were heavily reliant on agriculture. In the second stage, the period in which preconditions for take-off were met, modern science impacted industry and agriculture. Politically, a centralized national state was also often required. During the take-off stage, growth mounted, due to the accumulation of social capital and technological improvements in industry and agriculture, as well as the emergence of ambitious leadership. The drive to maturity consisted of an effort to extend modern technology to the whole of the economy. Finally, the age of high mass consumption saw a shift in leading sectors to production of durable goods and services. Japan's centralized, concerted efforts to apply technology across its industries indicated a desire to expand and maintain growth as laid out by Rostow.

W. Arthur Lewis constructed a theory based on a two-sector model of economic growth with an unlimited supply of labor in the agricultural sector (Lewis 1954). Surplus labor, in the industrial sector, is paid a subsistence wage, equal to average product plus a margin. Industrial expansion continues to employ additional workers as long as capital formation continues. Ranis applied Lewis's model to Japan, finding that some modifications needed to be made. Subsequently, Ranis and Fei (1961), fitting their model to the case of Japan, extended the Lewis model to account for continuing growth of the agricultural sector and a critical minimum effort to move away from economic stagnation.

The Lewis–Ranis–Fei model is laid out in detail in Ranis and Fei (1961). In this model, there are two sectors: one is a traditional agricultural sector with disguised unemployment; there is also a capitalist industrial sector that consumes surplus food produced by the agricultural sector. As the economy progresses, surplus labor moves from agriculture to industry. Figure 2.1 gives Ray's (1998) graphical presentation of the model, with the industrial labor force read from left to right, and the agricultural labor force read from right to left.

The bottom panel shows an agricultural production function drawn from left to right. The production function becomes flat at the phase of surplus labor, in the first section. Wages, determined by income sharing, are the average wage, or $\bar{\bar{w}}$. The second section shows a phase of disguised unemployment, since the marginal product of labor is lower than the average wage. The downward-sloping diagonal line in the bottom panel shows the entire wage bill; the vertical difference between the production function and the diagonal line is the agricultural surplus. The agricultural surplus divided by the number of workers who migrate to the industrial

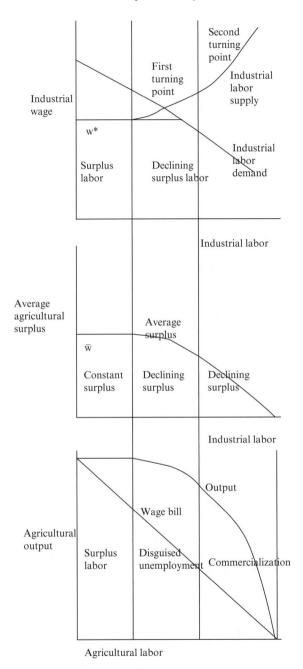

Figure 2.1   Lewis–Ranis–Fei model

sector represents the average surplus per migrant worker. The middle panel illustrates the average agricultural surplus available to industrial labor. The surplus is first constant during the surplus labor period, then declines over time.

The top panel illustrates what happens to the industrial wage at different points in the labor transfer process. The minimum industrial wage required for migrants to purchase their part of the agricultural surplus is described in terms of industrial goods, and therefore is w^*, or $\overline{\overline{w}}$ times the terms of trade between agriculture and industry. In the first phase of industrial development, labor is perfectly elastic, since it is in surplus. During disguised unemployment, as average agricultural surplus declines, food prices for industry start to rise, translating into rising industrial wages. When the supply curve of labor starts to slope upward, Ranis and Fei's (1961) "first turning point" has occurred.

At the "second turning point," disguised unemployment ends and the marginal product of labor exceeds the wage rate. Here, on the labor demand side, it becomes profitable to seek out labor since it is relatively cheap. This phase corresponds to the commercialization of agriculture, and agricultural surplus is declining even more. On the labor supply side, the industrial wage must compensate workers for a higher income they must pass up in the agricultural sector, indicating an increase in the industrial wage rate. The increase in demand curves in the top panel shows the resulting increase in demand for labor as profits are reinvested and capital expands. The decline in agricultural surplus inhibits further industrial employment, since it results in increased costs of hiring industrial labor.

Japan's economy was appropriate to the dual sector model, but in fact, agriculture and industry were more interconnected than was thought (Francks 1992). Although clearly industry demanded food and labor, farm households also demanded industrial products as inputs (such as fertilizer and machinery) and outside markets in which to sell their goods. Farmers' conditions were influenced by institutional changes set off by the growth of industry.

Moulder's (1977) dependency theory, for which Japan was a prime exception that proved the general rule, stated that Japan's development from the Meiji period onward was due to its ability to shield itself from colonialism. Other non-Western societies became colonized by Western powers, stunting their economic development. Moulder compares Japan to Imperial China, which was brought into dependency on Western powers in the nineteenth and early twentieth centuries, and therefore was sharply constrained in its growth.

After China's period of dependency, however, the country faced a period of reform and rapid growth. China, an original hybrid of a state and market-led economy, was for the first period of reform guided under Deng Xiaoping Theory. Deng Xiaoping Theory was not an economic theory per se, but incorporated Marxism and Mao Zedong Thought. Deng Xiaoping Theory emphasized constructing a market economy with a socialist political system. Marxism was applied to the development of society. Mao Zedong Thought was applied to the building of the Communist party. By appearing to continue along the same ideological lines that previously governed the country, Deng Xiaoping was able to move forward with his bold plans for opening up and reforming the economy.

Although it did not operate explicitly under a widely known development theory per se, China was also heavily influenced by the thinking of David Ricardo, particularly his theory of comparative advantage. Comparative advantage emphasizes the efficiency gains that result from trade, since countries or regions can specialize in an area in which they are comparatively more productive. This theory can be modeled as follows (as in Golub and Hsieh 2000). Unit labor requirements can be represented by *a* for sector *i* in country *j*:

$$a_{ij} = \frac{L_{ij}}{Q_{ij}} \tag{2.7}$$

where Q represents value added and L is labor employment. Unit labor requirements a_{ij} are constant with respect to L_{ij}. Wages are also a factor in determining comparative advantage between country *j* and country *k*, as is the exchange rate e_{jk}, denoted by common currency c_{ijk}, such that:

$$c_{ijk} = \frac{a_{ij}w_{ij}}{a_{ik}w_{ik}e_{jk}} \tag{2.8}$$

Country *j* therefore specializes in producing goods where $c_{ijk} < 1$ and imports goods where $_{cijk} > 1$.

The theory of comparative advantage influenced China's increased production and export activity in labor-intensive goods. This thinking was reinforced by China's "grand international cycle" theory, which asserted that because developed countries moved away from labor-intensive production, China should focus on labor-intensive production to support the upward movement of developed countries' economies (Fan 1997).

After the Washington Consensus period, political economists began talking about an alternative: the Beijing Consensus. The Beijing Consensus was considered an alternative type of development. Drawn out by Joshua Cooper Ramo (2004), the Beijing Consensus emphasizes the value of innovation, the importance of using measures other than gross domestic product (GDP) per capita, and the idea of self-determination. This theory was later criticized for emphasizing innovation for a country that grew through labor-intensive production, for holding up China's well-rounded development when China has been so focused on economic growth, and for underscoring the idea of self-determination, which does not say much about the development process itself (Kennedy 2011).

Beyond some generalizations of economic theory, economists have failed to classify China into one type of economic thinking or to show Chinese leadership as following a particular development theory. Chow (2007) asserts that China's economy contradicts economic theory by emphasizing public as well as private ownership of assets, maintaining a semi-formal legal system rather than a Western formal legal system, prizing the collective good rather than the solely individual good, and supporting a one-party rather than a multi-party state. Due to these characteristics, Chinese development has fallen outside of traditional economic thinking. Because of this, some analysts have referred to the "China Model," which more generally refers to "socialism with Chinese characteristics."

India was prompted to reform in 1991 by the International Monetary Fund (IMF), operating under neoliberal theory, but applied the theory selectively. Although some reforms occurred before the 1990s, extensive reform did not occur until 1991. Reforms promoted by the IMF in response to India's balance-of-payments crisis were applied selectively and gradually. What was applied was not Washington Consensus-style liberalization, which included elimination of capital controls and all-out privatization, but Chinese-style slow reduction of barriers to growth.

Even so, neoliberal reforms have been heavily criticized by some economists for their focus on growth rather than distribution or well-being. Bhattacharya (1999) offers some criticism of neoliberal policies, noting that small groups of Indian citizenry have benefited, while others have been passed over. Economic liberalization positively impacted the upper two income deciles of the population while underscoring existing poverty and widening inequality due to a weak and fragmented government (Sharma 1999). The state reduced its social safety nets, including spending on medical and public health, as inflationary pressures lowered real wages and raised food prices. Applying the neoliberal model to India wholesale does not necessarily do justice to its unique pattern of growth, however. There is currently no theory that can sufficiently describe India's growth trajectory.

Some analysts have highlighted general characteristics of India's development, which could be used as a basis for developing a formal theory. These elements include a reliance on domestic markets rather than export markets, consumption over investment, and high-technology sectors rather than low-skilled manufacturing (Das 2006). Success also occurred despite, rather than because of, government intervention; India's rise was centered on entrepreneurship rather than the state. This type of entrepreneurship-led model of reform and development does not yet exist in the scholarly literature.

The success of China and India and the failure of neoliberal liberalization policies applied wholesale to the Asian Tigers in the late 1990s opened the door once again to revisions in development theory. Development theory focused on "getting institutions right." "Getting institutions right" asserted that particular institutions, such as property rights, the rule of law, social insurance, civil liberties, and solid macroeconomic institutions, were essential to economic development (Rodrik 2004). Although helpful in pointing toward what might work or not work in promulgating growth, operationalizing "getting institutions right" often pointed toward improving governance, especially enforcement of property rights, without being necessary or easy to implement.

Also important in explaining development processes after the failure of neoliberal explanations has been work on coordination failures and multiple equilibria. Extensive work on coordination failure described the rise of externalities that occur for a variety of reasons, such as changes in information, effects of technology, and changes in markets (Hoff and Stiglitz 2001). Multiple equilibria may be achieved in the absence or presence of externalities such as research and development (R&D) spillovers, spillovers from rent-seekers, inequalities, and expansion toward a "big push."

OTHER ASIAN-INFLUENCED THEORIES

The East Asian developmental state theory was developed as the South-East Asian nations of Hong Kong, Singapore, South Korea, and Taiwan increased rates of growth through the 1990s. In all of these nations, the government played a large role in the reform and growth process. The East Asian developmental state theory has, at its base, the notion that late development has been purposefully contrived by the state in order to manipulate the international market forces such that they stand to benefit the nation (Öniş 1991).[1] Autonomous governments were integral to rapid industrialization because they blocked market forces from affecting the industrialization process. Within the countries themselves, private businesses were subject to rigid regulation and worked closely with the government bureaucracy to align with the government agenda. These countries largely ignored equality and social welfare for the sake of achieving economic goals.

More generally, some economists have emphasized the export-led growth model for Asian nations, citing Japan, South Korea, Taiwan, and

Hong Kong as prime examples. The Asian Tigers, especially South Korea and Taiwan, followed paths of export promotion, providing a desirable growth template for other nations. This model stressed import substitution industrialization followed by a shift to export-led growth, boosting the industrialization process through both means. Under the import substitution industrialization process, Asian nations built up manufacturing capacity to substitute domestic goods for imported ones in a protected economy; once that phase was exhausted, economies were to produce goods for export. This model was later questioned as export growth was limited by global demand under beggar-thy-neighbor, excess supply, and deflationary conditions (Palley 2003).

BOTTOM LINE

Various theories have grown out of economic development cases, and economic development and reform has also been influenced by development theory. This was particularly the case for Japan, which began its reform process quite early and served as an example of how an economy could successfully change itself, industrializing rapidly and accounting for its own comparative advantage. Gaps remain, however, in the creation of economic reform theory in general, and also in reform theory as it applies to the case of India. Difficulties in making generalizations occur with respect to China as well, since China based its reform process on pragmatism and, to a lesser extent, political ideology.

DISCUSSION QUESTIONS

1. Compare and contrast development theory used to justify reforms in China, India, and Japan.
2. What role, if any, did ideology play in the reform process in China, India, and Japan?
3. How is reform theory different from development theory? Do you believe that there is a need to build up a separate line of reform theory? Why or why not?
4. What are some other theories that can possibly explain reform and development in China, India, and Japan?
5. Explain how the flying geese theory may be applied to Japan.
6. Explain how Rostow's stages of growth may be applied to Japan, India, or China.
7. How did Deng Xiaoping Theory apply to China's reform process?

8. Describe Lewis's two-sector model.
9. For which country would the dependency theory play the weakest role in explaining economic development, and why?
10. Why do many economists argue that the "China Model" is not a development theory?
11. How does the "China Model" differ from the "Washington Consensus"?

NOTE

1. Paragraph attributed to Christine Kosmider, SUNY New Paltz Economics of Asia Class 2014.

3. An Asian leader: Japan's development trajectory

DEVELOPMENT INFLUENCES

Japan's development trajectory was heavily influenced by two factors: geography and foreign intervention. As a mountainous island nation, Japan lacked many natural resources and faced barriers to transportation, and was forced to make a concerted effort to industrialize. Japan was given impetus to develop after its negative experiences with traders from the United States, who forced Japan to open up to trade. This caused Japan to feel its own deficiencies painfully; with insufficient resource security and barriers to development, Japan had to seek innovative ways and obtain sufficient funds to industrialize.

Japan is an island chain in the North Pacific Ocean (Figure 3.1), east of Korea, Russia, and China (US Central Intelligence Agency 2012). With terrain that is mountainous and rugged, only 12 percent of Japan's land mass is comprised of arable land. The Japanese Alps on the main island of Honshu cover an area 140 miles long and 60 miles wide. Per capita land mass is the smallest of all G-7 nations. Because of Japan's mountainous terrain, it was not until the 1960s that Japan was able to build up its road network, and the main form of transportation remained the railways.

The country lacks its own energy resources and is the world's largest importer of coal and liquefied natural gas, and the second-largest importer of oil. Japan also has little iron ore and insufficient land on which to produce enough food for its population. Japan imports many goods, including raw materials for domestic production. Without natural resources, Japan was induced to export what it did have access to – silk and tea – and augment exports of these goods using technology to bring in foreign exchange to purchase imports. Unlike the resource-rich countries of China and India, Japan had to produce exports rapidly in order to import much-needed resources and technology for expanding development.

The other major influence upon Japan's development trajectory was the intervention of foreign powers. Japan's experience with Westerners was not positive and later produced determination in Japan's leadership to strengthen the economic and military power of the nation. Forced

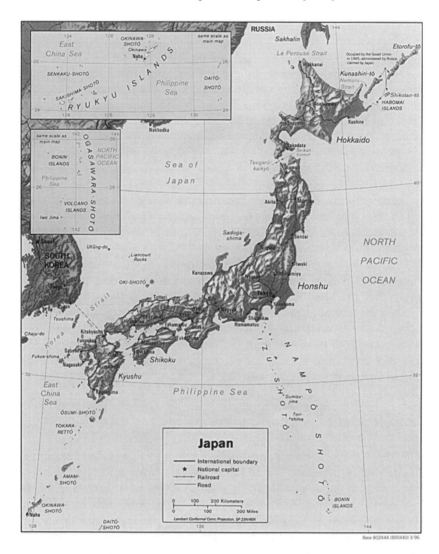

Source: Courtesy of the University of Texas Libraries, University of Texas at Austin.

Figure 3.1   Shaded relief map of Japan, 1996

opening of Japan by Commodore Perry and his "black ships of evil mien"[1] were not easily withstood by all Japanese. Young samurai overthrew the Tokugawa Shogun and installed the Meiji government, sweeping in what is now known as the Meiji Restoration.

Initial contact with Westerners occurred with traders from Portugal, the Netherlands, England, and Spain. Japan's shogunate was highly suspicious of these traders, and assumed that Europeans desired to colonize the country. Hence, throughout the later Tokugawa regime, the country was closed to trade with all except for Dutch and Chinese merchants (US Department of State 2011a). In 1854, US naval ships entered Shimoda Bay near Edo (now Tokyo) and demanded that Japan open its ports to American traders. Japan's relatively weak Shogun was forced to accede to the well-armed men, receiving heavy criticism from other *daimyo* (Rosenbluth and Thies 2010). A series of "unequal treaties" followed (Francks 1992).

Upset with this development, samurai and merchants conspired to get rid of the Tokugawa shogunate. Southwestern Han marched upon the shogunate and took control of the government, settling the new Meiji government in Tokyo. The rest is history.

Despite the large geographical barrier to development, Japan followed close behind Western nations in the industrialization process. One hundred years after the Meiji Restoration was established, in 1968, Japan's GNP became the second largest in the world. This was a year that Japan's interaction with the rest of the world changed; Japan had become a developed nation (Hamada 1996). Between 1891 and 1980, Japan's urban population had increased from 9.3 percent of the population to 76 percent of the population (Harris 1982; Honda 1997).

JAPAN'S REFORM PATH

The Meiji takeover was a time of foreign resentment and a deterioration in the balance of payments. When foreign powers had forced open Japanese ports, at least exports of Japanese silk to Europe were increasing due to a silkworm disease in Western Europe. However, by the time of the Meiji *coup d'état*, French and Italian silkworms had recovered, and Japan had even begun to import European silk (Francks 1992). The surge in imports shook the Japanese farm sector, upon which the government relied for tax income. Economic conditions soon improved under the Meiji regime.

At first, the Emperor Meiji (Box 3.1) abolished the domains and established new prefectures in order to create a more centralized political system. The process of moving the *daimyo*, or local governors, from their castle towns to Tokyo was accomplished peacefully, since several domains were indebted and all too happy to surrender their debts to the central government (Duus 1998). A modern monarch was established with a somewhat more visible Emperor as figurehead.

BOX 3.1 EMPEROR MEIJI

Emperor Meiji was Emperor of Japan from 1867 to 1912. He was a proponent of Japan's modernization process (*Encyclopædia Britannica* 2014). Meiji approved many changes that were under way, including the abolition of the feudal system, creation of a school system, creation of a cabinet in the government, and adoption of the constitution. Although the Emperor himself was not very powerful, he was an important symbol for the unity of Japan. Emperor Meiji proclaimed the Imperial Oath, intended to rally the population behind a common effort (Duus 1998).

Source: Photograph in public domain.

The new Meiji government quickly turned things around. Its motto was "rich country and strong army" (*fukoku kyōhei*). The four pillars of the *shokusan kōgyō* policy of the 1870s were to: (1) establish a national banking system; (2) develop transportation and communication networks; (3) create and subsequently sell public sector factories; and (4) lend to private firms. The Meiji government drew up a constitution in 1889 that gave power to the bureaucracy and the military, set up mandatory education and conscription, and promoted industry (Honda 1997).

The national bank system that was set up in 1876 resulted in a poorly managed financial system riddled with inflation. The central bank, the Bank of Japan, established in 1885, resolved the problem by removing unsound private and government paper notes from circulation (Duus 1998). The central bank eventually became a key part of a system of specialized semi-government banks. Dampened inflation promoted investor confidence and laid the groundwork for economic growth.

The Meiji government changed the tax system to obtain revenue from land rather than from production of crops, which provided the government with a steady stream of cash revenue. This system, devised by Ōkubo Toshimichi, a top government leader, used a national survey to determine the extent of cultivated land (Duus 1998). Without this reform of the government fiscal system, the new government would have continued to remain financially strained, as Japan continued to pay interest on samurai bonds and purchase goods from abroad.

Due to Japan's forced openness and increasing imports, the country focused on increasing competitiveness in domestic industries. Feudal institutions were eliminated, increasing employment based on merit rather than on title (Yoshihara 1994). Former samurai took up highly skilled tasks, as Japan imported technology to modernize its economy. Japan embarked on a policy of import substitution industrialization (*koku-sanka*), meaning "converting to domestic production" (Brown 2005).[2] By the beginning of the twentieth century, Japan was producing ships, chemicals, Western-style suits, watches, and even beer (Francks 2009). What is more, Japan went from being an importer of manufactured goods in the late nineteenth century, to being an exporter of manufactured goods by the time of World War I (Francks 1992).

Technology played an important role in Japan's economic reform process. In the 1870s, more than 3000 foreign engineers were hired by the government, and 2500 were hired by private industry to train Japanese scientists and engineers (Duus 1998). Young people went abroad on government scholarships to study and transfer their knowledge back to Japan.

Since the Meiji government inherited industrial enterprises from the Tokugawa government, the government continued to own most of the important industrial assets. However, by the 1880s the government sold most of its enterprises to the private sector. The government did not need to fully control enterprise, since businessmen and government officials, coming from the same samurai class, held the same goal of promoting industrial activity (Francks 1992). Private owners were able to make the enterprises newly profitable. By this time, private companies were allowed to deal directly with foreigners in trade (Francks 1992). Table 3.1 provides data to illustrate the transition from an agricultural-based economy to a manufacturing-based economy in Japan.

Infrastructure and the monetary and fiscal system were improved, streamlined, and geared toward facilitating private enterprise. Construction of railways began, increasing railway mileage. Issue of money was centralized and the yen was designated the central monetary unit. The fiscal system was streamlined and land taxation was put in place (Yoshihara 1994). The railroad system was later nationalized in 1906, and private railroads were purchased by the government to ensure uniform prices and guarantee transportation efficiency (Duus 1998).

The government also adopted a constitutional parliamentary government and a Western-style legal system. A gradual movement toward democracy was established (Rosenbluth and Thies 2010). Meiji scholars studied constitutions around the world to understand best practices in governance. Architects of the constitution proclaimed that the government was accountable only to the monarch, rather than to the general public. However, real accountability to the monarch was limited, since in fact Meiji oligarchs, acting as an advisory body, governed through the monarch.

Table 3.1   Growth and structural change, 1885–1920, 1970–2005

	GDP total (million yen)	Proportion (%) produced in:	
		Agriculture	Manufacturing
1885	3774	42.1	7.0
1890	4639	39.8	7.9
1895	5375	37.0	8.9
1900	5966	34.7	11.2
1905	6214	31.6	12.6
1910	7424	30.9	15.6
1915	8753	30.7	19.4
1920	10937	27.3	18.6
Data gap for 1925–65			
1970	74158136	6	45
1975	149971623	5	41
1980	242838700	4	41
1985	325401900	3	39
1990	442781000	2	39
1995	495165500	2	34
2000	502989900	2	32
2005	501734400	2	30

Sources: Francks (1992) from Ohkawa and Shinohara (1979), Table A.12: 278–9; World Bank (2014).

Japan focused on enhancing its textile and shipping industries. The Tokugawa regime had relied upon household production of silk and textiles (Figure 3.2). With increased competition in exports from Europeans, the Japanese silk industry increased mechanization under small enterprises while remaining in rural areas (Francks 1992). Japan's cotton industry also underwent increasing mechanization and became competitive in the 1880s, spurring further economic expansion.

The shipping industry, although slowly rising, faced competition from Western steamships, which accounted for most of the export shipping out of Japan (Francks 1992). Japan's desire to militarily back its claims on Taiwan forced recognition of the weakness of the Japanese merchant marine and resulted in both increased government policy focus on the shipping industry and development of a well-managed private shipping enterprise within the Mitsubishi *zaibatsu*. A major shipping company, Nippon Yūsen Kaisha, resulted from the merger in 1885 of Mitsubishi and Mitsui, a fierce competitor (Francks 1992).

At the end of the century, Japan went to war against the Chinese and

Source: Photographer: T. Enami. Photograph in public domain.

Figure 3.2   Reeling silk

Russians over Korea. The war with the Chinese occurred in 1894–95, while
the war with Russia occurred in 1904–05 (US Department of State 2011a).
Korea was important to Japan, which wanted to open up Korea for trade
and food production.

Improvements in agriculture occurred at the turn of the century, with new
types of rice allowing for higher responsiveness to fertilizer and increased
resistance to cold. More intensive use of fertilizer and improved irrigation
also enhanced agricultural growth. An industrial revolution, coupled with
technological improvements in agriculture, led to an increased movement
of individuals from rural to urban areas. The rural sector remained stable,
and agricultural growth prevented incidence of famine.

Small businesses grew up and performed better than larger firms in the
production of consumer products, for both domestic and foreign consumption (Francks 2009). These businesses used new technology, such
as the electric motor, and cooperated with local networks of producers,
to produce goods such as soap, bicycles, clothing, and food products.
Small businesses were popular with Japanese shoppers, who preferred to

purchase goods in neighborhood shops. Shopping centers grew up around train stations to cater for commuting workers.

A new school system was established after compulsory education was initiated in 1872. The ministry of education implemented a three-tiered structure of elementary schools, middle schools, and universities (Duus 1998). Compulsory education was close to fully implemented by 1910 and literacy rates thereafter increased (Honda 1997). Health scares in the form of epidemics resulting from contact with foreign countries, however, remained a problem from opening up in the nineteenth century through 1920. First cholera, then dysentery, typhoid, smallpox, and diphtheria, then influenza, ravaged the country. Without state-led medical care, commoners organized themselves into larger insurance and medical co-ops, called *mujin kaisha*, to combat these diseases. Public health was ignored while military health and technology were improved. The poor received little medical care and sporadic assistance, which could be cut to finance military expansion.

Heavy industry grew between 1912 and 1936 (Yoshihara 1994). During this time, Japan became engaged in World War I, on the side of the victorious Allies. The wartime boom brought about a large increase in industrial output, initiating a transformation from an agriculturally based economy to an industrial economy in a very short period of time (Francks 1992). The merchant marine fleet doubled in size to accommodate increased trade, as textiles and other light industries expanded production for export (Duus 1998).

During World War I, as Britain's productive capacity was shifted into war efforts, Japan was able to expand its export regime (Francks 1992). Shipping services expanded. As imports were cut off, domestic industries built up their ability to produce for the domestic market, allowing import substitution industrialization to finally occur. By 1920, industry, including primary and manufacturing industry, represented a greater share of production than did agriculture, and the industrial labor force had grown in step. Rising demand resulted in inflation and increasing pressure on real wages, causing social unrest in some places.

After the war, Japan's economy lagged as foreign powers resumed production and trade competition. Prices for major exports collapsed, resulting in bankruptcies and lay-offs. The Great Tokyo Earthquake of 1923, and the Great Depression of 1929, further dampened Japan's economy. The Great Tokyo Earthquake damaged bank financial and physical assets, and depositors feared bank losses (Shizume 2009). As a result, the government imposed a moratorium on payments and indemnified the Bank of Japan from losses incurred in rediscounting of bills in the affected areas, bringing about financial stability.

Under the Showa government, Japan faced the Showa financial crisis of 1927 and the Showa Depression of 1930–31. The former resulted from a build-up of bad loans by financial institutions after the Great Tokyo Earthquake, while the latter resulted from the Great Depression itself, as the world economy came to a grinding halt. Structural reforms imposed in 1927, and effected in 1928, allowed for the disposal of bad loans and imposed minimum capital requirements on banks, bolstering the banking sector. Japan's return to the gold standard in 1930 resulted in sharp appreciation of the yen, which compounded Japan's economic troubles as the Great Depression took hold. Japan experienced severe deflation and economic contraction at this time. Japan's departure from the gold standard on December 13, 1931 resulted in the depreciation of the yen and improved circumstances for the Japanese economy.

However, the significant industrialization of the economy allowed Japan to weather these crises (Francks 1992). The Japanese government sought to increase household savings by praising the practice of frugality and forgoing consumption (Francks 2009). The ability to save and undergo hardship became a patriotic characteristic.

Zaibatsu became increasingly important during the 1920s because politicians promised favorable regulation to *zaibatsu* firms in order to obtain campaign contributions (Rosenbluth and Thies 2010). This tied *zaibatsu* to politicians. Tying *zaibatsu* to banks was a shortage of capital, which led *zaibatsu* firms to banks to obtain preferential capital. *Zaibatsu* expanded as new technology became available, resulting in the growth of new industries.

In 1925, due to the growing role of industry in the economy, the Ministry of Agriculture and Commerce separated industrial and agricultural governance, and the Ministry of Commerce and Industry (MCI) was formed to address the industrial sector (Francks 1992). The new ministry sought to alleviate some of the economic pressures of the 1920s by improving management and technology, as well as by coordinating agreements to set boundaries on industrial capacity. The Temporary Industrial Rationality Bureau drafted the Important Industries Control Law of 1931, which allowed the MCI the ability to create cartel agreements with the consent of two-thirds of the firms in an industry (Francks 1992). This action strengthened the major *zaibatsu* firms and increased widening differentials in productivity and real wages between the modern and traditional sectors (Honda 1997). Figure 3.3 is a photograph of the employees of the Mitsubishi Heavy Industries.

Japan invaded China in 1937, in what is known as the Pacific War, the part of World War II that took place in the Asia-Pacific (Smitka 1998). Japan had built a colonial empire that included Taiwan, Korea, and

Source: Modern Business (Kodansha). Public domain photograph.

Figure 3.3   Employees of the Mitsubishi Heavy Industries, Ltd, July 1937

Manchuria (Honda 1997). In order to reduce inefficiencies and central-ize the economy to some degree during this war period, the Diet passed a National Mobilization Law that allowed a council to screen economic regulations while maintaining decision-making freedom for big business (Duus 1998). Supplies of consumer goods, including food, became increas-ingly scarce, and food rationing began in 1940. Families obtained food through neighborhood associations mobilized by the state (Francks 2009). Under the 1942 Food Control Law, agricultural output was purchased by the state and redistributed to the military and civilian populations. Black markets run by *yakuza* grew up to provide food and households goods that became increasingly hard to come by.

Japan had an economic and military infrastructure large enough to wage war on the Allies, but the United States enacted an embargo on aircraft and weapons materials to Japan. The war was unsuccessful and resulted in a severe economic downturn. Able agricultural workers had been drafted and natural resources became inaccessible, as Japan's colonies were taken away after the war. Basic products, including food, were hard to come by. Figure 3.4 illustrates Japanese soldiers on a flattop after the start of Allied Occupation.

After World War II, Japan was occupied by the Allies. Occupation

Source: US Navy. Public domain photograph.

Figure 3.4   Japanese soldiers on flattop, August 24, 1945

occurred from August 1945 to April 1952 and centralized control of the economy through the Economic Stabilization Board. An American-style constitution was grafted onto the Meiji constitution to reorganize the Japanese government along the lines of British parliamentary democracy (Kuwayama 1982). Hence democracy that had begun slowly during the Meiji Restoration was solidified because Americans wanted to reduce Japan's ability to gather forces for war.

At first, the Allies took no responsibility for ensuring the economic well-being of the Japanese people. The Occupation blocked Japan's heavy industry, including investment in steel, shipbuilding, and machinery, to stop its military expansion (Vestal 1993). Famine set in. However, the United States and other nations quickly changed course. With the increasing specter of the Soviet "threat," the United States in particular, along with the other Allies, committed to restoring Japan to its pre-war condition. Heavy industry was allowed to return in order to promote recovery.

Restructuring occurred in both rural and urban areas. First, land reform was carried out to equalize land holdings. Large landholders were forced to sell off one-third of land to their tenant farmers. Second, Japan's large corporations, or *zaibatsu*, were broken up into smaller companies in order to increase competition (Kuwayama 1982). About 1200 *zaibatsu* corporations were dissolved. In a period of upheaval and economic restructuring, the birth rate dropped dramatically between 1947 and 1957, from 34.3 to 17.2 per 1000 (Harris 1982).

Arisawa Hiromi, an economist at Tokyo University, played a key role in creating the first modern Japanese industrial policy, executed through the Economic Stabilization Board (Vestal 1993). Arisawa was able to identify bottlenecks in the economy, pointing out that the declines in coal production were affecting steel production as well as production of fertilizer.

Japan's democracy was created during the Allied Occupation. The Liberal Democratic Party, along with the Japan Socialist Party, were created, along with additional, smaller parties (Rosenbluth and Thies 2010).

Price controls and subsidies were provided for priority industries. The resulting increases in output helped to alleviate some of the cost-push inflation that occurred at the time, but it did not eliminate it (Vestal 1993). The Occupation therefore imposed a Nine-Part Interim Directive on Stabilization, which imposed austerity measures to stabilize the economy. The Directive was carried out under Joseph Dodge, and became known as the Dodge Line. Dodge demanded a government budget surplus, exposed previously hidden subsidies in the price control system, and called for a single exchange rate. New lending by the Reconstruction Finance Bank was ended. These measures reversed the inflationary trend and initiated a period of deflation and unemployment (Vestal 1993). As subsidies ended, firms went bankrupt and workers lost their jobs.

To combat the worst effects of the Dodge Plan, the Bank of Japan loaned large sums to banks, allowing financial institutions to assist flagging companies (Vestal 1993). Banks chose to lend first to their oldest companies, former *zaibatsu* group companies, which reinforced their relationships to one another. Bank lending also reunited *zaibatsu* links between companies, forming *keiretsu* with city banks at the center of the corporations (Vestal 1993). The Ministry of International Trade and Industry (MITI) tasked itself with coordinating industry to ease the pain of Dodge Line policies. MITI brought together businessmen, academics, and policy makers to lay out "rationalization" plans for industry. Companies that survived the subsidy cuts, in the long run, were forced to become more efficient. MITI's list of policy tools grew to include providing or removing tax incentives, government funding, cartelization, and control over technology.

The process of "rationalization" applied to industries, in the sense of choosing to support industries that were central to economic goals; choosing how many firms should operate within each industry; and increasing efficiency within companies by improving products and reducing costs (Vestal 1993). Small and medium-sized enterprises were not left out: they were supported through low-interest loans in order to maintain

employment. The steel industry was the first to undergo rationalization, from 1951 to 1952. The plan focused on a large increase in capital
expenditure. Rationalization plans for the coal, fertilizer, electric power,
and shipbuilding industries were also carried out.

The Dodge Plan ended with the onset of the Korean War (Vestal 1993).
The economy went from a period of austerity and contraction into a major
boom. Japan was a major supplier of trucks and equipment, a station
of rest and recreation for Allied troops, and a repair station for United
Nations forces (Kuwayama 1982). During the Korean War, demand for
Japanese goods increased and manufacturing output grew in step, by
44 percent between June 1950 and June 1951 (Vestal 1993). Lowered tariff
and non-tariff barriers as a result of the General Agreement on Tariffs and
Trade also helped to foment the export boom. A year into the war, although
there were concerns that the upturn could not be upheld, domestic consumption surged as pent-up demand for consumer goods, in combination
with continuing demand for Japanese exports, drove a continuing boom.

The post-Korean War period saw a year-long slump, followed by an
expansion that continued to focus on domestic demand (Vestal 1993).
A second round of rationalization was planned for multiple industries,
reducing existing inefficiencies. Global innovations changed the economy
in the last half of the 1950s, as synthetic fibers, synthetic rubber, plastic,
and aluminum were used to create new products. Industrial policy was
shaped to fit these new industries. The first five-year plan, laid out by the
Economic Planning Agency, was adopted in 1955 to promote trade and
technology, strengthen industry, and increase employment. Rather than
setting targets for growth, the plan sought to set directions for economic
development. Industries began to be promoted for their contribution to
trade and employment rather than for economic autonomy. Policies also
aimed to maintain employment and protect small and medium-sized enterprises. MITI spread technology among firms in an industry to prevent one
company from having an advantage.

In the 1960s, imports were liberalized (Vestal 1993). Capital expenditure
increased as part of growth policy. Even though workers earned only
10 percent of what US workers earned in 1960, consumers increased
demand for new products, such as vacuum cleaners, stereos, televisions,
washing machines, transistor radios, and refrigerators. At the same time,
however, surplus labor dwindled, and government policy toward smaller
enterprises increasingly promoted competition rather than passive support.
As oil became more widely available too, the coal industry was phased down.

A second agricultural revolution occurred in the 1960s, known as the
Green Revolution. The Green Revolution, like the first agricultural revolution at the turn of the century, resulted in improved seeds that were even

more responsive to fertilizer, and that were also high-yielding (Francks 1992). At the same time, policy toward agriculture supported employment rather than productivity.

During the late 1960s, corporate investment rose by almost three times (Vestal 1993). This was carried out in order to combat the threat of foreign investment that was on the rise after Japan agreed to meet international standards for trade and capital liberalization. Firm size increased since Japanese businessmen believed expanding firms would create economies of scale.

By the 1970s, Japan's economy was the third-largest in the world, measured by gross domestic product (GDP), behind only the United States and the Soviet Union (Kuwayama 1982). The Japanese were living at the same levels as the British. Japan was producing a larger percentage of machinery (32 percent of GDP in 1970) than of food products and textiles (19 percent of GDP in 1970).

US President Nixon's closing of the gold window in 1973 ended the period of controlled exchange rates, and Japan's currency appreciated substantially afterward, reducing demand for exports (Kuwayama 1982). Higher oil prices and increased competition from other Asian countries resulted in a sharp increase in bankruptcies. The Bank of Japan attempted to loosen monetary policy to increase domestic demand. With rising domestic demand came inflation. Monetary policy was then tightened, and Japan's economy began a recovery thereafter.

Japan's financial economy boomed in the 1980s, and particularly after the late 1980s when financial deregulation occurred. This led to a bubble economy during that decade, with large increases in real estate asset prices. Increasingly risky financial activities and less bank monitoring ability, coupled with the loss of technological innovation, set the stage for a financial crisis in the 1990s, followed by a long-lasting financial contraction. The financial crisis and its resulting contraction is not something that we study in this book, but it is perplexing that a country that rose from undeveloped to developed status over the course of a century, that was seemingly so unstoppable, should experience a more than 20-year economic malaise thereafter. At the time of writing in 2015, economists are still unable to ascertain ways in which the Japanese economy can exit dwindling economic growth.

POLITICAL ECONOMY OF REFORM

The political circumstances under which reform arose are essential to the process. Economic sluggishness was viewed as a political failure, and the feudal lords that had ushered in the Meiji Restoration were intent on changing the direction of the economy. This was the main target of the political coup.

During the Meiji period, the Emperor was restored as the head of Japan, but the reform process was guided in practice by the feudal lords who had overthrown the Shogun. The Emperor provided a symbol of Japanese culture and continuity, while the transition away from the feudal system induced increasing competition. Reduced restrictions on land use and land property rights in particular increased agricultural productivity and helped to generate revenue and free up labor for the industrial sector.

After the Meiji emperor died, the Taisho period began in 1912 and lasted to 1926. A political conflict at the beginning of the period resulted in reduced power to the old guard and increased power to the Diet. The Taisho Political Crisis of 1913 and the Rice Riots of 1918 revealed frustration with the government. Universal male suffrage was granted (Menton et al. 2003).

The Showa period began on December 25, 1926 and lasted until January 7, 1989, coinciding with the rule of Emperor Hirohito. This period also began with turbulence, as Japan was struck first by a financial crisis and then the Great Depression. Korekiyo Takahashi, Finance Minister, implemented fiscal policy rapidly to combat the crisis (Shizume 2009). Takahashi's aggressive debt-financed fiscal expansion has been rigorously shown by Cha (2003) to have saved Japan from the throes of the Great Depression. Using structural vectoral autoregression analysis, Cha finds that Takahashi's actions were indeed pivotal in preventing economic stagnation.

The early Showa period, which occurred until the end of World War II, saw the rise not only of financial crisis but also of militarism in Japan. In 1937, Japan invaded China as part of the second Sino-Japanese War. This followed the invasion of Manchuria in 1931. The second Sino-Japanese War lasted until the end of World War II. Japan became involved in World War II after bombing Pearl Harbor on December 7, 1941 to protest US opposition to negotiation on Japan's involvement in China. The United States declared war on Japan directly after this occurred.

The post-war Showa period was first dominated by the American Occupation. The Japanese government was reoriented, as the Emperor lost power and the parliament was given more power (US Department of State 2015). The Occupation lasted until 1952, when Japan once again became autonomous.

Japanese politics rose to the fore once more in the 1950s and 1960s. The Liberal Democratic Party (LDP) was backed in the late 1950s and 1960s by small businesses, farmers, and heavy industry (Rosenbluth and Thies 2010). The LDP protected small businesses from giant retailers. Heavy industry provided money for campaigns, while small farmers provided votes. The LDP government put into place the Large Scale Store Law of 1975, which allowed small stores to block the entry of larger firms into their neighborhoods. The government also supported farmers against foreign producers of oranges, beef, and rice.

INDUSTRIALIZATION

As mentioned above, Japan took on the industrialization process as a major state goal. Factory employment before World War I was low relative to employment in agriculture (Taira 1970), even though industrialization was a target of the Meiji government. Late-nineteenth-century factories organized around an experienced craftsman called an *oyakata*, who mentored apprentice workers in groups of workshops (Duus 1998). This later changed to a more modern factory system as better technology was introduced and more skilled workers were hired. Industrialization grew up by World War I from Tokyo in the eastern half of Honshu through Nagoya and Osaka in western Honshu, to Fukuoka in the northern part of Kyushu (Honda 1997).

Industrial power grew between 1881 and 1937, with horsepower growing consistently each decade at a rate of more than 9 percent (Minami 1977). This accompanied an increase in the capital stock, beginning with the textile industry, which led the industrialization process. Within the textile industry, the model for spinning was Osaka Spinning Company which was established in 1882 by Shibusawa Eiichi, a large, very efficient private enterprise (Ericson 2000).

TECHNOLOGY

Japan's comparative advantage lies in technology innovation. Japan was aggressive in ensuring that scientists were educated overseas, and in incorporating new technology into its production processes. This was notable, particularly in the Meiji era, as Japan was just emerging from a long period with little trade contact with the outside world, and therefore little contact with foreign innovation.

The Meiji government, and succeeding governments, instituted policy conducive to technological innovation. The government's policy was at first to import Western technology and to employ Western scientists and engineers in Japanese universities to teach students, who would later replace the foreign engineers (Fukasaku and Ishizaka 2005). Training and research were supported by government funding, and government officials themselves went abroad to study in Western universities (Francks 1992). In this way, Japan was able to catch up to Western powers in terms of its use and understanding of technology.

By the end of the nineteenth century, inventions such as scientific measuring instruments, armaments, and textiles and food industry inventions were created (Nicholas and Shimuzu 2012). Key technology investments were made by Tokyo Electric and Shibaura Engineering Works, Ltd, which were owned in part by General Electric. Inventions were also prevalent in the textile industry, in which the G-type automatic loom was created by the Toyoda family to increase productivity.

When World War I began, available imports declined, so that Japan was forced to produce many goods that it had previously imported from other nations. In order to develop industrial raw materials, the Chemical Industry Council was set up within the Ministry of Agriculture and Commerce in 1914 (Harayama 2001). The Institute of Physical and Chemical Research was established in 1917 with both public and private funding. The goal of these institutions was to enhance research and bring about innovation.

After World War II, additional technology was transferred to Japan from the West and reverse engineered to develop the ability of Japanese engineers to reproduce the products. Japanese workers were also hired during the Allied Occupation of Japan to work in factories on maintenance and repair of US equipment (Spencer 1969). Demand for high-technology military equipment and maintenance continued through the Korean War. Manufacturing capability for advanced fighter jets was established in 1955.

Japan incorporated technology through commercial channels, from investment of foreign companies. The 1960s also ushered in a trend in which private research companies set up their own research laboratories, called "Central Research Laboratories" (Harayama 2001). Private incentives were given to these companies via the Law on Industrial Technology Research Association of 1961, which encouraged private companies to participate in applied research activities. "Big Projects" were promoted for industry, university, and state cooperation by the Industrial Structure Council, which sought to embark on research of new technologies that could not be developed by the private sector alone, in sectors with large impact and many potential spillovers.

Social needs drove some technological innovation in the 1960s and 1970s, with regard to pollution, traffic, and water shortages. The oil crisis in the 1970s forced Japan to diversify its energy sources and to find new sources of energy. The main goal, however, was still to catch up to the West, particularly the United States. By the 1980s, this had more or less been accomplished.

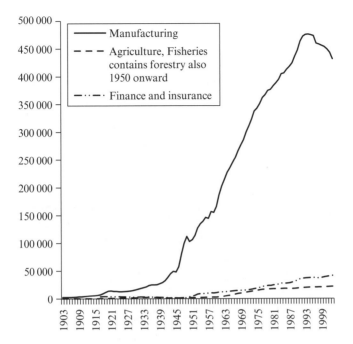

Source: Japan Ministry of Internal Affairs and Communications, Statistics Bureau.

Figure 3.5 Number of corporations by industry

DATA AND PATTERNS OF GROWTH

Data can help to illuminate Japan's pattern of growth. From Figure 3.5, one can see that the number of manufacturing companies skyrocketed in the post-World War II era, while growth in the agriculture and financial sectors was far slower. This illustrates Japan's dramatic take-off in the secondary sector after the war.

As Japan became more developed and urbanized, the number of railway passengers that it transported also grew. From Figure 3.6, it is clear that the number of travelers on the well-developed railway system increased steadily after World War I, through the 1990s.

The standard of living began to rise even during World War I, through 2000, as in Figure 3.7, as more and more households and firms obtained contracts for electric light and power. As industrialization, urbanization, and modernization occurred, more and more households had access to electricity and other modern amenities.

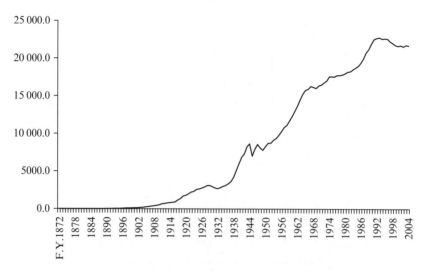

Source: Japan Ministry of Internal Affairs and Communications, Statistics Bureau.

Figure 3.6   Railway passengers transported (in millions)

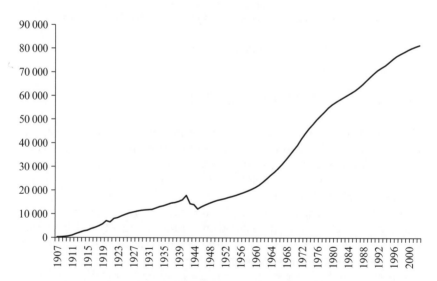

Source: Japan Ministry of Internal Affairs and Communications, Statistics Bureau.

Figure 3.7   Contracts for electric light and power (000s)

BOTTOM LINE

Japan developed over the course of a century in a concerted effort to industrialize and reinforce its comparative advantage in innovation. Despite having few natural resources and a mountainous terrain, Japan took advantage of internal and external circumstances to implement technology into its production processes and increase its export base. World War II boosted the reform and development process under Allied Occupation by enhancing Allied support, over time, for the critically located island nation. Technology transfers, strong government policies, and hard work allowed Japan to officially "catch up" to the West by the 1970s or 1980s. Japan is a prime example of how targeted reform policies can bring about real changes in economic development status.

DISCUSSION QUESTIONS

1. What reforms did Japan's Meiji government (1868–1912) implement? In what ways did these contribute to Japan's future success?
2. What component(s) of reform was essential to Japan's success? Are there elements of Japan's reform process that were not essential to Japan's success? Please justify your answer.
3. Discuss two turning points in Japan's history that resulted in the greatest economic growth. Explain.
4. What prompted Japan's Meiji Restoration?
5. How did World War I benefit Japan? Explain.
6. How did the Allied Occupation work for or against Japanese reform goals? Explain.
7. In what ways did Japan develop technology innovation as its base of comparative advantage?
8. Why were the four pillars of the Meiji Restoration important in the reform process?

NOTES

1. From a Japanese ballad entitled "Black Ships."
2. Thanks to Ahmet Can Kucukagiz, in the SUNY New Paltz Economics of Asia class of 2014, for this contribution.

4. The waking giant: China's development trajectory

CHINA'S GEOGRAPHY

By contrast to Japan, China was a nation rich in natural resources at the outset of reform. China contains resources such as coal, zinc, copper, tin, and mercury. China is also large in geographical area, and is about the size of the United States, although China is more mountainous. The nation has a long coastline, while the western region is landlocked. Elevation rises to the west of the Aihui–Tengchong line; therefore, much of the population lives to the east of this line, where far more of the land is arable (Naughton 2007).

China (Figure 4.1) is divided into 31 administrative divisions, with 22 provinces, 5 autonomous regions, and 4 municipalities under direct control of the central government. Western provinces face barriers to development due to their geography, including lack of access to transportation and water, as well as lack of access to energy resources in the south-west, and poor agricultural climate in the north-west. Much of China's development has taken place in the eastern coastal region, which through its water-borne shipping routes has easy access to foreign markets.

China's uneven development has resulted in plans to encourage development of the interior, but due to geographical realities, particularly a dry climate and high elevation in the west, these plans have met with limited success. In the next section, we discuss the "China Model" and China's reform trajectory. As will become evident, China's manufacturing and export-intensive model of reform favored the eastern coastal region, placing strain on the prospect of installing a balanced development trajectory.

THE CHINA MODEL

China's development process is now often referred to as the "China Model," which combines a market economy with an authoritarian state. The China Model is viewed as distinct in being guided by pragmatism over ideology

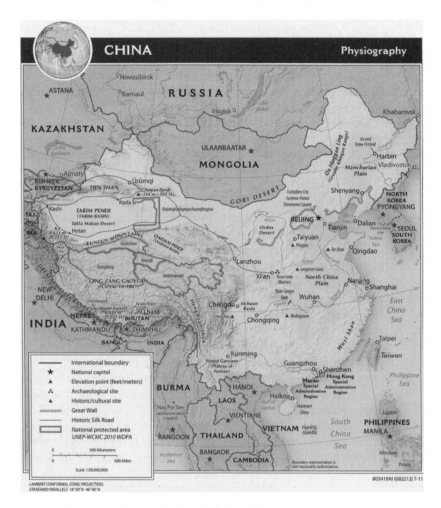

Source: University of Texas Libraries. Public domain image.

Figure 4.1   Geography of China

in economic development; leadership by a strong, pro-development state; and selective learning from liberal Western models (Zhao 2010). The China Model focuses on equitable growth, and rejects outright privatization and free trade.

The China Model asserts that the Chinese development path is not only viable, but worth imitating. The China Model calls for government protectionism and government support of experimentation and innovation.

Economics and governance serve to improve society; the China Model is also sometimes referred to as the "Beijing Consensus" (Ramo 2004).[1] The China Model and the Chinese reform process did not arise overnight, however.

China's experience with foreign powers heavily influenced the manner in which it reformed. China was a world power for centuries before it rose again in the twentieth century. A master of trade and war, China's economy dominated in the East until the Opium Wars starting in 1839, when Western powers grew strong and forced the country to open to trade. The bitterness of this experience led the country to seek shelter behind the closed doors of Communism in 1949.

During this period, China barely engaged in trade with the outside world and produced solely for its own planned economy. Production was geared toward, and resources mobilized for, heavy industry. The planned economy encouraged rapid industrialization. Job creation was not a priority, and retail and service businesses were discouraged (Naughton 2007). Private enterprise was illegal. Outright suppression of human rights became a fact of life, made starkly evident in the Cultural Revolution and grain famine during the Great Leap Forward. The Cultural Revolution sought to remove all capitalist and cultural elements from society through violence, and many people were tortured or executed, while the Great Leap Forward attempted to foment rapid industrialization and brought about agricultural collectivization and the transfer of food from rural to urban areas.

The Communist Party became decreasingly popular, particularly in the wake of the Cultural Revolution. The government was strong-handed but the economy was weak. Despite the fact that the Chinese leadership did not want to experience subservience to foreign trading powers, the lack of trade had left the economy stunted. The need for strong leadership continued even after Mao Zedong (Box 4.1) became increasingly unable to

---

BOX 4.1   MAO ZEDONG

Mao Zedong founded the People's Republic of China in 1949 after a civil war between the Communists and the Kuomintang (BBC History 2014). Industry was placed under government control and agriculture was organized into collectives. Mao ruled by suppressing opposition and following his own interpretation of Marxist-Leninist policies. Political suppression resulted in the infamous Cultural Revolution, in which millions of individuals were persecuted or killed.

Source: Photograph in public domain.

govern, while the potential for the government to instill economic reform policies grew simultaneously. The "Gang of Four" had overseen the last stages of the Cultural Revolution and later paid the price for these crimes. After Mao died and the Gang of Four were prosecuted, a large vacuum developed in China's political leadership. Hence the potential for the China Model, which couples strong political leadership with experimental economic policies, arose.

CHINA'S REFORM PATH

After Mao died in 1976, a leader needed to be chosen to lead the country forward. The planned economy had proven itself cumbersome and inefficient, and memories of the Cultural Revolution were fresh and distressing (Chow 2004). At the Third Plenum in December 1978, there was a sense of frustration with strong ideologies and international disengagement. The new leadership, under Deng Xiaoping, was open to change and economic growth. A decision was made to start a reform process referred to as "socialism with Chinese characteristics" (Naughton 2007). Deng aimed at bringing back the import-substitution strategy that had succeeded at the beginning of the Communist period, in the 1950s (Sen 2001).

Chinese reform policy was successful because leaders were bold and willing to begin reform without knowing the direct consequences of each stage of reform. This process was known as "crossing the river while groping for stones." Changes were made in ideas about economic development strategy, economic institutions, and legal rules (Garnaut 2004).

The first sector to undergo change was the agricultural sector (Figure 4.2). Before reform, farmers worked collectives that distributed a fixed number of work points to each individual, regardless of how hard they worked. This system resulted in great inefficiencies in productivity. After reform, and under the household responsibility system (approved of in 1981), communes were broken up into individual plots of land, which were leased to farmers. In addition, price incentives given to farmers were improved, mandatory production planning was eliminated, and township and village enterprises were allowed to fill consumer demand. The aim of agricultural reforms was diversification of the rural economy and expansion of free markets (Lin 1988). Zhang and Carter (1997) find that institutional reform in the agricultural sector was responsible for about 38 percent of agricultural production growth between 1980 and 1985, and the estimate is even higher in other studies.

Agricultural prices were gradually changed. The government increased basic agricultural procurement prices in 1979 by 17.1 percent, while selling

Figure 4.2 Agriculture in China

the goods at a lower price to urban residents at a loss (Mackerras et al. 1998). The system was changed in 1985 so that the government purchased 70 percent of agricultural goods at a higher above-quota price, and 30 percent at a below-quota price, and was no longer required to purchase surplus grain at guaranteed prices.

Indeed, the rural sector was considered a key to reform, particularly until the late 1990s. Rural enterprises, particularly township and village enterprises (TVEs) (called commune and brigade enterprises until 1983), opened up options for consumers and increased competition. Township and village enterprises promoted development particularly in coastal regions. By 1996, TVEs were producing 40 percent of the gross national product (GNP) and 55 percent of gross industrial output value (Lai 2006).

Decentralization was a key element of reform. As reform began, local governments were given the ability to better finance their needs. Local governments were also able to support enterprise development in their areas (Wu 2009) and also to collect revenues.

Also critical to reform was the dual-track system of production, in which farmers and state-owned enterprises were allowed to sell goods on the market after meeting production targets. This system was an important means of expanding markets at the beginning of the reform period and through the 1980s. Price system reform was very gradual, allowing some goods with controlled prices to continue to be effectively subsidized, while slowly growing the ability of markets to determine prices. Urban workers were able to maintain their apartments associated with their employment, while prices gradually increased as wages rose (Chow 2004).

The beginning of reform also brought about some changes in state-owned enterprises, in which most urban workers were employed. The process began with giving a small amount of autonomy to a few enterprises in Sichuan province at the end of 1978. The experiment was successful and was expanded to 4200 enterprises by the end of 1979 (Wu 2009). Through the 1980s, however, reform was slow, starting with changing internal governance of state-owned enterprises and introducing a contracting system under the Contract Responsibility System which required managers to meet targets for sales and profits (Garnaut et al. 2006). This process was effective in making state-owned enterprises more efficient. Leasing, by which private individuals could lease state-owned enterprises, and private shareholding, by which employees could purchase part of enterprise shares, were introduced in the late 1980s. By 1991, state-owned enterprises continued to employ 73 percent of all urban workers (Perkins 1996). Starting in 1994, the Company Law stipulated that state-owned enterprises should be restructured and gradually listed on the stock market (Naughton 2007). The Company Law also introduced various types of corporate legal concepts such as limited liability, share capital, and boards of directors.

Outright private ownership was allowed in the 1980s, with restrictions on public enterprise hiring removed in 1983 (Wu 2009). Private industry grew twice as fast as state-owned industry. However, although the political climate in terms of privatization improved in the late 1980s, privatization was not a clearly politically endorsed policy until Deng Xiaoping traveled to the Special Economic Zones in 1992 and publicly supported production for the private economy. Private firms were kept small in the early 1980s but allowed to grow somewhat larger in 1987 and 1988 (Lai 2006).

In the 1990s, reform moved from the hands of Deng Xiaoping to Zhu Rongji. Zhu speeded up the reform process. In the state-owned enterprise sector, Zhu followed a policy of "grasping the big, and letting the small go," starting in 1995 (Zheng and Chen 2009). This translated into cultivating strong, large firms and transforming them into multinational firms, while privatizing small and medium-sized enterprises. Management buy-out was the most common way of privatizing the small and medium-sized enterprises (Garnaut et al. 2006). This policy resulted in the creation of overly large firms making monopoly profits, and massive lay-offs from state-owned enterprises in the late 1990s.

The privatization process resulted in stock listing of medium-sized and large state-owned enterprises (SOEs) and the sale of a small proportion of shares to individual investors (Huang and Wang 2011). When this first occurred, most shares were held by SOE parent companies. Later, some firms became fully privatized. Ultimate privatization may occur when all shares are sold to private entities. This has been shown to improve firm performance in terms of efficiency.

As the environment became more competitive, the dual-track system of production and pricing was eliminated, and products were sold on the market only. The privatization of township and village enterprises resulted in increased efficiency among these entities, after a one-year transition period (Li and Rozelle 2000).

Policies toward privatization were unclear until 1992, when the Communist Party declared that it was working toward a socialist market economy and that various types of ownerships were acceptable (Lai 2006). The 1990s ushered in a more liberal mentality. In 1997, Jiang Zemin even defended the Party's promotion of private and foreign enterprises, even as these were under attack by critics. The "Three Represents" ideology adopted in 2000 allowed private entrepreneurs to become Communist Party members. This policy later became part of the constitution, and legal rights and recognition were extended to private entrepreneurs. As a result, the private economy's share of retail sales more than doubled during the 1990s and into the 2000s.

Trade liberalization occurred slowly over the reform period and was an important driver of growth. This occurred under the so-called "Open Door Policy." Trade decentralization through the 1980s assisted with this process. First, trade administration was moved from the central to the local level, so that local state-owned trading companies could make international trading linkages (Zhang and van Witteloostuijn 2004). No longer was the Ministry of Foreign Economic Relations and Trade in control of all trade. Second, more decision-making power was given to trading companies through a contracting-out system. Third, trading companies were allowed to retain part of the foreign exchange they earned, so that they could make a profit and operate in the foreign exchange market. Fourth, a small group of import tariffs were reduced. In the 1990s, tariff and non-tariff barriers were further lowered. The trading system also became increasingly transparent.

China has attracted a large amount of foreign direct investment, particularly in Special Economic Zones and Export Processing Zones, reaching $105.7 billion in 2010. Special Economic Zones were created in 1980 in Shenzhen, Zhuhai, Shantou, and Xiamen, and another 14 port cities were opened in 1985 (Wu 2009). The Special Economic Zones were at first experimental, and were carefully calculated in terms of political viability, location, and scale. The zones were placed so that foreign nationals such as the Japanese and Koreans could witness the success of investment and trade in China. The zones were also regions with an entrepreneurial culture and centuries of experience with trade, poising them for success before the program was even implemented.

The Special Economic Zones (SEZs) were successful despite some difficulties with smuggling (Lai 2006). Fiscal revenue in the zones increased rapidly and living standards in these regions improved dramatically. SEZs became attractive ways to grow local economies and to gain revenue, as well as to earn foreign currencies, and after just two years of the SEZ experiment, other provinces were asking the state to set up their own Special Economic Zones.

The banking system was transformed from a mono-bank to a multi-branch, credit-lending banking system. Separation of central and commercial banking functions also occurred, such that a hierarchical, multifunctional system was created. The People's Bank of China became the central bank at the top of the hierarchy, while beneath it were three policy banks: the State Development Bank, the Agricultural Development Bank, and the Export–Import Bank; four state-owned commercial banks: the Bank of China, the Industrial and Commercial Bank of China, the Agricultural Bank of China, and China Construction Bank; nationwide commercial banks; regional commercial banks; and non-bank financial institutions (Wu and Chen 2010). China's banking system has been so gradually reformed that it has become an albatross around the neck of enterprise. The system is dominated by the state-owned sector and banks are restricted to deposit and loan business; and non-performing loans extended to state-owned enterprises that do not repay the loans continue to plague the books of state-owned banks. Banking efficiency has improved but is one area that continues to hold back the growth process.

The standard of living increased dramatically after reform. Between 1981 and 1990, the nominal share of basic necessities in total expenditure declined in both rural and urban areas, falling by half in urban areas (Zhang 1996). Farmers and enterprises alike gained more autonomy over making production decisions. Life expectancy continued to rise along with gross domestic product (GDP) per capita.

Structural reforms were carried out in order to increase productive efficiency. The textile industry faced major restructuring, and millions of spindles were put out of use and hundreds of thousands of workers were laid off (Jha 2002). Coal mines were shut down to reduce excess production. Workers were laid off en masse in the petroleum, petrochemical, and metallurgical industries.

By the 1990s, however, it became clear that certain facets of development were suffering. Although under the commune system rural residents had access to health care, both in the form of "barefoot doctors" that could provide basic medical care and in commune health centers and county hospitals, health care in rural areas after reform began was lacking; no health insurance scheme existed for rural residents until 2003. Inequality between rural and urban areas became vast and problematic; articles such as Knight and Song (1993) brought to light problems of spatial inequality that were subsequently incorporated into policy objectives in the 2000s. The quickened pace of reform had brought about concentrated growth in coastal areas, as well as concentrated social spending for urban coastal residents that did not reach the western expanse of the country. Riots due to land seizures by the government in western China erupted periodically and highlighted the need to improve living standards in China's interior. These issues were not addressed until later, in the Eleventh and Twelfth Five-Year Plans. The early 2000s were thus fraught with social unrest.

China's road to World Trade Organization (WTO) accession on December 11, 2001 was gradual, and the country continued to reduce tariffs and decentralize authority. China went from having a closed economy at the outset of reform, to becoming the "world's factory" as a relatively open economy (Naughton 2007). China's accession as a member of the General Agreement on Tariffs and Trade (GATT) in the 1980s was denied after the Tiananmen Square incident in 1989, which was considered a prodigious violation of human rights. The WTO's Uruguay Round which emphasized a "grand bargain" between developed and developing countries, which would allow for more protection in production for developing countries in exchange for more protection for developed countries' firms in developing countries, facilitated China's acceptance to the WTO. Trade liberalization only continued after accession, and trade itself greatly expanded. Large increases in exports followed as China became one of the largest trading bodies in the world. Figure 4.3 is a photograph of one of the many shipping boats carrying freight for export from China.

Trade and growth expanded until 2007 or 2008, when the global financial crisis impacted all countries, hitting China through trade channels. Exports slowed dramatically at the end of 2008 and beginning of 2009, and many rural migrants to urban areas were laid off from their jobs and had to return to their relatively poorer villages. To combat the crisis, China announced a $586 billion stimulus package to stimulate domestic demand by expanding infrastructure and improving social welfare programs. The stimulus package focused on spending, over two years, on health care, education, low-income housing, environmental protection, programs to promote technological innovation, transport and other

Source: Eustace Bagge. Public domain photograph.

Figure 4.3   Chinese shipping boat

infrastructure projects, and reconstruction after the Sichuan earthquake (*The Economist* 2008).

CHINA'S STAGES OF DEVELOPMENT

China's development trajectory has undergone several stages, as has been extensively discussed in the literature. These can be grouped by five-year plans.

The latter part of the Fifth Plan, the Sixth Plan, and the Seventh Plan can be grouped together under the process of agricultural reform, the dual-track system of producing for plan and market, and relative absence of privatization (Naughton 2007). In this book we refer to this period as the Dawn of Reform. Agricultural reform began spontaneously as farmers in Anhui seized individual plots of land, calling for the end to farmed communes. What followed was the dismantling of the commune system and a shift to the household responsibility system, as families became responsible for their own plots of land. Farmers produced crops for the plan and sold the remainder on the market. State-owned enterprises did the same, as market prices were allowed to flourish. Privatization remained *verboten*, but government-owned enterprises produced increasingly for consumption and profit.

To begin this period, the Fifth Plan, from 1976 to 1980, was interrupted by the change in direction induced by the appointment of Deng Xiaoping as leader of the Communist Party. The third plenary session of the Eleventh Central Committee of the Chinese Communist Party resolved, on December 18, 1978, to reform all backward activities and thinking, and Deng's appointment indicated a shift toward economic reform. The Fifth Plan was altered in accordance to focus on modernization.

With the Sixth Plan came the shift of focus from the rural sector to the urban industrialized sector of the economy. The Sixth Plan, from 1981 to 1985, focused on improving the supply and quality of consumer products, strengthening production, and controlling population growth (China. org.cn 2013a). The Seventh Plan, from 1986 to 1990, focused on reform, including the modernization process of industry and economic efficiency (Gov.cn 2006a). The plan attempted to improve science and technology, and to meet consumer demand. Through the 1980s, China's economy was increasingly industrialized and modernized. The benefits of the household responsibility system declined after 1984, while the manufacturing sector began a steady ascent.

A second grouping of five-year plans can be made to encompass the Eighth Plan and the Ninth Plan, through the decade of the 1990s. This period we dub the Rise of the Market. Over this period, the dual-track system was eliminated and economic forces became increasingly competitive, culminating in mass lay-offs of state-owned enterprise workers in the late 1990s and progress toward WTO accession in 2001. Privatization became acceptable, even encouraged, by the end of the decade.

The Eighth Plan, from 1991 to 1995, brought an accelerated pace of reform and increased opening up to the outside world. Outputs of televisions, coal, cement, and cotton were the highest in the world (China. org.cn 2013b). Fixed investment and infrastructure were also strongly emphasized.

The Ninth Plan, from 1996 to 2000, strove to further the modernization process and to reduce population growth. The plan also sought to reduce poverty while increasing per capita GDP. The plan was interrupted when, starting in 1997, the Asian financial crisis provided a "vivid, invaluable, and 'free' lesson" (Gao 1999). As a response to the crisis, scholars encouraged market forces, cautioning against government overintervention in the market, strong interrelations between banks, government, and enterprise with the inclusion of soft budgetary constraints, persistence of state-owned banks' non-performing loans, lack of risk management, and market pessimism. The need to remain competitive, and to allow market forces to arise, was underscored by the fallout from the crisis that China escaped.

The Tenth and Eleventh Plans constitute a third period of China's development, which we refer to as the Arrival on the World Stage. China's preparations for and accession to the WTO in 2001 served to focus attention on necessary reforms. WTO accession secured China's rank among the most powerful nations. The Tenth Plan, from 2001 to 2005, attempted to increase employment and improve the livelihood of the people (China.org.cn 2013c). Enhancing the social security system and support for new farming technologies were also focuses. The latter would be achieved by commercialization of the agricultural sector.

The first plan to focus on the human aspect of development rather than economic growth alone was the Eleventh Plan, from 2006 to 2010, which sought to build a "new socialist countryside" and a "harmonious society" (Gov.cn 2006b). The plan focused on improving economic welfare in underserved areas. The plan also focused on structural upgrading and enhancing the services sector.

The global financial crisis that began in the USA in 2007 and 2008 left few countries unscathed. China's exports suffered from contraction in the US and European economies, and the government sought remedies to improve the flagging economy. Fiscal stimulus was the first order of the day, and helped to maintain acceptable rates of growth for two to three years following its passage. However, as it appeared that the Western economies would remain in a slump, China attuned its Twelfth Plan to address this issue.

The Twelfth Plan, from 2011 to 2015, the beginning of what we call the Balanced Growth Period, aims at increasing domestic consumption, developing the service sector, shifting to higher-value-added manufacturing, and improving the environment (Casey and Koleski 2011). The intent to expand domestic consumption resulted to a great degree from the global crisis that dragged down global demand for Chinese exports.

POLITICAL ECONOMY OF REFORM

China's political economy of reform is complex, and has relied on a process of coalition building and political maneuvering over time. At the outset of reform, reformist leaders have had to build coalitions with conservatives to ensure political palatability of reforms. The gradual approach was first adopted in part because a more sudden strategy would have been rejected by much of the leadership. Some major political constraints were therefore overcome after the reform process began in 1979.

Political barriers to reform included opposition to more extensive marketization at the outset of reform, the population's unhappiness with slow income growth, dominance of the Communist Party, and provincial variation in attitude toward reforms (Lai 2006). The first barrier to reform, opposition to more extensive marketization, was overcome by undertaking slow, gradual reform. Slow income growth that resulted brought about unrest among the population, and negative attitudes toward the so-called reform process which was in reality slowed by conservatives. To combat this view, and prevent the loss of momentum among popular support for reform policies, reformists sought to implement reforms in regions that would experience large economic successes as a result. This helped to maintain public acceptance of the reform trajectory.

Others were against reform, and viewed modernization as a path to capitalism. They believed that reform could lead to corruption, instability, and inflation (Mackerras et al. 1998). They also believed that reform could undermine the power of the Communist Party and eventually destroy the fabric of the state. Those opposed to reform lost out to forces in favor of economic growth.

Dominance of the Party was used as an asset rather than a liability, as the Party was used to advance the reform cause (Lai 2006). The dominance of the central government within the Party was used to promote local leaders whose reform policies were successful. Finally, the barrier of provincial variation in attitudes toward reform was overcome in much the same way that discontent with sluggish growth was combated: leaders chose provinces that were most receptive to reform, which brought about requests from other provinces to receive reforms in turn.

In order to uphold the process of reform, China needed a strong leader. Deng Xiaoping was a strong-minded individual but amenable to economic change. He had been an ally of Mao from the 1930s until the 1960s, when he was purged twice from the Party. Due to his experiences with the Cultural Revolution, he decried the movement. Since many conservative Party members remained in office and continued to idolize Mao (they were called "Whateverists," as in following whatever Mao said), Deng was smart to maintain Chairman Mao's reputation while acknowledging Mao's mistakes. Deng was supported by Zhao Ziyang as Premier and Hu Yaobang as CCP Chairman in the 1980s (Mackerras et al. 1998).

Through the 1980s, some believed that under Deng, political change toward a democratic environment would become possible. However, it became clear after the crackdown on protesters at the Tiananmen Square incident on June 3–4, 1989, that Deng Xiaoping was not at all in favor of political change. Deng had viewed the student protests as "turmoil," but believed that some evil individuals had taken advantage of students and convinced them to protest. In Deng's mind, the unrest expressed leading up to the Tiananmen Square incident was the beginning of a counter-revolutionary uprising that would result in the collapse of the Communist Party, and he believed he was forced to halt the activity (Mackerras et al. 1998). Deng's health deteriorated thereafter.

The Fourteenth Congress of the Chinese Communist Party in 1992 reaffirmed Deng's trajectory and continued to approach reform toward a "socialist market economy" (Mackerras et al. 1998). Jiang Zemin began a ten-year term as President and continued the reform process. After Zhu Rongji became Premier, the reform process sped up considerably, as both leaders were strong reformists (Jha 2002).

As the reform process sped up and the standard of living rose under Jiang Zemin and Zhu Rongji, less political suasion was needed to justify reforms. China followed the "Three Represents" which stated that the reform process must always represent the development of productive forces, promotion of China's advanced culture, and the promotion of the interests of the people (Narayanan 2006). In 2000, capitalists were allowed to join the Communist Party.

Due to the transition over the Jiang Zemin period to a focus on successful economic growth as an outcome of reform, President Hu Jintao and Premier Wen Jiabao were less encumbered by persuading other cadres in favor of reform. However, Hu was confronted with reconciling the desires of the pro-development liberals and the pro-social justice new Left (Zheng 2007). Hu's answer to this was social democracy, which emphasized rural democracy, grassroots participation, and intraparty democracy. President Hu emphasized collective over charismatic leadership, which increased his rate of approval even while constraining his freedom (Duchâtel and Godement 2009).

President Xi Jinping and Premier Li Keqiang came to power in 2013 and focused on reducing corruption within the Communist Party while continuing the reform process. President Xi inherited an economy undergoing structural change, from a labor-intensive manufacturing economy to a skill-intensive manufacturing and service-based economy. The economy was also slowing, experiencing a decline in real estate prices and a build-up in debt on the part of local governments and real estate developers. President Xi led the reform process by declaring continued financial and economic reform. By dubbing slower growth the "New Normal," President Xi bypassed social frustration about the slowing economy and promoted a psychological transition toward a more consumption, service-based economy.

DATA AND PATTERN OF GROWTH

China's growth process continued from the outset of reform and continues today. This is illustrated by the amount of electricity used per capita, in Figure 4.4.

Despite the fast pace of growth, however, in the 1990s, the coastal region became significantly wealthier, in terms of GDP per capita, than the western, inland region (Table 4.1).

China's growth trajectory can also be viewed by sectoral changes (Figure 4.5). China's agricultural sector as a share of GDP declined from 30 percent in 1980 to 10 percent in 2010. The industrial sector as a share of GDP declined from 48 percent in 1980 to 45 percent in 2010. China's services sector as a share of GDP climbed from 22 percent of GDP in 1980 to 45 percent in 2010. China now has an industrializing economy instead of an agriculturally based developing economy.

In addition to sectoral changes, employment in state-owned enterprises declined from 78 percent of all workers in 1978 to 26 percent in 1997 (Sachs and Woo 2000). Trade, including both imports and exports, rose from 10 percent of GDP in 1978 to 36 percent in 1997, and reached 55 percent in 2010 (World Bank 2012a).

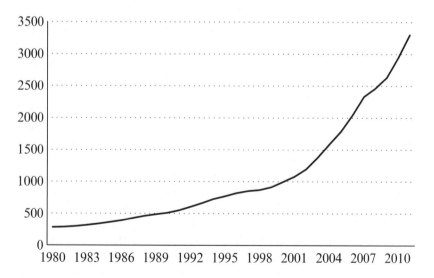

Source: World Development Indicators Database, World Bank.

Figure 4.4   Electric power consumption (kWh per capita)

Table 4.1   GDP per capita, 1997

Region	Urban income per capita	Rural income per capita	Coastal/inland
National total	5188.54	2090.13	NA
Guangdong	8615.86	3467.69	Coastal
Shanghai	8475.50	5277.02	Coastal
Beijing	7861.74	3661.68	Coastal
Zhejiang	7366.19	3684.22	Coastal
Tianjin	6621.47	3243.68	Coastal
Fujian	6201.00	2785.67	Coastal
Jiangsu	5807.35	3269.85	Coastal
Yunnan	5616.21	1375.50	Inland
Chongqing	5343.12	1643.21	Inland
Hunan	5248.93	2037.06	Inland
Shandong	5217.18	2292.12	Coastal
Guangxi	5139.52	1875.28	Inland
Hebei	4982.43	2286.01	Coastal
Hainan	4917.55	1916.90	Island
Xinjiang	4878.52	1504.43	Inland
Sichuan	4787.86	1680.69	Inland
Hubei	4693.82	2102.23	Inland
Anhui	4619.95	1808.75	Inland
Liaoning	4547.23	2301.48	Coastal
Guizhou	4458.29	1298.54	Inland
Jilin	4206.04	2186.29	Coastal
Henan	4111.54	1733.89	Inland
Heilongjiang	4110.08	2308.29	Coastal
Jiangxi	4090.74	2107.28	Inland
Shaanxi	4022.20	1273.30	Inland
Qinghai	4015.50	1320.63	Inland
Shanxi	4007.86	1738.26	Inland
Inner Mongolia	3968.09	1780.19	Inland
Ningxia	3863.65	1512.50	Inland
Gansu	3613.43	1185.07	Inland
Tibet	NA	1194.51	Inland

Source: National Bureau of Statistics.

BOTTOM LINE

China has been a prime example of a successful reform process. Its reform process was guided by pragmatism, and focused on developing

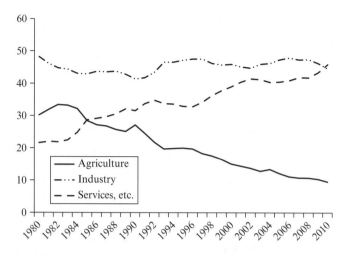

Source: World Development Indicators Database, World Bank.

Figure 4.5   China's sector value added (% of GDP)

the economy rather than on reforming the political system. Reform was carried out in many areas, including in finance, trade, agriculture, and manufacturing. China became a key player in the globalization process, producing many goods for export to the rest of the world. The China Model of development has come to symbolize a strong government, coupled with a market economy.

DISCUSSION QUESTIONS

1. What are some reasons for and obstacles to China's growth? Elaborate on these.
2. How did reform in China proceed in the 1980s and 1990s? What reforms were implemented and why?
3. What factors influenced China in embarking on a program of reform?
4. How did the political leadership handle the reform process?
5. What were some major setbacks to reform in China?
6. How did SEZs contribute to China's economic growth?
7. How did the geography of China influence its development?
8. Explain China's comparative advantage: what is it, and what role did it play in the reform process?

9. Discuss two main differences between Deng's and Mao's rule.
10. Describe the role the household responsibility system played in China's reform process.
11. What was the effect of the elimination of the dual-track system in China?
12. What was the impact of opening up to global trade in China?

NOTE

1. This sentence is attributed to Christine Kosmider, SUNY New Paltz Asian Economics student, Spring 2014.

5. Gradual growth: India's development trajectory

DEVELOPMENT INFLUENCES

As in Japan and China, India's reform process was also influenced by geography and colonial history. India's coastline has been a boon to development. A long history of British colonialism motivated many Indian leaders to reform. Colonialism gave rise to Mahatma Gandhi, who urged protest against British rule, and Gandhi in turn helped to shape the regimes that came thereafter.

India is a country in South Asia, bordered by Pakistan in the north-west, and by Nepal, Bhutan, Myanmar, Bangladesh, and China in the north and north-east. Its lower portion is surrounded by oceans, with the Arabian Sea to the west, the Indian Ocean to the south, and the Bay of Bengal to the east. A large number of sea ports have allowed India to engage in large-scale seafaring trade for centuries. About 95 percent of trade in goods is seaborne.

By contrast to China and Japan, other elements of India's geography, though positive, have resulted in a negative impact on growth. First, although about half the land is considered arable, many Indians remain small-scale farmers. Because the number of individuals employed in the agricultural sector is large in relation to the amount of output it produces, most of India's farmers remain poor. Issues remain with agricultural pricing, research and development, and presence of rural infrastructure.

Second, despite the fact that India is rich in natural resources, over- or underexploitation of resources has stymied growth. India is home to many resources, including coal, iron ore, natural gas, limestone, manganese, mica, bauxite, and petroleum (US CIA 2012). However, transporting resources from one location (particularly in the north-east) to another is problematic and expensive, given a lack of infrastructure. Illegal practices in the mining industry have intermittently led to bans on mining of particular metals in certain states, stopping production. Further, while the rate of exploitation of metal resources is high, water is currently the most depleted resource today. Many of India's rivers and waterways are polluted with toxic substances.

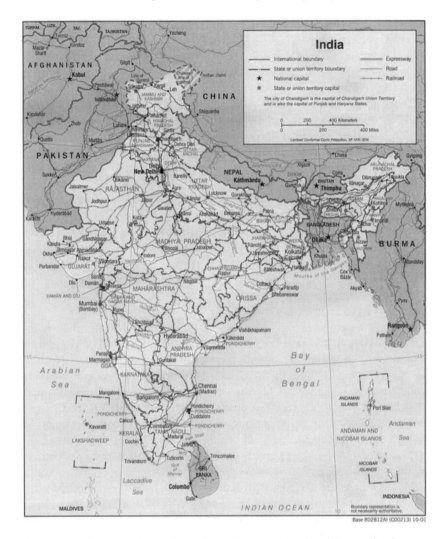

Source: Courtesy of the University of Texas Libraries, University of Texas at Austin.

Figure 5.1 *Political map of India, 2001*

Figure 5.1, a map of India, shows the country's landlocked northern region and the coastal southern region. India contains 29 states and is the second most populous nation after China (Thaper 2015). One-third of the nation is bordered by coastline, and the rest is bordered by six nations, including Pakistan, Nepal, China, Bhutan, Myanmar, and Bangladesh. India's land is divided into three regions, the Indo-Gangetic Plain, the Himalayas, and the Peninsula region.

Sixteen states account for more than 90 percent of India's gross domestic product (GDP). These are Andhra Pradesh, Assam, Bihar, Gujarat, Haryana, Himachal Pradesh, Karnataka, Kerala, Madhya Pradesh, Maharashtra, Orissa, Punjab, Rajasthan, Tamil Nadu, Uttar Pradesh, and West Bengal (Anand et al. 2014). The north-eastern states, as well as Jammu and Kashmir in the north, account for less than 10 percent of India's GDP. The states of Bihar, Orissa, Uttar Pradesh, and Madhya Pradesh in the central and north-eastern region account for more than half of India's poor.

India was first colonized for trade reasons, and over time, the English East India Company's ventures in India set the stage for British rule. Britain exercised political control over India from 1757 until 1947. After the company's victories in the Battle of Plassey in 1757 and the Battle of Buxar in 1764, the company was given control of Bengal and Bihar in eastern India (Iyer 2003). Much of the rest of India was annexed over the following decades. In 1858, the British Crown took control of the Indian polity from the East India Company.

Some states continued to be de facto ruled by native Indian rulers, comprising almost half of the India territory in 1911 (Iyer 2003). The native states were limited in the size of their armed forces, and were required to pay an annual tribute to the British government. British rule was not widely accepted, and peasants rose up in rebellion many times through the eighteenth and nineteenth centuries (Raychaudhuri 1990). Some were unhappy due to dislocation, seizure of cultivation or hereditary rights, or indebtedness to moneylenders, all of this resulting in economic decline.

Mahatma (Mohandas) Gandhi had long encouraged peaceful protest against British rule in the movement for Indian independence. India achieved independence from British colonial rule in 1947, six months after which Gandhi was assassinated. Jawaharlal Nehru, Gandhi's protégé in the Indian independence movement, became the first Prime Minister of India. After independence, India turned inward, beginning with the implementation of five-year plans in 1951. India had been stuck for decades in a cycle of poverty under low per capita consumption and low income under colonial rule, and was determined to instill growth through careful planning.

INDIA'S REFORM HISTORY

After independence from Britain in 1947, India was able to reverse trends of declining consumption of grains and to gradually increase per capita income (Alagh 1992). The Indian economy was controlled for three decades after independence under the auspices of Nehruvian Socialism, which emphasized generating capital accumulation and savings (Kapila 2008a). Planning was a part of improving economic growth, and attempted to redirect capital and technical skills to areas that already had labor and natural resources. Strong government intervention in the economy persisted from the time of Nehru through the administration of Indira Gandhi.

Foreign investment was encouraged, and increased in the 1950s (Panagariya 2008). Industrialization was the focus, and in order to accomplish this in part, particular sectors were chosen to be maintained under state control. Industries of national importance such as atomic energy, arms, and railways were maintained under state monopolies. Distribution and price controls were also used to guarantee availability of inputs for key industries.

The first three five-year plans experienced growth in per capita incomes as well as growth in industrial output, comprising the first post-independence growth period through 1964 (Alagh 1992). Agriculture, however, was not a focus (Panagariya 2008). The so-called land reform of the 1950s was roundly criticized for failing to redistribute land to the farmers, but rather gave land to small landlords who then leased their land to tenants (Jha 2002). The mid-1960s brought droughts and foreign exchange crisis. Armed conflicts with China and Pakistan, as well as reductions in foreign aid, exacerbated the economic situation (Kapila 2008a). Famines that resulted from the droughts in northern India, coupled with the sudden reduction of food aid, resulted in the political popularity of food security policy to ensure that such dire circumstances would not happen again. In 1972, however, another drought occurred and resulted in high inflation and an increase in exports, while the global oil crisis resulted in a large increase in oil prices in 1973, which created shortages in foreign exchange reserves (Jha 2002). As a result, a general economic decline continued from 1964 through 1974.

Devaluation of the rupee, decreased import protection, and increased export taxes in the mid-1960s coincided with crop failures and famine, which caused a recession in the industrial sector. This made the policy that enhanced attractiveness of imports relative to domestic goods quite unpopular, since the domestic economy was already under stress (Panagariya 2008). Exports also suffered as a result of the recession and of the increased export taxes. Foreign investment was also discouraged, further slowing growth. By 1971, import controls and export subsidies had been put back into place.

Growth subsequently improved between 1974 and 1988. The Fifth

Five-Year Plan in 1974 focused on anti-poverty programs in order to stimulate the lagging economy. Subsequent plans focused on infrastructure and less on heavy industry. Exports increased through the 1970s. The Sixth Five-Year Plan, in 1980, set the goal of reducing poverty, while industrial policy reforms were laid out to promote competition, improve technology, and improve productivity. Rural poverty programs were implemented, while in urban areas, many industries were subsequently delicensed. Taxes were reduced, imports were liberalized, and government controls on industries were reduced (Dutta 2011). Quantitative allocations were reduced. The main goal of the Seventh Five-Year Plan was, accordingly, to improve industrial growth. Industrial growth increased over the 1980s because of these policy changes.

Rajiv Gandhi's reforms implemented in 1985 resulted in relaxed industrial licensing and reduced import duties on capital goods. Crucial sectors, including the machine tools, computers, and drugs sectors, were deregulated (Guha 2007). These were carried out under the Finance Minister, V.P. Singh. The policies were widely accepted by businesses and the middle class. A market for consumer durables expanded and new businesses opened at a faster pace. The real estate market experienced a boom, and overall, the economy grew at a faster rate. Despite this success, the policies were criticized by some, who stated that there continued to be a lack of focus on exports and opening up of trade to the outside world (Jha 2002). Reform was therefore only partial, it was said, and the balance-of-payments gap was covered by borrowing. In addition, reforms did not raise the standards of living for all Indians; droughts in Orissa in 1985, and in Orissa, Gujarat, and Rajasthan in 1987, caused many villagers to suffer or starve. In March 1989, Rajiv Gandhi reversed his middle-class-focused policies, increasing taxes on consumer durables while introducing rural employment schemes (Guha 2007).

Despite some growth, the first three decades of planning have been referred to as the "License Raj," resulting in the "Hindu rate of growth" of the late 1960s and early 1970s. In other words, industrial and other activities were subject to licensing (permits for myriad business activities) and rigid capacity controls, as well as rationed inputs and capital goods (Athreye and Kapur 2006). Licenses served the purpose of protecting some industries over others, and ensuring that industries could achieve satisfactory geographic diversification. During this period, India remained poor, with a relatively low GDP growth rate of 3.6 percent, and with 40 percent of its population living on less than $1 per day (Dutta 2011). India's state of technology fell far behind that of the rest of the world. Many had no access to safe drinking water, health care, or education. Total factor productivity growth remained low.

The 1991 debt crisis was one of twin deficits: a growing debt on the

Source: UN data.

Figure 5.2 Current account balance, 1980–2000 (million US dollars)

part of the government, and an ever-increasing current account deficit (Figure 5.2). The twin deficits, and slowing economic growth, interacted in a negative way to foment this crisis. First, the decline in economic growth in the late 1980s led to a sharp fall-off in government revenue. Government expenditures did not decline in step, so that the government debt only mounted (Bajpai 1996). This was financed by borrowing from private lenders. Second, the current account deficit mounted as India continued to import defense-related goods and as oil prices increased. Remittances from other nations dropped off. Third, the drought of 1987–88 resulted in a decline in growth in the agricultural sector and required government subsidies to assist rural residents. A slowdown in industrial growth further worsened both deficits.

These elements were made even starker by a sudden drop-off in foreign exchange. By January 1991, foreign exchange reserves were sufficient to cover the cost of imports for only 13 days (Dholakia 1991). The Indian government was forced to sell several tons of gold in London to obtain foreign exchange. Political uncertainty did not inspire confidence; churning of the leadership, leading eventually to the assassination of Rajiv Gandhi in 1991, increased economic instability (Cerra and Saxena 2000). Rising inflation due to monetization of the deficit in the 1980s eroded purchasing power.

As a result of the crisis, the IMF intervened, providing $1.8 billion in January 1991 under the Compensatory and Contingency Financing Facility and a First Credit Tranche arrangement (Acharya 2002). Under the arrangement, India agreed to reduce imports, but still non-resident Indian (NRI) deposit outflows accelerated in the second quarter of 1991, reflecting a crisis of confidence, as mentioned above. A swathe of measures was instituted in 1991 to reform the economy, in response both to industrial stagnation beginning in 1988, and to the balance-of-payments crisis. India implemented this series of reforms under the New Economic Policy to further liberalize the economy to foreign trade.

The New Economic Policy focused on devaluing the rupee, increasing interest rates, cutting the union budget as well as subsidies and transfers to public enterprises, abolishing many industrial and import licenses, liberalizing trade policy, and strengthening capital markets. Although these kinds of neoliberal measures had a negative impact in other countries, India's economy largely benefited. Foreign investment, exports, infrastructure, and consumption all grew as a result.

In addition, the Planning Commission "planned" its own role reduction. The Planning Commission became, during and after the Eighth Five-Year Plan, a body that constructs indicative plans rather than hard targets. Since then, the electronics sector, the fastest-growing subsector of Indian industry, has been delicensed, and foreign investment has been liberalized (Dutta 2011). Large firms have subcontracted to smaller firms through the adoption of flexible production processes, increasing growth of the informal sector and employment (Rani and Unni 2009).

Central public sector enterprises continue to occupy a relatively large share of state-owned enterprise assets, accounting for 85 percent of these assets in 2005 (Panagariya 2008). Many of these produce basic goods and services such as steel, cement, boilers, and electricity as well as telecommunications and tourism. Privatization has taken the form of share issues, asset sales, and voucher issues. Share issues occurred largely between 1991 and 2000, when the government sold shares of companies to institutional investors. The government carried out more strategic sales between 2000 and 2004 to sell off nonstrategic firms. From 2004 and 2005 onward, privatization slowed down, and the government focused on the sale of minority shares.

To aid growth, particularly in the services and manufacturing sectors, the banking system was reoriented. When India opened up in 1991, the weakness of its financial sector came to light, and the country was unable to attract foreign investment (Mishra et al. 2010). The banks were weighed down with too many non-performing loans and old practices and technology. Private bank branches had been growing prior to reform, but the largest private banks were nationalized in 1980. Measured by percentage of deposits held, government ownership of the banking industry dominated, at 83 percent (Banerjee et al. 2004).

In order to address this issue, the Indian government allowed new banks to enter the market more easily (Panagariya 2008). Six new private banks opened for business in 1994–95, and four more opened for business the following year. Up to 12 foreign bank branches were allowed to enter the market. Improved prudential regulations were also put into place; in 1997, India's central bank implemented the CAMELS (capital, asset quality, management, earnings, liquidity, sensitivity) system of regulation and supervision.

Before India's information technology (IT) explosion, telecommunication bandwidth was scarce and expensive. India was viewed as a difficult location for foreign investment (Dossani and Kenney 2009). The labor force available for foreign investment was viewed as confined to a very small number of activities. However, by 2000, India had deregulated its telecommunications sector, and bandwidth blossomed. The year 2000 (Y2K) problem placed a great burden of demand on businesses for programming capabilities. Indian software service providers were able to offer low-cost programming services. Since 2001, India has focused on growing its IT-enabled services that focus on people-intensive services delivered over telecom networks or the internet. India's provision of data exports (sometimes in the form of voice streams) represents the first time in history that a developing country has stimulated vast growth by providing services (Dossani and Kenney 2009). Before the advent of India's IT service sector export growth, export of data streams and offshoring of high-skill industry was unforeseen (Dossani and Kenney 2009). Figure 5.3 shows new construction for high tech company buildings in Pune, Maharashtra, India.

By 2007, firms were relocating entire processes, rather than just parts of processes, to India. Indian operations therefore became a large component of global operations. Indian corporations adopted foreign quality standards such as the Capability Maturity Model for software process maturity and International Organization for Standardization (ISO) initiatives. What is more, a start-up culture was emerging (Dossani and Kenney 2009).

Outside of the service export sector, much of India's growth has been built on entrepreneurship. Goods and services are sold daily by small businesses, often micro-enterprises with less than nine employees, to domestic customers (*The Economist* 2010). Businesses are often local, particularly since road infrastructure is often insufficient, due either to heavy traffic in urban areas or to unpaved roads in rural areas.

India weathered the global economic crisis of 2008 well. However, since the corporate sector depends to some extent on foreign capital, the crisis

Source: Author's photograph.

*Figure 5.3   New construction of high-tech company buildings in Pune,
            Maharashtra, India*

was not entirely avoided. Trade channels also transmitted the crisis and
resulted in economic weakening at the end of 2008 (Herd et al. 2011). The
impact of drought in 2009 on the agricultural sector exacerbated matters.
Expansionary economic policy assisting the health, education, and infrastructure sectors, and loose monetary policy, helped to combat some of the
worst effects of these negative shocks.

Some economists have pointed out that India passed from an

agriculture-based economy to a service-based economy without experiencing an appropriate industrial revolution, as has been carried out in China. This is in large part due to government restrictions that barred large companies from participating in particular industries, and overregulated the economy (Das 2006). It is also due to extensive labor regulations that prevent large firms from employing unskilled labor; additional requirements on these firms govern the relations between workers and management (Panagariya 2008). A lack of manufacturing jobs has left many low-skilled workers without decent work. While more highly educated Indians are able to obtain jobs in call centers or the IT industry, rural Indians are left to remain in poverty.

This is a serious problem. Small enterprises attempting to enter the formal sector are subject to paying higher wages, enforcing overtime and safety regulations, offering mandatory health insurance at 50 workers or more, losing the right to fire workers at 100 workers or more, and providing pensions for workers (Panagariya 2008). This is far beyond what ordinary business can endure. At the same time, the Industrial Disputes Act restricts large firms from entering unskilled, labor-intensive sectors. Therefore neither small and medium-sized firms nor large firms are able to hire unskilled workers for labor-intensive production in the formal sector, creating a large bottleneck to bringing about industrialization.

Lack of infrastructure is also a serious problem. India lags behind many other Asian nations in terms of railroad infrastructure development, port infrastructure development, and air transport infrastructure development (Sahoo 2011). Highways are narrow and congested, and not of high quality. Fewer than half of all roads are paved. Railway density has not increased in step with railway traffic (Figure 5.4). Pressure on the capacity of port and air transport infrastructure has also created hurdles to development.

India faces barriers to growth in many areas, including poverty, unemployment, education and health care, infrastructure, energy and the environment, and agriculture. The young population will allow the labor force to continue to expand, while the growing middle class will push forward domestic demand as well (Urata 2009). Policies that use the latter positive forces to counteract the former negative forces can help India continue to grow.

In addition, although increased employment among small businesses and households is a positive development, there is evidence of some exploitation of informal workers. Among these, women are predominant and engage in work that is monotonous, repetitive, and low-skill-intensive for little pay. About 81 percent of all female workers and about 46 percent of male workers were home-based workers in 2000–2001 (Rani and Unni 2009).

Source: Public domain photograph.

Figure 5.4   Bombay train station

Today, India faces issues with high inflation and interest rates, while experiencing a slowdown in the pace of economic reforms. A decline in economic growth set in during 2011–12, and continued through 2013. Rising fiscal and current account deficits have once again become a concern. Analysts believe that India's young population, coupled with policies that can improve the lot of the poor, build infrastructure, and reduce the twin deficits, will allow its growth rate to rebound.

FINANCIAL REFORMS

Since the 1990s, the Indian financial system has experienced several important liberalization measures. First, interest rates have been deregulated. Second, banks have allowed for new competition to enter the market. Third, stock exchange and derivatives markets have emerged. And finally, a vibrant microfinance sector has emerged (Herd et al. 2011).

Currently, the Indian financial system consists of commercial banks, including public sector and private sector banks, foreign banks, and co-operative banks; financial institutions at the central and state levels, as well as the State Industrial Development Corporation; non-banking financial companies; and capital market intermediaries (Banerjee 2011). Public sector banks are subject to intense regulation by the Reserve Bank of India (RBI).

Constraints continue to exist in the financial sector, however. Lending from the dominant public sector banks is rigid, as the RBI continues to direct funds, resulting in underlending to private enterprises (Banerjee et al. 2004). What is more, the government bond market is underdeveloped, and the regulatory framework for the financial system is outdated. Further financial sector reform is therefore necessary to expand economic growth.

RURAL REFORMS

India's rural sector also underwent development after reforms began. The 1949 constitution gave states the power to enact land reforms (Besley and Burgess 2000). Therefore states have been carrying out land reform since independence, into the 1990s and 2000s. As landlessness is the main cause of rural poverty, most land reform Acts were aimed toward poverty reduction, and in this they appear to be successful, or at the minimum to be correlated to poverty reduction.

The Green Revolution positively impacted India in the 1960s, varying in success at each locale according to government policy and weather conditions. Government policy that assisted the Green Revolution includes lifting restrictions on specific imports and developing and disseminating complementary inputs. State-level governments have been responsible for irrigation, power, agriculture, health, co-operatives, rural development, and much more (Fan et al. 1999). Most expenditures, then, on agriculture and rural areas are undertaken by state governments. The expenditures that grew most rapidly between 1970 and 1993 were on welfare and rural development. State development expenditure accounted for 75 percent of the budget in 1993, with social and economic services each comprising about half of development spending.

Crop yields have expanded greatly, particularly since 1980, and rural incomes have increased based on better farm productivity as well as increased opportunities for off-farm income (Foster and Rosenzweig 2004). The sales and distribution system for agricultural goods was changed, from a non-transparent system in which prices were privately negotiated with state-owned Agricultural Produce Marketing Committees and produce was sold to wholesalers, to a more competitive system in which farmers have other channels through which to sell their goods (Panagariya 2008). Farmers were allowed to sell their goods directly to consumers, to licensed firms, or to a contract farming sponsor from their fields. New entities for buying agricultural goods rose up immediately thereafter.

The number of villages with banks increased. Through a government program that attempted to reduce poverty in rural areas, families with incomes below the poverty line were able to obtain a bank loan that was subsidized by the government (Mahajan and Laskar 2010). Although more than Rs 19 500 crore was lent between 1982 and November 1998, the Integrated Rural Development Programme was successful in assisting only 20 percent of borrowers to cross the poverty line.

The Agricultural and Rural Debt Relief Scheme sought to provide debt relief to rural residents of up to Rs 10 000 per borrower, starting in 1990. However, through this program, rural borrowers seeking debt relief were labeled as "defaulters" by banks and prevented from obtaining loans in the future. In 2003, rural lending was again emphasized in a policy that required commercial bank branches to enroll at least 100 new farmers as borrowers per year. Some of the lending was risky, and in 2008, Rs 72 000 crore were written off as bad debts.

CASE OF ANDHRA PRADESH

Andhra Pradesh, an underdeveloped state in south India, has been noted by many analysts as a leader in modern economic development. The state has grown rapidly during and since the reforms of the 1990s, using policy campaigns that were successful in creating an enthusiastic drive toward change (Mooij 2007). Andhra Pradesh integrated economic development policies into its larger governance program. GDP per capita grew in Andhra Pradesh at a faster rate than that of India as a whole from the beginning of reform onward (Centre for Economic and Social Studies 2007). In addition, the state enjoyed the largest proportional increase in economic and business freedom between 2005 and 2009.

Andhra Pradesh is home to about 70 million people and is agriculture-based. During the 1980s, the government put in place a well-received food distribution program which was cut in 1989 when the ruling political party, the Telugu Desam Party (TDP), lost in the elections, but was reinstated in 1994 when the TDP was elected once again (Mooij 2007). The party was in power until 2004.

Andhra Pradesh was also a first-mover in bringing about technology-based industrial growth after it became possible in 1991 (Mooij 2007). The government set about creating schemes to attract non-resident Indians, establishing a software technology park in Hyderabad. Hyderabad was promoted as an IT city and currently houses more than 800 companies.

Software exports increased from about US$13 million in 1995–96 to more than US$1 billion in 2003–04. A new Indian Institute for Information Technology was opened in 1998 (Ramachandraiah and Bawa 2000).

Public expenditure in Andhra Pradesh also increased in the mid-1990s, particularly in the areas of poverty alleviation (subsidizing rice, and the expansion of District Poverty programs), health reforms (to upgrade services), and rural development (the Janmabhoomi program). The government also attempted to privatize power and health care and to improve government performance through assessment. Road and power infrastructures were developed. Finally, the state government, until the 1990s, focused on improving irrigation; the policy was reversed in the 1990s and then reinstated in recent years in order to improve the status of agriculture.

Growth in Andhra Pradesh took place mainly in the service sector, and secondarily in the industrial sector, particularly in construction-related activities. The agricultural sector has lagged behind. While a middle class emerged in urban areas, farmers continued to suffer and even commit suicide due to severe deprivation, excess debt, and food price inflation. The urban–rural divide has therefore increased income disparities. Regional disparities due to uneven growth have also emerged, with seven districts of Telangana and two districts of north coastal Andhra displaying higher than state average growth rates, and all the districts in south coastal Andhra and Rayalaseema, three districts of Telangana and one district of north coastal Andhra demonstrating lower than state average growth rates (Centre for Economic and Social Studies 2007).

The goal in any development situation is to "climb up" the ladder of life. In Kamalapur, Andhra Pradesh, the ladder of life is as follows:

- Step 6. Landlords: Employ servants to cultivate their lands; own huge buildings; command high respect in the village. Only 2 families in the village are at this step.
- Step 5. Big farmers: Own 15–25 acres of ancestral property and 4–5 houses, plus motorbikes, fans, and cattle. Cultivate crops like cotton, chilies, soybeans; land gives good yields. Banks provide loans. Educate their children and can live without working.
- Step 4. Medium farmers: Own 5 acres of land. Some have government jobs. Own houses with cement walls, cattle, borehole wells, televisions, fans and cots. Eat fine rice. Women wear gold ornaments, and children study in good schools. Banks provide loans.
- Step 3. Small farmers: Own 3–5 acres of land. Own houses and cattle but do not have wells. Their lives depend on rainfall. During periods of drought, they migrate to towns or work as agricultural labor. They are a little bit educated.
- Step 2. Laborers and small landholdings: Own 1–2 acres of land. Land is rarely fertile, and they have to do wage labor; some serve as bonded labor.

Don't have proper houses. They are illiterate and belong to backward and scheduled castes. Every day is a struggle.

- Step 1. Landless laborers: Lack proper food, proper clothes, and proper houses. Don't find work regularly and are able to work only 12–15 days a month. They are usually illiterate, and their children cannot attend school because they have to work. (Narayan et al. 2009)

The study found that some households stagnated in their position, while others were able to move up the ladder of life (Narayan et al. 2009). Another recent study found that of 36 villages in three districts of Andhra Pradesh, 14 percent escaped poverty, while 12 percent fell into poverty (Krishna 2006). The villages defined local poverty as being unable to purchase food, make minor house repairs, make regular debt payments, and purchase some clothing to wear outside the home. Reasons for escaping poverty include diversify income sources and land improvements. Reasons for falling into poverty include high health care costs, drought, high social costs (payment for funerals, and so on) and repayment of high-interest debts.

Although Andhra Pradesh has improved greatly in recent years, it still lags behind in some areas. The state is one of the worst performers in its treatment of women. The state recorded the highest number, out of all states, of crimes against women (Masoodi and Ratan 2014). These include rapes, kidnapping, dowry deaths, domestic abuse by husband and in-laws, and assault. Dash (2006) conducted interviews in five villages of Andhra Pradesh on violence against women, finding that the most common age group of women to suffer from domestic violence was between 25 and 30 years. More than half of the women in the study lived in one-room homes and close to half were verbally abused, slapped, kicked, or beaten. Another issue is child poverty, with about one-third of children experiencing stunted growth. Undernutrition is higher in rural than in urban areas, and children from Scheduled Tribes in Andhra Pradesh are the worst off. In response to gender and child disadvantages, Andhra Pradesh has implemented the Girl Child Protection Scheme to empower and protect the rights of girls (Galab et al. 2011).

POLITICAL ECONOMY OF REFORM

The pre-1991 period informed the post-1991 reform period, as India became independent, but implemented policies that resulted in growth stagnation. India transitioned out of colonialism in 1947 and chose Jawaharlal Nehru as its first prime minister. Nehru was considered to be the political heir of Mahatma Gandhi, as he was a leader in India's

Source: Photograph in public domain.

Figure 5.5   Jawaharlal Nehru and Mahatma Gandhi, 1942

independence movement, and aimed at uniting India across differences in language and religion (see Figure 5.5).

Prime Minister Nehru was a beloved leader who controlled the Congress Party. He held a sophisticated, modern view of what India could become, and emphasized building heavy industry as well as cottage industry in the 1950s (Panagariya 2008). However, he was biased against competition, which created barriers to future growth. As Das (2002) writes:

> Nehru taught us all our good and bad habits. He taught us to be liberal and tolerant (of Muslims, especially). He inculcated in us a respect for democracy

and a loathing for feudal behavior. He infected us with his idealism. But he also reinforced our prejudice against businessmen and profit. We never learned about the virtues of entrepreneurship and competition and we paid dearly for this blind spot.

Nehru's economy had focused less on the factory goods sector and elevated the investment goods sector. Under his rule, the government directed businesses to where they could invest and what they could produce. The government was involved in production and selling as well as regulation of the private sector (Wheelan 2005). The government expanded in size, and dominated the economy.

Nehru's death occurred in May 1964, and Lal Bahadur Shastri in turn briefly became the Prime Minister. While Nehru's polices had emphasized industrialization, Shastri placed more focus on agriculture (Panagariya 2008). In January 1966, Indira Gandhi, Nehru's daughter, became Prime Minister until 1977, and again from 1980 until her assassination in October 1984. The Gandhians were in favor of increasing protection to traditional industries and were hostile to modern industries (Das 2002). This prevented modernization of the economy and economic reform.

When famine occurred in 1965–67, Indira Gandhi faced a contentious relationship with the United States, which provided food aid subject to constant threats of suspension (Panagariya 2008). The US forced its way into domestic policy in this way, leaving Gandhi and the Indian public with ill feelings toward the Western nation. This reinforced Gandhi's socialist beliefs and moved her further away from capitalist practices. Oil price shocks in the 1970s that brought high inflation persisted since the economy continued to be highly controlled.

Until this point, India's political leadership was poised against free markets in practice. The prominence of the government in economic activities, extensive regulation of private businesses, inward-looking import substitution policies, and trade protectionism resulted in slow growth. Nehru and Indira Gandhi were both a part of this, resulting in three decades of underdevelopment. Things changed somewhat with the advent of Rajiv Gandhi to power.

Rajiv Gandhi was the first post-independence leader who implemented growth-oriented reforms. As Prime Minister, he reduced licenses and quotas and modernized the telecommunications system. Gandhi also increased science and technology initiatives. Growth took off, but fiscal and current account debt mounted, setting the stage for the debt crisis of the early 1990s.

The debt crisis occurred while the V.P. Singh government was collapsing in 1990, and a very weak government, under Chandra Shekhar, came to power (Jha 2002). Chandra Shekhar was not able to put into place structural adjustment measures that he had proposed, and he resigned in March 1991. The country had a caretaker government for three months thereafter, as the crisis worsened.

Narasimha Rao came into power in June 1991 and launched liberalization reforms. The reforms supported by the International Monetary Fund (IMF) led to some economic stabilization and to a rise in foreign currency reserves, as the current account deficit declined (Jha 2002). The Rao government, like other governments before it, was unable to put into place reforms without full political consensus, since as a democratic entity it was forced to service both the external constituency of creditors and the internal constituency of voters. Rao was able to devalue the rupee and consolidate the exchange rate, reduce import duties and quotas, and lower the excise duty. However, he was defeated for re-election in 1996. Das (2002) attributes this to his lack of confidence and inability to embrace his own accomplishments.

India's political economy of reform has reflected its status as a democratic nation. Reform took place gradually and as a result of consensus created in committees and discussions (Panagariya 2008). Rao's government took pains to build consensus by slowing the pace of reforms, properly sequencing reforms, strengthening existing state institutions rather than shutting them down, and acting transparently (Jha 2002). Even so, however, consensus was largely created among the elite at the top of the social and political structure, rather than the masses at the bottom.

Guha (2007) categorizes the economic debate today as that between reformists and populists. While reformists believe in free market forces, and decline of state participation in the economy, populists argue for restrictions on foreign investment and the protection of workers and small business owners. The arguments are carried out in the media, in parliament, and in the streets.

DATA AND PATTERNS OF GROWTH

India's GDP per capita has increased rapidly since the 1990s (Figure 5.6). This illustrates the positive impact of economic reforms on the average standard of living. However, although GDP growth itself has increased in India, its pattern of growth may be of concern since it is mainly in the skilled services and manufacturing sectors. As Kochhar et al. (2006) emphasize, the pattern of growth stemmed from policies that originated before reforms began. Reforms, then, provided growth opportunities within this context. Policies that created this pattern include: (1) government investment in capital goods; with (2) regulatory constraints on very

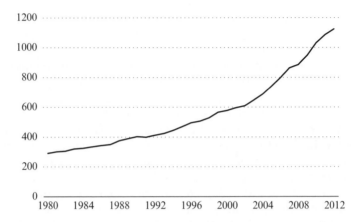

Source: World Development Indicators Database, World Bank.

Figure 5.6   India's GDP per capita (constant 2005 USD)

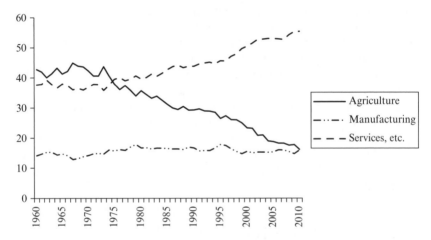

Source: World Development Indicators Database, World Bank.

Figure 5.7   India's sector value added (% of GDP)

large enterprises; and (3) rigid labor laws that constrained labor-intensive
practices. By 1981, India's share in services was below that of other developing countries.

After reforms were implemented, India's skill-intensive sector grew.
Skill-intensive, rather than unskilled labor-intensive, activities grew, particularly in the information and communication technology (ICT) industry.

The vast majority of the Indian population engages in relatively unskilled labor, and low literacy rates permeate society. Hence the pattern of growth has not built upon India's comparative advantage in low-skilled labor. Much of this low-skilled labor (about 60 percent) continues to be employed, at poverty wage, in the agricultural sector.

This can be viewed in Figure 5.7, which shows that India experienced a dramatic increase in the size of the services sector (from 37 percent to 55 percent) and a large decline in the size of the agricultural sector (from 43 percent to 16 percent) between 1960 and 2010, while the manufacturing sector generally remained the same size.

In addition, much of India's economy is not part of the formal economy. That is, many businesses are unregistered, and therefore regulations applied to this sector are not enforced. The unorganized sector is not negligible. In 1999–2000, the unorganized sector accounted for 39 percent of sector GDP in the manufacturing sector, and 49 percent of sector GDP in the services sector; and 96 percent of total employment in all sectors (Bosworth et al. 2007). Because GDP has grown largely in formal sectors, many workers have been left out of the growth process. This is of grave concern with regard to future development.

India's informal sector includes a wide range of activities. Part of it acts as subcontractors to the formal sector, particularly in the manufacturing industry, and a fraction of that has succeeded in reaping modernization benefits from acting as subcontractors to the formal sector (Moreno-Monroy et al. 2012). Other informal sector workers act as day laborers, paid domestic workers, or employees in informal enterprises.

Inequality between states also illustrates the problem of unbalanced growth. One can also compare states in terms of the Human Development Index (Table 5.1), which contains measures of health, education, and standard of living.

India's growth is remarkable yet unbalanced. I discuss India's struggle with poverty and inequality in the following chapter.

BOTTOM LINE

India's economic growth has been remarkable since reform began in 1991. Ushered in by a debt crisis, the liberalization reforms were surprisingly successful. Much of India's growth has been generated by growth in the services sector, particularly in information and communications technology. This has biased India's pattern of growth. However, India's leadership continues to attempt to improve rural development, with some success. The current slowdown in economic growth has been attributed

Table 5.1   Indian states' Human Development Index, 1996 and 2006

State	HDI 2006	HDI 1996
Chandigarh	0.784	0.723
Goa	0.764	0.709
Kerala	0.764	0.736
Delhi	0.740	0.687
Puducherry	0.725	0.676
Andaman & Nicobar Islands	0.708	0.678
Manipur	0.702	0.610
Nagaland	0.700	0.653
Daman & Diu	0.700	0.569
Lakshadweep	0.697	0.686
Maharashtra	0.689	0.629
Mizoram	0.688	0.618
Dadra & Nagar Haveli	0.677	0.573
Punjab	0.668	0.621
Himachal Pradesh	0.667	0.590
Tamil Nadu	0.666	0.589
Sikkim	0.665	0.582
Tripura	0.663	0.579
Uttarakhand	0.652	0.487
Haryana	0.643	0.570
West Bengal	0.642	0.573
Gujarat	0.634	0.574
Meghalaya	0.629	0.595
Karnataka	0.622	0.558
Assam	0.595	0.543
Jammu & Kashmir	0.590	0.542
Andhra Pradesh	0.585	0.519
Jharkhand	0.574	0.434
Chhattisgarh	0.549	0.451
Arunachal Pradesh	0.547	0.549
Rajasthan	0.541	0.472
Orissa	0.537	0.461
Madhya Pradesh	0.529	0.433
Uttar Pradesh	0.528	0.458
Bihar	0.507	0.430

Source: Ministry of Women and Child Development, Government of India (2009).

to a decline in the pace of economic reforms, but additional policies are expected.

DISCUSSION QUESTIONS

1. How did reform in India unfold, and what are the reasons that it developed in this way?
2. Describe and discuss barriers to development in India. How have these barriers stood in the way of proper reform?
3. What rural reforms were most beneficial to rural residents? Justify your answer.
4. What impact did India's political leadership have on the reform process?
5. Discuss India's twin deficits and how they came about.
6. What sort of reforms did India implement after 1991, and were they effective?
7. Describe India's informal sector and its impact on the reform process.
8. What was the impact of the Green Revolution in India?
9. How did India's infrastructure hinder its early development?
10. How might India have started large-scale reforms before its debt crisis occurred?
11. Did India truly industrialize? Explain why or why not.

6. Poverty and inequality in China, India, and Japan

Poverty is the condition of being poor, through income, health, education, or choice. China, India, and Japan have all experienced a dramatic reduction in poverty and an increase in the standard of living. Still, poverty remains a problem in China and India. At the same time, inequality is on the rise. Inequality is a relative measure, looking at the gap between society's rich and poor. Inequality is increasing in China and India, and has created resentment among the poor of the burgeoning wealthy and middle classes. In this chapter, we discuss the situation of poverty and inequality in each country, looking first at poverty and inequality in development theory.

POVERTY AND INEQUALITY IN DEVELOPMENT THEORY

Poverty and inequality can be viewed through the lens of development theory that focuses on why some households fail to raise their standard of living. First, theory has informed the way in which poverty is measured. This measurement has changed from one of relative income gaps to multidimensional indices of poverty. The theory behind this states that poverty is not merely a measure of how much money a household takes in, but also of individuals' well-being or capabilities.

Amartya Sen (Box 6.1) believed that well-being should be understood in terms of how much freedom individuals have rather than in terms of gross domestic product (GDP) per capita, which he viewed as merely a means to an end. Sen viewed wealth as potentially inefficient, and saw development planning as essential. Individual freedoms, he believed, were embodied in functionings, from basic functionings such as being able to feed oneself, to more sophisticated functionings such as being able to obtain self-respect (Sen 1990). Capabilities were derived from functionings and reflect a person's freedom to choose how they live. Sen's analysis induces scholars to examine a range of indicators for their poverty implications, as opposed to looking solely at income. Going even further, Sen's measurement of

---

BOX 6.1   AMARTYA SEN

 Amartya Sen was born in Dhaka, now the capital of Bangladesh, as the son of a university professor. He studied economics and philosophy at Trinity College, Cambridge. Sen combined the two fields to write about social choice in *Collective Choice and Social Welfare* (1970). These topics were later applied to poverty and inequality in the concept of capabilities, focusing on individual freedoms. In this work, Sen proposed an alternative measure of national success other than economic measures alone (Sen 1998).

Source: Photograph in public domain.

---

poverty in terms of freedom and capabilities can be contrasted to other approaches that look at utility, or pleasure, as the poor may be forced to derive pleasure from the smallest things. The focus on freedom also overcomes the problem of accounting for how different people in similar circumstances may choose different life circumstances. Measures of their real freedom helps to surmount this problem.

There are also other theories surrounding poverty and inequality. One strain of poverty theory has attempted to revise views of the poor as a distinct group, rather than a socially constructed phenomenon (Yapa 1998). This theory states that one must examine wider social conditions that give rise to poverty to understand how poverty is created. Production relations result in poverty for some rather than others. Another type of poverty theory makes the distinction between transient and chronic poverty, where the transient poor are those who can be classified as poor in some periods and not in others (Hulme and Shepherd 2003; Baulch and Hoddinott 2000).

Another widely cited poverty theory was proposed by Ravallion (1988), in which he finds an expected value of a poverty measure which results from changes in a welfare indicator. This theory has been applied to a number of different countries (Ravallion 1988; Jalan and Ravallion 1998; Gibson 2001). Ravallion's (1988) model follows.

Household welfare is an increasing function of random variable η, such as good weather. Poverty is a function of η, $P(\eta)$, and is strictly decreasing and twice differentiable. Household welfare y depends also on x, such that:

$$y = \varphi(x,\eta),(\varphi_x > 0, \varphi_\eta > 0) \tag{6.1}$$

where φ is at least twice differentiable. A simple version of this function is:

$$y = \varphi[x + v(\eta)] \tag{6.2}$$

where x is steady-state income and v is some increasing function. Poverty measurements can be written as a sum of different measurements, such as the headcount index, for example, such that:

$$P(\eta) = \int_0^z p(y,z)\,dG(y), (p_y < 0, p_z > 0) \tag{6.3}$$

where z is the fixed poverty line, G is the distribution of y, and poverty of each individual is represented by $p(y, z)$. This equation can also be stated as:

$$P(\eta) = \int_0^{\zeta(\eta,z)} p[\varphi(x,\eta),z]\,dF(x) \tag{6.4}$$

where ζ is the poverty line in terms of x and F is the distribution function of x.

From the last equation, Ravallion (1988) derives a number of poverty measures, including the headcount index and the Atkinson class of poverty measures, as functions of welfare. He proposes that an increase in risk will increase the expected value of the poverty headcount ratio or Atkinson poverty measures under certain conditions. The model shows how riskiness of income (here affected by weather) can increase poverty.

Second, inequality theory has various explanations for how inequality arises. One theory finds that inequality persists due to credit market imperfections since poor individuals lack collateral and other types of positive indicators to obtain loans in the credit market. Another explanation for inequality finds that quality of institutions impact distribution and vice versa (Chong and Gradstein 2007). Using the cases of Russia in transition, where political and income inequality blocked implementation of good institutions, and of some Latin American countries, in which the interests of ruling elites and large corporations subvert the power of smaller businesses, giving rise to a large informal sector, Chong and Gradstein create a theoretical model in which individuals allocate resources among consumption, productive investment, and unproductive investment in rent seeking.

Galor and Zeira (1993) lay out a model of income distribution and inequality which determines the future poverty status of households. In this model, individuals live for two periods in overlapping generations, and can be unskilled in two periods, or unskilled in the first period and skilled in the second period.

Production in the skilled labor sector is:

$$Y_t^s = F(K_t, L_t^s) \tag{6.5}$$

where Y_t^s is output at time t, K_t is capital input, and L_t^s is labor input. Production in the unskilled labor sector is:

$$Y_t^n = w_n \cdot L_t^n \tag{6.6}$$

where Y_t^n and L_t^n are output and unskilled labor, and w_n is the marginal productivity of unskilled labor. Individuals live two periods in overlapping generations, with utility functions as follows:

$$u = \alpha \log c + (1 - \alpha) \log b \tag{6.7}$$

where c indicates consumption in the second period, b is bequest, and $0 < \alpha < 1$. Individuals vary in bequest, and not in abilities or preferences.

Capital is assumed to be mobile, and the world interest rate $r > 0$ and constant. Borrowers can evade repayment by moving, but this is costly. While lenders spend amount z tracking the borrowers, borrowers can default at a cost of βz, where $\beta > 1$.

Because firms can borrow at interest rate r and since there are no adjustment costs to investment:

$$F_K(K_t, L_t^s) = r \tag{6.8}$$

The constant capital–labor ratio determines the wage of skilled labor, which is constant and depends only on r and technology.

An individual who chooses to work as an unskilled laborer has lifetime utility:

$$U_n(x) = \log[(x + w_n)(1 + r) + w_n] + \varepsilon \tag{6.9}$$

where $\varepsilon = \alpha \log \alpha + (1 - \alpha) \log(1 - \alpha)$. The unskilled worker leaves a bequest as follows:

$$b_n(x) = (1 - \alpha)[(1 + r)(x + w_n) + w_n] \tag{6.10}$$

The skilled worker with $x \geq h$ has lifetime utility:

$$U_s(x) = \log[w_s + (x - h)(1 + r)] + \varepsilon \tag{6.11}$$

and bequest:

$$b_s(x) = (1 - \alpha)[w_s + (x - h)(1 + r)] \tag{6.12}$$

While a skilled worker with $x < h$ has lifetime utility:

$$U_s(x) = \log[w_s + (x - h)(1 + i)] + \varepsilon \qquad (6.13)$$

where i is the borrowing interest rate. This individual leaves a bequest of:

$$b_s(x) = (1 - \alpha)[w_s + (x - h)(1 + i)] \qquad (6.14)$$

Therefore borrowers will invest in human capital as long as $U_s(x) \geq U_n(x)$, that is:

$$x \geq f = \frac{1}{i - r}[w_n(2 + r) + h(1 + i) - w_s] \qquad (6.15)$$

Individuals who inherit wealth smaller than f choose to work as unskilled; therefore, the amount of inheritance determines whether or not individuals will invest in human capital. The initial distribution of wealth therefore also influences economic performance, determining aggregate output.

Galor and Zeira go on to show that under a dynamic equilibrium, the economy converges to different levels of wealth for skilled and unskilled workers, and again the long-run equilibrium is dependent on initial conditions of wealth. In an economy with many unskilled workers who receive less than the bequest at the "tipping point" (which determines whether individuals will invest in human capital), inequality arises as an unequal distribution of income is propagated. Initial factors, and the initial distribution of wealth, are critical in determining the level of inequality.

POVERTY IN INDIA

Despite increased economic growth after the reform period of the 1990s, India remains home to 20 percent of the world's poorest people, living on under $1 per day (Siggel 2010). India's poor are largely found in rural areas and tend to be of lower castes (Polaski et al. 2008). Indeed, the persistence of the caste system cannot be ignored, even though both religious and political mandates have striven to eliminate caste discrimination. Caste had existed for centuries but was solidified into a system under British colonial rule (Rai 2009). This system of social and economic hierarchy is enforced by caste violence, particularly against the "untouchables."

Poverty has been accompanied by child malnutrition. A 2006 UNICEF study found that 47 percent of children under five were underweight. Malnourishment within the population as a whole is also a concern.

Protein malnourishment is twice as high in India as in sub-Saharan Africa (Kapila 2008b).

Education was a large cause of poverty before liberalization. In the 1990s, however, the government attempted to universalize education through the District Primary Education Programme, implemented in 250 districts in which female literacy was below average. Later, the Sarva Shiksa Abhiyan program was put in place, and funds for education were increased (Guha 2007). Non-governmental organizations (NGOs) have also worked to improve education, helping those, for example, who entered school late, or who live in slums. Variations in school quality, however, can be dramatic between and within states.

India's poverty situation is desperate in some regions. For some farmers, food intake has declined so severely that they have been driven to suicide. More than 1000 farmers committed suicide between 1998 and 2002 (Vakulabharanam 2005). Policy reforms that swept India attempted at first to relieve poverty, as noted above, but the heart of the reforms affected the industrial sector. The rural, agrarian sector was left behind.

India agreed to liberalize agriculture in 1994 under the Agreement on Agriculture. Agriculture liberalization in India remains a goal of the World Trade Organization. As an example, in the state of Andhra Pradesh, export-oriented farming and capital-invested agriculture became a goal (Vakulabharanam 2005). At the same time that liberalization was occurring, many government input subsidies were cut. Power subsidies were cut, adversely affecting farmers with small landholdings.

There has been some debate about whether agricultural productivity improvements have had a large impact on rural poverty reduction. Rural areas that have been successful in reducing poverty through agriculture have benefited more from irrigation infrastructure, due to better agro-climatic conditions combined with appropriate policies (Palmer-Jones and Sen 2003).

Land reform is one policy that has had a positive impact on poverty reduction, since landlessness is a key determinant of poverty and low social status (Deininger et al. 2009). Reform had three main goals: (1) elimination of intermediaries (that is, landholding by *zamindari*), just after independence; (2) improvement of tenure contracts by registering tenants and restricting the amount of rent paid; and (3) restriction of landholdings through ceiling laws that set a maximum amount of land that could be owned before it is redistributed to the poor. State-level passage of laws that required land reform did not necessarily translate into action.

Land redistribution programs were implemented at the state level, rather than the central level, resulting in positive impacts on income, consumption, and asset accumulation, according to a study performed by Deininger et al. (2009). Deininger et al. base the findings on data collected from two rounds of the ARIS/REDS10 survey conducted by India's National Council for Applied Economic Research (NCAER) in 1982 and 1999. Still, a lack of clear, state-guaranteed property titles presents a barrier to borrowing against land collateral and clarifying ownership (Panagariya 2008). This, coupled with restrictions on land use and conversion, has resulted in the lack of ability by landowners to efficiently utilize land as an asset. What is more, the ongoing ability of the government to seize land for its own use or for assignment to another party such as a corporation has resulted in violent protests.

There is also debate as to whether non-agricultural reforms have exacerbated or dampened poverty. At the country level, poverty in terms of caloric intake has declined, while in some states poverty increased over the period of the 1990s, particularly in rural areas (Kumar et al. 2009). The debate about whether reforms have had a positive or a negative impact on poverty stems from different interpretations of the poverty statistics (Siggel 2010).[1] Deaton and Drèze (2002) proposed an adjustment that would allow the 55th round of surveying by the National Sample Survey Organization (NSSO) to be comparable to the 50th, the previous large round using a specific group of goods that remained the same between both rounds, and that is highly correlated to total expenditure (from Siggel 2010). They also use, rather than the Consumer Price Index for Agricultural Labourers (CPI-AL) used by the official estimate, a Tornqvist price index. Deaton and Drèze find overall poverty estimates similar to official estimates, but a higher poverty gap between urban and rural areas.

The Planning Commission uses the United Nations Development Programme's (UNDP) human development framework in its National Human Development Report (NHDR) (Siggel 2010). This accounts for additional measures of well-being such as education and health. The Planning Commission uses somewhat different indicators of education, health, and command over resources. For education, it uses literacy rate at age seven and intensity of formal education, rather than school enrollment and adult literacy rate. For health, it uses life expectancy at age one and the infant mortality rate instead of only life expectancy at birth. For economic well-being, it uses per capita real consumption expenditure adjusted for inequality instead of real GDP per capita in purchasing power parity (PPP) dollars (Siggel 2010). Equal weights are given to each of these measures. The resulting index, the Human Poverty Index (HPI), is translated into the Human Development Index (HDI) by Siggel (2010), who shows that Bihar performed the worst in 1981, 1991, and 2001, while Kerala performed the best over the period.

Siggel finds very slightly improving circumstances in terms of well-being between 1981 and 1991, along with increasing inequality. For the whole period, about a third of the population lived in the three poorest states: Bihar, Uttar Pradesh, and Madhya Pradesh in 1981 and 1991; and Bihar, Uttar Pradesh, and Assam in 2001 (Siggel 2010). Fifteen percent or less of the population lived in the three richest states, which were Kerala, Punjab, and Maharashtra in 1981; and Kerala, Punjab, and Tamil Nadu in 1991 and 2001. Siggel still finds poverty reduction, although at a lower pace than other authors predict.

A new census on those living under the poverty line was approved in 2011 and was carried out by Ministry of Rural Development, Housing, and Rural Poverty Alleviation, and the Registrar General of India (SECC 2015). The census gathered information on poverty, caste, and religion. Electronic handheld devices were used to collect data. This combined Socio Economic and Caste Census was carried out once more in 2015.

INEQUALITY IN INDIA

Indians maintained an attitude of austerity with regard to consumerism in the early years of independence, but particularly with the liberalization measures in the 1990s, consumerism expanded greatly (Guha 2007). This gave rise to a new middle class, and to a widening inequality, with some able to afford luxury goods, and others still barely able to consume a sufficient amount of daily calories.

Because India's growth has been concentrated in skill-intensive sectors, while poverty persists, economic inequality has been on the rise. Rising inequality harms the growth process politically and economically by reducing popular support for growth policies, and by reducing or maintaining low levels of opportunities for poorer individuals.

Rural casual labor is the largest segment of the Indian workforce (Sarkar and Mehta 2010). Wages for rural casual labor as compared to urban casual labor have been declining over time, as shown in Table 6.1.

Looking at urban or rural areas alone, the Gini coefficient is higher by about ten points in urban areas. That is to say, the range of inequality in urban areas is higher than that in rural areas. The state with the highest urban and rural Ginis was Tamil Nadu in 1999–2000 (Sen and Himanshu 2004). The Gini corresponding to inequality across all India, whether rural or urban, has been rising as well.

Women also face gender discrimination, despite the fact that the constitution of India lays out equal rights for women, while the Tenth Plan, from 2002 to 2007, strove to provide social empowerment, economic empowerment, and gender justice for women (Ganesamurthy 2008). Women often

Table 6.1   Rural and urban labor, wage per day

		Wage per day (rupees)		
		1983	1993	2004
Regular	Rural (R)	40	57	78
	Urban (U)	59	77	101
	Total	51	69	92
	R/U ratio	1.5	1.4	1.3
Casual	Rural (R)	17	21	29
	Urban (U)	24	30	36
	Total	17	22	30
	R/U ratio	1.4	1.4	1.2

Source: Sarkar and Mehta (2010).

do not attend secondary school or high school; today there are more than 200 million illiterate women in India (Velkoff 1998).[2] What is more, women have faced declining real wages in rural regions through the 1980s and the 1990s (Albin 2008). Women dominate the unpaid labor segment of the economy despite their rural or urban status. In order to combat gender discrimination to some degree, the government, working with NGOs and civil society, has attempted to promote the status of women in small subsistence farming households, as well as in the garment and textiles industry.

POVERTY IN CHINA

Like India, China continues to face both high levels of poverty and growing inequality. The number of people living in extreme poverty has declined, but the difference between income growth in rural versus urban areas is stark. Income has grown several percentage points faster per year in urban areas than in rural areas (Naughton 2007).

China's reported statistics are unreliable since incidences of poverty may be understated and reports of productivity may be overstated. Due to difficulties with data and varying measures of poverty, the positive impact of reforms on poverty reduction was, for some time, overstated. China's participation in the International Comparison Program (ICP), which collects primary data on prices for an internationally comparable list of goods, revealed in 2005 that poverty reduction has been overstated (Chen and Ravallion 2008). There was found to be 130 million more poor (in consumption) using this data and the standard of the international poverty line at $1.25 per day at 2005 purchasing power parity. The study also found larger poverty reduction since 1981 than official figures had indicated.

As in India, poverty tends to be a rural phenomenon, and poverty begets undernutrition and vice versa. China's improvements in the 1980s with the household responsibility system, in which farmers were allowed to farm and keep the yields of their own lands, helped some farmers move out of poverty. At the same time, as prices on agricultural products were lifted and the supply of farm inputs was increased, farmers were able to produce more food, which gradually was allowed to be sold on the market (Naughton 2007). Poverty reduction declined in the late 1990s due to lack of resources in remote areas, and environmental degradation. The rural standard of living has risen from US$20 per capita in 1978 to US$604 in 2007 (*Beijing Review* 2008), accompanied by a rising cost of living, particularly on health expenditures. Large households and households with non-working members are more likely to be poor (Meng et al. 2007). Food price increases over 1986–93 also contributed to poverty. State sector lay-offs between 1994 and 2000 contributed to poverty increases over this period.

Contributing to persistent rural poverty is the presence of thin land markets and the prospect for administrative reallocation of land, which prevents farmers from being able to sell their land for a profit (Jalan and Ravallion 2002).

A story told by Anthony Kunn (2006) with National Public Radio (NPR) illustrates rural poverty:

> The village of Dalaochi is the only settlement along a stretch of road in mountainous northwest Gansu province. The village's mud-brick buildings seem to be a continuation of the khaki-colored earth on which they're built. Farmer Wei Zijian squats at the entrance to the village, sipping from a jar of green tea. The reason he's not out planting wheat, corn and potatoes is simple. "They won't grow," he says. "There hasn't been enough rain this year." In fact, there hasn't been enough rain here for 10 years . . . Life in poverty-stricken Dalaochi exemplifies how far some rural areas lag behind China's cities. It also illustrates the tremendous challenges the Chinese government faces in improving life for Chinese farmers.
>
> To eke out a living in these barren badlands of soaring cliffs and plunging ravines would appear to be an amazing feat of survival. But people have farmed the land here for at least 2000 years, terracing the hills into a landscape of giant steps. On the rare occasions when it does rain, locals catch water in concrete cisterns built outside each home . . . Agriculture doesn't yield enough to live on, and Wei and other locals subsist on government handouts. Traditionally, the majority of loess plateau inhabitants lived in caves dug into the hillsides . . . The good news for Wei is that he's moved out of his cave and into a new, one-room house just steps away. He bought it for about $350. Another source of pride for Wei is his two teenage children's academic achievement; he beams as he displays their certificates for excellence in school. Wei himself never learned to read or

write. To pay for the children's school fees, Wei says his wife has been working as a migrant laborer for the past 10 years. She makes $70 to $80 a month weaving grain sacks, twice as much as what Wei earns from farming . . .

Things have definitely improved in Dalaochi. In the past decade, the village has gotten electricity and most families now have televisions. Yet many older village residents have never seen a train or airplane. Most are so poor they can't afford to eat meat except at Chinese New Year. China's government has recently outlined its vision of building a "new socialist countryside" that is clean, prosperous and democratic. Dalaochi shows just how far they have to go.

INEQUALITY IN CHINA

China's Communist past harbored relative equality. Modernization and opening up to trade and investment have dramatically increased inequality. Before 1978, when reforms began, inequality was not a major issue. Most people were relatively poor and did not own land or other assets. As China opened up, its urban coastal areas flourished, leading to rapid growth in those regions, while rural areas grew much more slowly. What is more, for some time, urban residents continued to receive state-subsidized housing through state-owned enterprises, as well as subsidized health and pension programs. A study by Kanbur and Zhang (1999) reveals that for the period 1983 to 1995, the urban–rural income gap dominated the inland–coastal income gap, although both increased over the entire period. After this period, these gaps continued to grow.

Economic inequality became a major social issue starting in the mid-1990s, as agricultural incomes declined (Benjamin et al. 2005). Growth generated by the household responsibility system slowed. As mentioned previously, sectoral shifts away from agriculture and toward the industrial sector created an urban bias. Concentrated growth in the urban sector, with barriers to migration through the *hukou* system, made it insurmountably difficult for many to obtain decent employment (Knight and Song 1993). Differences in consumption patterns between urban and rural households can be viewed in Table 6.2.

There is a positive trend in openness to trade as well as in the reduction of the inland–coastal disparity. As Wei and Wi (2001) find, the correlation between rural and urban inequality and trade openness is negative; that is, as cities show an increase in the trade-to-GDP ratio, they show a corresponding reduction in urban–rural income inequality.

Inequality was greater not only between urban and rural, and coastal and inland areas, but also between women and men (with women paid less than men) and educated and non-educated individuals (Knight and Song 2003). Labor restructuring in the latter half of the 1990s also contributed

Table 6.2   Ownership per 100 households, urban and rural households

	Urban households			Rural households		
	1990	2000	2009	1990	2000	2009
Color TV	59	117	136	5	49	109
Cars	–	0.5	11	–	0.1	0.7
Motorcycles	2	19	22	1	22	57
Computer	–	10	66	–	0.5	8
Washing machines	78	91	96	9	29	53
Refrigerators	42	80	95	1	12	37
Air conditioners	0.3	31	107	–	1.3	12

Source: Tobin (2011).

greatly to inequality, as state-owned enterprise workers were laid off en masse (Meng 2004).

Government policies are able to influence inequality. Fan et al. (2002) find that, for 1997, government policies that contributed most to inequality reduction were those that focused on spending in western regions, while spending in eastern or central regions worsened existing regional inequalities. Government spending on agricultural research and development improved agricultural production and reduced poverty and inequality, as did expenditure on rural education and infrastructure.

POVERTY IN JAPAN

Under the feudal system in Tokugawa Japan, peasants suffered from famine, as variations in regional market access combined with exogenous shocks led to suffering in less integrated locations (Bassino 2007). Most peasants were normally close to poverty, so that crop failure often led to starvation.

The Meiji Restoration changed the social structure. However, despite the fact that the Meiji Restoration eliminated the very unequal feudal system, which kept social groups separated by castes, some stratification remained (Chūbachi and Taira 1976). Poverty remained a problem for much of the population in the lower class of society, while the middle and upper classes fared better. The poor were classified as fishermen, small tenant farmers, small merchants, the unemployed and underemployed, and seasonal workers. The poor also included scavengers, beggars, traveling entertainers, and soothsayers.

Poverty in Meiji-era Japan was studied by Masana Maeda (reprinted in Maeda 1971), who wrote in the 1880s about three grades of living standards, including superior, intermediate, and inferior (Chūbachi and Taira 1976). The inferior group was classified as spending half their income on rice. The qualification for public relief for elderly adults from the Meiji period through the 1930s was one-half of Maeda's inferior standard. Another Meiji-era scholar, Mikio Sumiya (reprinted in Sumiya 1976), showed that poverty worsened between 1883 and 1885 in Yamanashi prefecture due to ongoing deflation. Poor individuals lacked proper food and clothing. More than half the population lived in either inferior or poor circumstances, either being born into the poor stratum or falling down the socio-economic ladder over time. A 1912 Tokyo survey showed that poverty arose due to poor health, aging, personal deficiencies, natural calamities, and economic failure.

Chroniclers of the poor appeared in Meiji-era Japan and set out to located areas of poverty, usually ghettos, to portray the lives of the poor (Chūbachi and Taira 1976). Ghettos were unsanitary, and poor residents ate food left over from military mess halls and low-quality restaurant leftovers that would otherwise go to pigs. The Home Ministry later undertook surveys of the poor in Tokyo in order to enumerate them and improve the urban area. The Great Earthquake of 1923 burned the Tokyo ghettos down and resulted in reconstruction of the area with improved housing. Similarly, by World War I, Osaka had also eradicated most of its worst housing structures.

By the 1930s, a more sophisticated understanding of class differences had evolved (Chūbachi and Taira 1976). Workers referred to themselves as the proletariat and viewed their struggle as that against the bourgeoisie, in Marxist terms. Labor unions bargained on behalf of workers and were often associated with the Japan Federation of Labor. Poverty was viewed then as something to combat. Social welfare laws, including a labor exchange law, a national health insurance law, and a minimum age law, were passed through the mid-1920s as a result of this class awareness (Duus 1998).

INEQUALITY IN JAPAN

Inequality in gender-based earnings was present at the outset of reform. As can be seen in Table 6.3, wages varied greatly in Japan depending on the type of work performed and the worker's gender. The worst gender bias occurred among textile weavers in 1905, when female workers earned less than 40 percent of what male workers earned.

Table 6.3   Employment earnings by type of work

	Farm employment (sen per day)			Textiles weavers (sen per day)			Domestic servants (yen per month)		
	Male	Female	% F/M	Male	Female	% F/M	Male	Female	% F/M
1885	15.1	9.7	64.2	12.3	7.5	61.0	1.38	0.75	54.3
1892	15.5	9.4	60.6	12.0	8.4	70.0	1.55	0.82	52.9
1895	18.5	11.3	61.1	18.3	11.6	63.4	1.64	0.90	54.9
1900	30.0	19.0	63.3	33.0	20.0	60.6	2.70	1.56	57.8
1905	32.0	20.0	62.5	34.0	13.0	38.2	3.22	1.79	55.6
1910	39.0	24.0	61.5	49.0	27.0	55.1	4.56	2.96	64.9
1915	46.0	29.0	63.0	46.0	30.0	65.2	4.97	3.13	63.0
1920	144.0	92.0	63.9	175.0	95.0	54.3	28.86	22.68	78.6

Note: 1 yen = 100 sen.

Source: Utsumi (1959).

In the early twentieth century (1923), Japan's Gini coefficient was relatively high, at about 0.56, and increased through 1937 (Minami 2008). Income inequality increased due to lagging incomes and productivity in the rural sector, as contrasted with minimum wages in the growing urban sector, a side-effect of industrialization similar to that in China today. Income comparisons can be viewed in Table 6.4.

Notice the clear difference over the early twentieth century in agricultural versus manufacturing wages. Prices were also divergent between rural and urban areas, but the gap narrowed at the turn of the nineteenth century as railways developed (Ono and Watanabe 1976).

The trend in inequality changed after World War II, due to growing equality or reduced inequality in urban and rural areas (Minami 2008). This change stemmed from destruction due to the war and from economic democratization measures after the war, particularly dissolution of the *zaibatsu*, levying of taxes on the rich, and land redistribution in rural areas. Former tenant farmers were allowed to purchase land at very low prices.

Japan was a relatively egalitarian society after World War II through the 1970s, when the country began to regard itself as "all middle class" (Minami 2008). This lasted until the 1980s, when changes due to globalization created higher demand and wages for skilled labor and lower wages for unskilled labor. Currently, Japan has been ranked sixth among Organisation for Economic Co-operation and Development (OECD) nations for its high level of inequality (Tachibanaki 2006).

Japan struggled with gender inequality, as even through the 1980s

Table 6.4   *Income and wage gaps between agriculture and industry in the*
interwar period and causes thereof

	1910	1915	1920	1925	1930	1935
Per capita real incomes (yen/year)						
Farming	602	655	700	653	571	593
Non-farming	1024	1124	1317	1352	1489	1593
Farming/non-farming	0.59	0.58	0.53	0.48	0.38	0.37
Real wages (yen/day)						
Agricultural day laborers (male)	0.93	0.95	1.17	1.21	1.10	0.89
Non-agricultural laborers (male)	1.06	1.00	1.41	1.77	1.64	1.34
Agricultural/non-agricultural	0.88	0.95	0.83	0.68	0.67	0.66
Real wages (yen/year)						
Agricultural annual laborers (male & female)	126	122	145	167	153	131
Manufacturing workers (male and female)	214	229	336	400	439	436
Agricultural/manufacturing	0.59	0.53	0.43	0.42	0.35	0.30
Real labor productivity (yen/person)						
Primary industry	161	182	197	203	210	225
Non-primary industry	517	571	678	729	777	862
Primary/non-primary	0.31	0.32	0.29	0.28	0.27	0.26

Source: Minami (2008).

women faced lower attendance at junior colleges and four-year universities, as well as lower labor force participation. The separation of unskilled
female labor from skilled male labor at the outset of reform continued
until World War II. Female workers from rural areas were thought to be
excellent workers due to their relative poverty and docile nature. Female
workers often worked 12-hour shifts with limited rest. A bias toward
male workers continued after World War II – despite the fact that during
the war women increasingly began to work, particularly in the munitions
industry – since women often quit their jobs upon marriage.

POVERTY AND INEQUALITY POLICY

All three countries have sought to alleviate poverty and inequality through
various means. Assistance to the poor has helped to reduce poverty,
through a variety of programs including food for work, employment
assistance, food subsidies, and direct government assistance. Where government assistance was taken from progressive taxes, relief for the poor

was redistributive and reduced inequality. We discuss these policies in turn, looking first at poverty policies, then at inequality policies.

In India, several policies were used over time. The Integrated Rural Development Programme in the 1970s sought to increase income for small farmers and landless laborers. The goal was to provide credit and training, but the program fell short of success because often laborers lacked sufficient ability to run their own businesses, and banks remained unwilling to lend to them (Yesudian 2007). This program was replaced by Swarnjayanti Gram Swarozgar Yojana (SGSY) in 1999, which strove to assist self-help groups rather than individuals. Wage employment programs under the National Rural Employment Programme and the Rural Landless Employment Guarantee Programmes were launched during the Sixth and Seventh Plans to improve employment in lean agricultural seasons. These were later merged under Jawahar Rozgar Yojana in 1989.

A new public distribution system which sought to target poverty alleviation was created in 1997. This program provided subsidized food grains to poor households. The social security program also provided additional means for poor individuals. The National Social Assistance Programme, created in 1995, provided old-age pensions, family benefits to widows, and subsidies to pregnant women living in poverty (Yesudian 2007).

China's largest reduction in rural poverty was carried out at the beginning of reform, 1979–84, as growth increased incomes. Over this period, policies focused on agriculture and rural areas, introducing the household responsibility system and diversification to higher-value produce, both of which boosted incomes.

Before the mid-1980s, China used social welfare and relief funds to provide subsidies for poor families (Fan et al. 2002). The first program specifically targeted to alleviate poverty was introduced in China in 1986. This program sought to designate funds to counties that were designated as poor, through budgetary grants, targeted loans, and rural development projects. The program's success was dampened by leakage of funds to other entities (Park et al. 2002). The "Food for Work" program was also introduced in 1986 and lasted through 1997, focusing on building up infrastructure in poor regions (Heilig et al. 2005).

The "Grain for Green" program was initiated in 1999 and focused on reforestation or conversion of grassland to forest to prevent erosion. Farmers who set aside crop areas for conversion were compensated with cash, grain, and seedlings. The Minimum Living Standard Scheme in China, mainly funded by city governments, is determined by city governments. Due to a lack of funds, the coverage falls short of reaching all poor households.

Japan offered assistance to the poor for some time. In the Meiji period, starting in 1874 under the Relief Regulations, the government issued relief to people 13 years and older who were chronically ill and those who were 70 years of age or older (Chūbachi and Taira 1976). Individuals had to be very poor and without family, and were required to prove their inability to work (Garon 2002). The Veterans Assistance Law of 1917 also extended relief to disabled veterans and their families. Prefectures set up their own welfare commissions.

The Relief and Protection Law enacted in 1929 sought to provide benefits for medical care, childbirth expenses, occupational rehabilitation, and funeral costs. Relief was reserved for those who were not employable and who lacked family. Japan's Daily Life Security Law of 1946 (revised in 1950) provided financial aid to households in the form of monthly living allowances, housing allowances, medical assistance, and scholarships to children, and still forms the basis for public assistance policy (Garon 2002). All needy individuals were eligible for this program by law, but in reality need had to be clearly proven.

Inequality was also reduced in Japan, China, and India using specific, targeted policies. In Japan, inequality was reduced as a result of the General Mobilization Act, which regulated rents, dividends, wages, and bonuses from 1939 to 1945. Property tax rates also became heavy and more progressive between 1946 and 1951 (Moriguchi and Saez 2008). Occupation policies also reduced inequality through land redistributions in 1947–50 and the dissolution of *zaibatsu* in 1948, which reduced the concentration of property and business holdings and opened up the rural and industrial arenas to competition.

China began to implement policies to address the inequality issue starting in 1999, with the Open Up the West program. This policy aimed to develop infrastructure, improve education, and increase foreign investment in the poor inland provinces. The program included a 15 percent tax rate for domestic and foreign-funded enterprises; a two-year exemption and three-year half deduction for firms in transportation, power, water conservancy, postal service, and radio and television; exemption from import tariffs for projects conducted in the western area; exemption from income tax for rural credit co-operatives between 2003 and 2005; and preferential tax policies for key infrastructure construction projects (Lu and Deng 2011).

Hand-in-Hand Aid was also implemented to pair different regions or industries together based on the needs and advantages of the pair. The Three Gorges Dam area, Tibet, Xinjiang, and earthquake-hit areas in Sichuan were beneficiaries of the Hand-in-Hand Aid program. The East–West Interaction policy promoted the flow of production factors from region to region (Lu and Deng 2011). The Chinese government has also stressed the importance of and promoted rural development. China's annual Number One Policy Documents have pledged to address several issues in turn, including increasing farmers' incomes, improving agricultural production, building a "new countryside," developing modern agriculture, resolving rural problems, stabilizing agricultural prices, and promoting rural development (Long et al. 2011).

India reduced inequality by promoting caste equality. Through the reservation system, India has attempted to end the caste system through a system of quotas to promote access to political participation, education, and state employment (Grinsell 2010). However, in practice, Indian courts as well as society have perpetuated the caste system. *Dalits*, or untouchables, continue to reside in the lowest class of the social sphere, continuing to a large extent to hold the filthiest occupations. *Dalits* are usually disadvantaged on social, cultural, and economic levels. The practice of land reform has also been ongoing since 1949. One type of land reform focused on redistributing land to the landless, although progress has slowed since the 1970s and 1980s. Deininger et al. (2009) also find that the *zamindari* (land intermediary) land tenure system has imposed a long-term detrimental impact on growth of income, consumption, and assets by rural households. Both the caste system and the land tenure system, while becoming somewhat more equal, need further attention to reduce inequality.

BOTTOM LINE

China, India, and Japan all have suffered from issues of poverty and inequality during the process of reform and development. Poverty in all three countries was a product of urbanization, and inequality arose as a result of the urban–rural divide as well as differences between income groups in urban areas. Each country dealt with poverty and inequality in different ways; poverty was addressed through relief programs and other measures, while inequality was addressed through land redistribution or other targeted policies. While Japan reduced inequality as it went through the reform process, China and India continue to struggle with deepening inequality and persistent poverty.

DISCUSSION QUESTIONS

1. Compare and contrast the poverty situation in China, India, and Japan.

2. Compare and contrast the inequality situation in China, India, and Japan.
3. What types of poverty policies were the most effective? Explain.
4. What types of inequality policies were most effective? Explain.
5. How can Sen's theory be applied to China, India, and Japan?
6. What does Ravallion's theory state about poverty?
7. What does Galor and Zeira's theory state about inequality?
8. What have been the reasons for Japan's low poverty rate toward the end of its industrialization period?
9. What type of policy changes have been made to reduce inequality in all three countries?

NOTES

1. Indian poverty statistics are made available by the Planning Commission, which uses data collected from the National Sample Survey Organization (NSSO), which conducts household expenditure surveys continuously (Siggel 2010). Large surveys are conducted every five years. The national poverty line is determined by the Planning Commission, and people living below the poverty line specific to the state and sector in which they live are enumerated and used to calculated the poverty headcount ratio, the number of poor to the number of the entire population. In addition to the household surveys, the National Accounts Statistics (NAS) reports data collected by the national statistical system on the standard of living. The NSSO and the NAS define consumption differently and therefore arrive at different numbers. Confusing matters further was the redefinition by the NSSO of consumption expenditure, which computed consumption as higher starting in 1999 (Siggel 2010). Since many were already living close to the poverty line, when their consumption was calculated as higher, they moved above the poverty line and were no longer included. Finally, the NSSO data was formerly adjusted by the NAS data, but this practice was abandoned in the 1990s, producing two very different data sets on poverty which provide a basis for controversy.
2. Fact contributed by Pinar Ok, SUNY New Paltz Asian Economics Class.

7. Urbanization and migration

The forces of urbanization and migration have shaped the development and reform process in China, India, and Japan. This is because modern industries tend to develop in urban areas, pulling residents from rural areas to rapidly growing cities. Problems associated with rapid movement of people tend to arise as the infrastructure of cities often remains insufficient to support all human activities for some time. Studies of megacities and the urbanization and planning processes have arisen as a result. We now turn to the phenomenon of urbanization in the context of the reform process.

URBANIZATION

Urbanization has been an essential component of the reform process in China, India, and Japan. Urbanization is the process through which people settle in a city, and the way in which cities physically expand as a result. Where there are proper mechanisms in place, such as urban planning, institutions are usually created as people congregate in a particular city, although creating institutions sufficient to satisfy the needs of all urban residents has presented a challenge for some time. Institutions relating to building proper infrastructure and education, health care, and employment are necessary to provide for the well-being of urban residents, and cities may lack the funds or governance structures to carry out necessary plans.

Urbanization in developing countries is of a different nature than that in developed countries, since proper infrastructure and critical services may be lacking in the former. Urban residents may be left to their own devices to find and pay for public goods such as clean water and waste services. Even so, in the present-day developing countries of China and India, the global pressures to migrate are greater and the pace of urbanization more rapid than they were in the United States and Europe during their industrialization processes. Even Japan, a relatively poor country just before the Meiji era, experienced a pace of urbanization that was relatively slow compared to that in China and India. Pressures to provide goods and services for developed nations, and to catch up to developed nations, are strong in China and India.

The urbanization process has had both positive and negative impacts in all three nations under study. In general, cities grow bigger during the industrialization process and afterward, since there are benefits to agglomeration of economic activity (Henderson 2002). There are spillover effects from other firms, of information and know-how, labor markets, and suppliers. Individuals, firms, and other institutions, such as universities, benefit from locating in cities. Agglomeration effects of urbanization can be seen in China, India, and Japan, as large companies outsource to smaller ones, companies connect with one another and find pools of labor to source, and public services and infrastructure are built up to accommodate the growing needs of urban firms and workers.

Negative implications of living in urban areas include higher costs of living, denser living spaces, and pollution. In the early stages of reform, development has had deleterious impacts on the environment. Urban residents live in crowded living spaces, even urban slums. Individuals face very poor sanitation and living conditions, but they remain in cities and even migrate in order to take advantage of the opportunities they see in these areas.

Figure 7.1 shows the level of urbanization in all three countries, from 1960 to 2012. Japan's level of urbanization was already high by the 1960s, but it continued to grow through the present day. India's steady upward pace of urbanization, which began after independence, can be seen as well. China's low level of urbanization continued until reform and opening up, growing rapidly thereafter.

Next, I look at the urbanization processes in each individual country, starting with Japan.

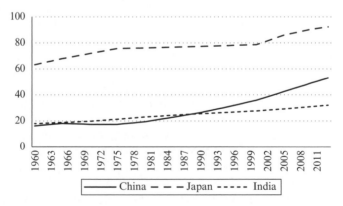

Source: World Development Indicators Database, World Bank.

Figure 7.1   Urban population in China, India and Japan (% of total)

URBANIZATION IN JAPAN

In Japan, the urbanized share of the population grew from 11 percent in 1867, just before reform began, to 32 percent by 1932 (Kawabe 1989). Urban areas remained unplanned from the Meiji Restoration through World War I. During this period, a process of industrial urbanization occurred in Japan during the reform process, growing out of existing land use patterns. The central part of Tokyo became a base of industrial production that later diffused to other areas (Waley 2009). By 1920, about 2500 factories had grown up in the Honjo and Fukagawa wards. Electrical machinery dominated the southern industrial wards, while the northeast of Tokyo became a food processing center in the 1870s. Large state enterprises were also located in the north-east of Tokyo.

Japan remained relatively agrarian until 1920, as most of the population lived in the country or in small towns and villages. However, urban planning began after 1919 with the City Planning and Land Readjustment Act and resulted in planning for purposes other than industrialization alone (Mizuuchi 2002). In the 1930s, local administrations were put under state control. The government managed intra-city street networks and land readjustment. Infrastructure was well planned in response to the urbanization and industrialization processes. Central Tokyo, in the early twentieth century, developed a subway system that expanded over time, easing the urbanization and industrialization process. In addition, areas surrounding major railways were designated as "downtown" and infrastructure was regulated to allow for taller buildings and intensive commercial development.

New munitions-producing cities were built in the 1940s, but many towns were destroyed by Allied bombing during World War II. Urban planning was used after World War II as a means for reconstruction, as urban space was reorganized and many citizens relocated. By the 1950s, reconstruction was mainly complete, and urban and suburban areas were developed as a period of prosperity blossomed.

Japan's first Comprehensive National Development Plan was created in the 1960s to aid regional development by promoting urbanization of suburban areas through attracting enterprises (Ding and Zhao 2011). This proved unsuccessful, as citizens continued to move to already urban areas. A series of these plans followed. The second plan attempted to build up new cities in order to spread urbanization out and prompt industrial relocation. This plan was also relatively unsuccessful, as improved transportation systems designed to attract industrial relocation were used by residents to get to urban areas, further increasing the size of major cities.

By the 1970s, population density per square kilometer was 280, up from 191 in 1950 (Bennett and Levine 1977). The percentage of residents living in cities of more than 100 000 people rose from 12 percent in 1920 to more than 50 percent by 1970. In 1970, there were 103 cities and metropolitan areas with populations of more than 100 000. A strip of urbanized areas ran from Tokyo in the east through Nagoya and Osaka to Kobe in the west, becoming known as the Tōkaidō Megalopolis.

Land was reused more efficiently in the 1980s to accommodate a growing population, creating more living spaces and improved infrastructure and other public provisions (Nagamine 1986). This allowed urban spaces to be greatly extended, especially in the 1970s and 1980s.

URBANIZATION IN CHINA

China's urbanization and migration processes are even more closely linked than those in other nations, for the reason that migration is strictly control-led, and some residents have clear access to cities through the urban *hukou*, or residential permit, while some do not. Because of this, China continues to be considered under-urbanized, since many citizens are unable to move to cities due to this government control. Compared to other nations, China's level of urbanization is lower, despite the fact that the importance of urbanization as a component of growth has been highlighted in the economics literature.

China's urbanization process was virtually halted under Mao, but restarted in 1978 as market forces were able to mobilize factors of produc-tion into urban, industrialized areas (Yeh et al. 2011). The Tenth Five-Year Plan included urbanization as a specific development strategy for the first time. Urbanization continues to be viewed as an important means to increasing economic growth and prosperity, and China is in the accelera-tion phase of urbanization.

During the decade of the 1980s, urbanization was not so rapid, as many reforms focused on improving the lives of rural residents, through the household responsibility system decollectivization process, and through the establishment of profitable township and village enterprises. Urbanization occurred during this period in a more natural way, with some rural areas building up industry, and some smaller urban areas becoming industrial zones.

In the 1990s, however, the urbanization process sped up quickly as indus-trialization increased rapidly. Factories in eastern coastal regions attracted many workers from the interior. Urbanization of land increased, and many peasants migrated to cities despite their rural *hukou* status. Large cities grew quickly due to migration or annexation of territory, while small cities grew as a result of an increase in industrialization or policy mandate (Chan 2010).

One of the main focuses of the current reform agenda is to increase the urban population, in order to build a more modern, consumption-oriented economy. A number of new cities have been built, and existing cities continue to expand. Social, economic, and environmental pressures have, however, resulted from the urbanization process, as more individuals live in a crowded space and compete for jobs and scarce resources. Many rural residents have had their land seized with insufficient compensation in order to accommodate pressures to urbanize.

Scholars who have been against rapid urbanization in China have mainly examined environmental degradation as a result of urbanization. Chinn et al. (2013) find that China has urbanized rapidly in recent years, and needs to focus on urbanization quality rather than quantity; Siciliano (2012) and Zhang and Lin (2012) find that urbanization strategies have been associated with an increase in consumption of fossil fuels and strain on the environment; Chen (2007) argues that rapid urbanization has resulted in rapid soil pollution through waste disposal and acid deposition from urban air pollution; Li et al. (2011) make the case that urbanization of rural areas has resulted in increased waste in these regions, resulting in strains on the environment; Wu and Tan (2012) examine water management and shortage issues during the urbanization process in Shandong; Shen et al. (2005) argue that without higher energy consumption levels and resource utilization rates, China will be unable to meet its current urbanization goals; Bao (2011) writes that urbanization has focused on generating income while failing to account for sustainability; and Zheng et al. (2011) conclude that policies that encourage urbanization in China's north-eastern cities are likely to increase carbon emissions.

Rural residents who have lost land due to forced urbanization have often found themselves members of the urban unemployed, resulting in falling standards of living, even if they received compensation for the land (Lou 2006). Zhang (2011) asserts that urbanization should occur in conjunction with proper concern for the rights of rural residents, and the modernization of agriculture through a type of household-based co-operative approach that allows for economies of scale to be achieved.

Going forward, it is essential that China undertakes an efficient and sustainable urbanization process. Maximizing the use of factors of production such as land, labor, and capital is essential, as is preserving the natural environment as much as possible. Not only has factor use become less productive over time, but sustainability has become a pressing issue, as the environment becomes more polluted.

Agglomeration effects are important to the services sector, which China is increasingly emphasizing (World Bank and DRC 2014). This means that many businesses will coexist in close proximity. Less emphasis on physical capital accumulation and more emphasis on using capital wisely to produce higher rather than lower levels of output is key to China's urbanization future. Migration and efficient land use will also help to spur productivity in urban areas, generating growth and urban expansion. Increased consumption will complement the urbanization process and encourage the growth of the services sector.

URBANIZATION IN INDIA

Although the pace of urbanization is slower in India than in China, it has been steady, beginning even before the reform process, and continuing today. India's population has more than doubled in the past 50 years, but the urban population has increased more than fivefold (Taubenböck et al. 2009). The percentage of urban population was 31 percent in 2011 (Ghosh and Kanjilal 2014). As cities have grown in India, population pressures on urban infrastructure and employment have increased alongside them. Cities are unable to provide sufficient clean water, waste removal, roads, and upkeep for the millions of urban residents, and municipal governments have insufficient funds to cover improvements. Urban governance is weak. The energy supply struggles to keep up with the rising urban population, and political and development barriers have discouraged sufficient investment in the energy sector.

The three largest cities include Mumbai, Delhi, and Kolkatta, while the cities of Chennai, Bengaluru, Hyderbad, and Ahmadabad have between 5 and 7 million urban residents. Cities of between 2.5 and 5 million residents include Poona, Surat, Kanpur, Jaipur, and Lucknow (Taubenböck et al. 2009). The largest cities have a growing percentage share of the urban population as well as a growing physical footprint, while smaller cities have experienced a decreasing percentage share of the urban population. This is called dualism, as urbanization at the macro level is decelerating but accelerating in Class I cities (Kundu 2011). Expansion of the urbanization process in large cities would have been greater, but for the lobbying efforts of environmental groups to situate some industrial areas outside of cities.

Rapid growth of cities has led to intensive pollution, as coal remains a primary source of energy and vehicle emissions comprise a large percentage of gas pollutants. Average per capita carbon emissions are higher in larger cities, since these areas have more transportation services (Sridar and Kumar 2012). Seventy percent of effluent in water goes untreated as treatment capacity is severely lacking. This presents serious challenges to cities, especially poorer ones.

Economically advanced states within India show higher levels of urbanization than less advanced states (Bhagat 2011). The southern states, as well as Punjab, Haryana, Gujarat, Maharashtra, and West Bengal, have higher than average levels of urbanization. Tamil Nadu is the most urbanized state in the country. As the rates of urbanization are projected only to increase, pressures on urban infrastructure and services will mount, as access to water supply, transportation, and treated sewage continue to lag behind. The demand for affordable urban housing also must be addressed in order to accommodate a growing urban population.

Because urban infrastructure is lacking, many migrants are temporary rather than permanent migrants to cities. Many of the migrants join the informal sector, increasing the slum populations. "Low-value" users of urban land markets have been forced into marginal land areas, segmenting the city areas (Kundu 2011). This is one aspect of inequality in urban development.

MEGACITIES

Megacities are cities with populations of more than 10 million people. As a result of the reform and urbanization processes, all three countries have experienced the growth of megacities. Some megacities have better infrastructure and fewer slums than others. China's strict migration control system has led to under-urbanization, which translates into fewer pressures on urban infrastructure, particularly by contrast to India, whose megacities are excessively crowded, congested, and polluted. Below, we describe the megacities of China, India, and Japan.

China's megacities have been growing rapidly, and the urbanization rate has sped up. Currently, there are megacities located along the coast, in Beijing, Shanghai, on the Shandong peninsula, and increasingly in the Greater Guangzhou region, Greater Shenyang, and Shenzhen. Several new megacities are emerging inland, and possess a younger population and less wealth than the large urban areas on the coast (Economist Intelligence Unit 2012). These include Chongqing, Wuhan, the Hefei region, Greater Zhengzhou, Greater Xi'an, Chengdu, and the Changsha–Zhuzhou–Xiangtan area.

Shanghai is a megacity that sits on China's eastern coastline where the Yangtze River pours into the sea (Zhu and Qian 2003). Shanghai has well-developed transportation networks due to its location and also to favorable policy. The city was designated a Special City from 1927, and municipal development moved rapidly thereafter. After reform and opening up began in 1979, the population of the city grew rapidly, and is now at about 24 million. Transportation and housing infrastructure was built to accommodate the expanding population pressures.

Beijing also grew rapidly after reform and opening up, responding to both population pressures and economic development. The current population is about 21 million. As in Shanghai, infrastructure was built to accommodate the urbanization process. However, Beijing, more than other cities, suffers extreme problems with air pollution. What is more, migrant dwellings on Beijing's fringe are ghetto-like and lack access to proper infrastructure (Deng and Huang 2004).

The Shandong peninsula includes the cities of Qingdao, Yantai, Weihai, Rizhao, Weifang, Jinan, Binzhou, Dongying, and Zibo and possesses a total population of 17.9 million (Economist Intelligence Unit 2012). Shandong has focused on industrial development to spur its economy, and the urbanization rate has increased in step. Shandong is working to expand public services such as higher education and pensions to all urban residents (NPC 2013).

India contains several megacities that face severe sanitation problems. Population pressures are so great, and infrastructure so lacking, in the megacities of Mumbai, Delhi, and Kolkata, that slums are a persistent problem (Box 7.1). Additional megacities are expected to arise in the coming years, in Bangalore, Chennai, and Hyderabad (Taubenböck et al. 2008).

Mumbai is the largest city in India, with a population of 13 million. Population pressures have created extreme challenges for the city's infrastructure. Most commuters walk to work, although there is high demand

---

BOX 7.1   DHARAVI SLUM IN MUMBAI

Dharavi is a slum in Mumbai, and is the largest slum in Asia. Dharavi houses more than 1 million residents and notoriously contains cramped quarters and open sewers. Dharavi provides housing for migrants who are unable to afford the cost of housing in Mumbai. The slum is also home to many manufacturing businesses that generate more than $650 million per year (BBC 2015).

Source: Photograph in public domain; attributed to Padmanaba01.

for train and automobile transportation (Rode 2009). Although personal living space is already very low at under 3 m^2 per person, the population is expected to surge to 34 million by 2031.

Development of Delhi began with the Delhi Development Act 1957, followed by the Master Plan of Delhi in 1962 (Delhi Development Authority 2009). The aim of the latter was to ensure proper development of land with infrastructure and services. However, well-planned housing remains a problem for the city, whose current population registers at 16.75 million. Slums continue to plague this megacity.

Kolkata is a city somewhat close to the coast, about 145 km away from the Bay of Bengal (Dasgupta et al. 2013). The urban built-up land area comprises 54.2 percent of the Kolkata Metropolitan Area, with the rest made up of agricultural land and wetlands. The area is prone to flooding due to its flat topography and insufficient drainage and sewer system. In Kolkata, there are large officially authorized slums called *bustees*, as well as squatter settlements (Kundu 2003). As in other slum areas, residents do not have access to sanitation or water. Some of the slums, such as those located in the city center, are more than 150 years old.

Japan's megacities grew over the twentieth century. These include Tokyo and Osaka, which were strongly impacted by the industrialization process. Tokyo was one of the largest cities in the world by the early 1700s, when it was known as Edo (Okata and Murayama 2010). Tokyo was modernized by 1910, with the introduction of railways, trams, water supply, and modern parks. By 1920, Tokyo was growing beyond its fringes, and heavy industry located in suburban areas. In 1920 the population was 3.7 million (Ministry of Internal Affairs and Communications 2012). The population exceeded 11 million people by 1970.

Osaka experienced industrialization in the 1880s as it was a major spinning industry city. The spinning sector was placed within the city near the poor quarters. Osaka grew in the 1900s as industrialization continued to take root, and as administrative urbanization and military development expanded (Mizuuchi 2002). A lack of urban planning in Japan's early stages of development is reflected in insufficient areas for housing and narrow roads, particularly along what is now the JR Osaka Loop Line railway.

Urban planning and government control have played an important role in enhancing the urbanization process, particularly in megacities. A lack of organization and insufficient presence of public goods is most visible in India, while it is least visible in Japan, which built up infrastructure and began the urban planning process early in its reform process. China's phenomenon of under-urbanization and control over migration has prevented excessive pressure on cities, and the nation has attempted to build up appropriate infrastructure in an ongoing fashion.

I now turn to migration, which has heavily influenced the urbanization process. I first look at migration in theory, then turn to the specific cases of China, India, and Japan.

MIGRATION IN THEORY

Migration from rural to urban areas has been a main feature of development in China, India, and early modern Japan, and has strongly impacted the urbanization process. Wage – and expected wage – differentials motivate migration.

Two important theorems that are used to explain migration were developed in the 1930s and 1940s: the Heckscher–Ohlin theorem and the factor price equalization theorem. The Heckscher–Ohlin theorem states that a country will export goods that make use of the country's abundant factors. The country is exporting the product of labor and, in some sense, the labor itself (Borjas 1989). The factor price equalization theorem states that free trade in goods equalized the prices of factors over all trading countries. Wages will in this case be equalized across nations. These two theorems can be applied to international and domestic internal migration, as shown by Mundell (1957), to help understand why individuals choose to migrate and how wages are determined after migration occurs. Mundell (1957) used the Heckscher–Ohlin framework to show that trade and factor movements are substitutes. Economists following Mundell have asserted that both international and internal migration can be motivated by wage differentials.

Indeed, this concept has been applied to internal migration (which we focus on in this text) in the work of Reed (1994) and Andrienko and Guriev (2004). Reed (1994) finds that income and wealth shocks in the poor north-east of Brazil result in increases in internal migration to São Paolo, the wealthiest state. Similarly, Andrienko and Guriev (2004) show that an increase in source-region income raises migration within 78 regions in Russia, particularly for the poorest regions.

Migration has also been discussed in Chapter 2 in the context of the Lewis–Ranis–Fei model of development. In this model, the rural sector provides labor for the transition to an industrialized nation. Surplus labor in the rural sector allowed rural residents to migrate to urban areas at relatively low wages. This model was applied to Japan and is also applicable to China and (to a somewhat lesser extent) India. One of the most interesting discussions surrounding the Lewis model is about when a country has reached the so-called "Lewis turning point," at which the surplus labor from the rural sector is completely absorbed into the urban sector. Scholars disagree on when this occurred in Japan, and whether or when this has occurred in China.

Perhaps one of the most widely used models is the Harris–Todaro model, which was created in 1970 to explain rural-to-urban migration. This model states that the decision to migrate is based on expected income, rather than actual income, in urban areas. Those who fail to obtain a job in the urban formal sector remain unemployed or get a job in the informal sector. Equilibrium in the model is reached when the expected urban wage is equal to the marginal product of an agricultural worker.

The Harris–Todaro model of internal migration states that urban to rural migration in time period t is a function of the difference between the urban expected wage and the rural wage:

$$M_t = f(pW_u - W_r) \tag{7.1}$$

where:
M_t = the number of rural to urban migrants in time period t;
p = probability of finding an urban job;
W_u = urban wage;
W_r = rural wage.

In the migration decisions, the worker compares what they can be expected to earn in the city with what they earn in the rural sector. Workers are assumed to be risk-neutral. The urban expected wage is the weighted average of the urban wage, under the probability of finding a job, and the urban wage if unemployed, such that the expected urban wage is:

$$pW_u + (1 - p)0 = pW_u \tag{7.2}$$

where $1 - p$ = probability of not finding an urban job.

The probability of finding a job in the urban sector (p) written as:

$$p = \frac{E_u}{E_u + U_u} \tag{7.3}$$

where:
E_u = the number of urban employed;
U_u = the number of urban unemployed.

The model finds the decision to migrate, even in the face of unemployment in the urban sector, to be rational. People migrate if the expected urban wage is higher than rural wage.

George Borjas and others also present a model of internal migration. Borjas et al. (1990) lay out a theory of internal migration based on wage differentials in between regions. The model is as follows. Suppose a country is divided into k regions denoted by $i = 1, \ldots, k$. Individuals migrate to other regions after birth based on earnings opportunities. At the time of birth, individuals are heterogeneously located across regions. The population log earnings distribution for region i is:

$$\log w_i = \mu_1 + v_i, \quad i = 1, \ldots, k \tag{7.4}$$

where μ_1 is mean income in region i with no internal migration and v_i is a random variable with mean 0 and variance σ_i^2 of individual deviations from the mean income. Population income distributions are shaped by regional differences in resources, capital, and economic incomes rather than initial allocations of skills. Individuals chose to migrate to region j when:

$$\log w_j > \max_{r \neq j}[\log w_r] \tag{7.5}$$

Assume that individual earnings are perfectly correlated across regions, such that $Corr(v_i, v_j) = 1$ for all i and j. The population income distribution for region i is thus:

$$\log w_i = \mu_1 + \eta_i v, \quad i = 1, \ldots, k \tag{7.6}$$

The factor of proportionality is η_i or the skill rate of return for region i.
Equilibrium skill-sorting across k regions is:

$$\text{Choose region } i\colon -\infty < v < \min_{i=2,\ldots,k} \frac{\mu_1 - \mu_i}{\eta_i - \eta_1} \tag{7.7a}$$

Choose region j $(1 < j < k)$: $\max_{i=1,\ldots,j-1}$

$$\frac{\mu_i - \mu_j}{\eta_j - \eta_i} < v < \min_{i=j+1,\ldots,k} \frac{\mu_j - \mu_i}{\eta_i - \eta_j} \tag{7.7b}$$

$$\text{Choose region } k\colon \max_{i=1,\ldots,k-1} \frac{\mu_i - \mu_k}{\eta_k - \eta_i} < v < \infty \tag{7.7c}$$

Those with positive v values gain most by migrating to regions with highest η, and those with negative v values gain most by migrating to regions with lowest η.

A necessary condition for region j to be populated is $\frac{\mu_{j-1} - \mu_j}{\eta_j - \eta_{j-1}} < \frac{\mu_j - \mu_{j+1}}{\eta_{j+1} - \eta_j}$. This can be referred to as the "existence condition." The pairwise comparisons can therefore be rewritten as:

$$\text{Choose region } i\colon -\infty < v < \frac{\mu_1 - \mu_2}{\eta_2 - \eta_1} \tag{7.8a}$$

$$\text{Choose region } j \ (1 < j < k): \frac{\mu_{j-1} - \mu_j}{\eta_j - \eta_{j-1}} < v < \frac{\mu_j - \mu_{j+1}}{\eta_{j+1} - \eta_j} \qquad (7.8b)$$

$$\text{Choose region } k: \frac{\mu_{k-1} - \mu_k}{\eta_k - \eta_{k-1}} < v < \infty \qquad (7.8c)$$

Income-maximizing behavior results in a positive correlation between average skill level and rate of return to skills in the region. Two-way population flows occur because individuals are born in regions where skills and rates of return are often mismatched.

We next turn to the migration context of China, India, and Japan. While reading this section, we can consider how and to what extent theories of migration apply.

MIGRATION IN CHINA

For China, both urban earnings and expected earnings have played a role in the migration decisions. Residents in rural regions, mired in poverty, migrated to urban areas in order to seek better incomes, much of which were often remitted back home. The agricultural sector has also been viewed as boasting surplus labor, which provided a labor base for the urban sector.

China has experienced a large amount of migration since reform began. Rural-to-urban migration has brought rural residents to cities such as Shenzhen in Guangdong province, Xiamen in Fujian province, Shanghai, and Beijing. This has occurred despite barriers to in-country migration, in particular the *hukou* system of registration. The *hukou* identifies individuals as rural or urban residents in their area of origination.

The *hukou* was first created under the early Communist system to control movement of people from one region to another, and has persisted through today. A *hukou* is necessary to establish identity and citizenship. Under the early Communist system, urban areas were prioritized over rural areas as priority sectors (Cheng and Selden 1994), so that urban residents received more funds and benefits than rural residents. While rural residents farmed within communes and received grain allocations for their households, urban residents were organized into work units that were provided with housing, food, and social services. Today, the *hukou* continues to prevent rural residents from moving permanently to urban areas, and from receiving urban benefits and obtaining better jobs and housing.

Rural-to-urban migration accelerated in the 1990s after township and village enterprises (TVEs) in rural areas declined in terms of competitiveness. During the 1990s, surplus rural labor moved to cities to find employment, rising from 30 million migrant workers in 1989 to 62 million in 1993 (from 2 million in the late 1970s) (Shi 2008). At the same time, lay-offs in urban state-owned enterprises increased the pool of unemployed workers in the cities. City governments forced enterprises to lay off rural migrant workers and to hire local urban workers instead. In the early 2000s, rural-to-urban migration increased again (Shi 2008). The number of rural migrants rose to 120 million in 2004 and to 132 million in 2006. Jobs in the construction and manufacturing sectors were dominated by rural migrants by 2000.

Migration occurs due to large disparities in wages between rural and urban areas. While rural areas have lagged behind urban areas, starting particularly in the late 1980s due to a relative lack of job opportunities, urban areas have flourished as the manufacturing sector has prospered. The type of migration that has occurred encompasses both push factors from areas of rural poverty, and pull factors from areas of plenty. Remittances from rural migrants to urban areas to families left behind in rural areas have often provided a much-needed source of income.

Migrants who come to urban areas often tend to reside in peri-urban regions which are forms of "urban villages," known as *cheng zhong cun*. These places are known as China's urban slums because the village-style housing lacks sufficient facilities, which creates health problems. These places also harbor social problems because the overcrowding results in an increase in crime and drug and alcohol abuse. Low-income migrants live in these places while working or searching for jobs in urban areas (Zhao 2012).[1]

Rural migrants have been estimated to account for up to one-third of the population in Beijing and one-fourth of the population in Shanghai (Appleton et al. 2002). In addition, the urban population increased to almost half of the country's population, accounting for much of the country's wealth. The income and wealth gap between rural and urban areas grew over the 1990s and 2000s and became a serious source of social instability and therefore political concern. Rural areas lack means of production, particularly since agricultural prices have declined relative to prices of manufactured goods (in urban areas). Hence urban areas became much more attractive to rural residents than their own rural homes.

Migrants are typically younger, with close to half being under 26 in 2004, and 84 percent under 40 (Shi 2008). Migrants also tend to be male (about two-thirds) and to have relatively low levels of education, with 83 percent of migrant workers having nine years of schooling or less.

Rural migrants in China typically lead difficult and challenging lives. Because rural migrants are for the most part unable to obtain urban status (*hukou*), the jobs they are able to obtain are poorer and pay less, with long working hours, greater instability, and more dangerous working conditions. If employers are unhappy with workers' performance, they may withhold workers' pay.

Migrants live with a lower level of happiness than urban or rural residents (Knight and Gunatilaka 2010). Rural migrants are often unable to afford or obtain proper housing. Rural migrants normally cannot obtain housing of any quality due to differences between housing prices in rural and urban areas, and lower pay for rural migrant workers. Migrants live in inferior circumstances, often sleeping at their work sites. According to a study performed in 1997 by the Administration Bureau of Household Registration, most rural migrants live in inferior accommodation provided by their employers (Shen 2002). This type of housing varied from sleeping on construction sites to staying in company quarters. Rural migrant housing often lacks a toilet or proper bathroom facilities.

MIGRATION IN INDIA

Migration in India occurs as a result of push and pull factors, as individuals migrate for reasons of poverty, to obtain jobs in other areas. India's colonial period concentrated population and commodity flows toward ports and administrative towns (Kundu 2011). The extractive nature of the colonial period resulted in insufficient job creation and therefore insufficient support for rural migrants to urban areas. The change after independence was not enough to create large-scale employment for low-skilled labor. This is particularly evident in less-developed states, where small and medium-sized towns experienced rapid urban growth due to extreme poverty in rural areas. In developed states, the situation was far better, as they experienced more industrialization and development of infrastructure. India's urbanization process continues to lag behind as infrastructure falls short of human needs and the industrialization process moves slowly. Migration trends can be viewed in Table 7.1.

Migration in India occurs due to both pull factors (the promise of better income in urban areas) and push factors (below-subsistence-level agricultural wages in rural areas). Many migrants are pushed out from poor states where there is a lack of job opportunities, take up seasonal work in urban areas and then return to their homes thereafter. Seasonal work is available in both agriculture and manufacturing. Most seasonal migrants work in cultivation, brick kilns, construction sites, fish processing, and quarries, while others work in urban informal manufacturing or services sectors (Deshingkar and Start 2003).

Table 7.1   Decomposition of urban growth in India

	1961–71	1971–81	1981–91	1991–2001
Natural increase	64.6	51.3	61.3	59.4
Population of new towns	13.8	14.8	9.4	6.2
Increase due to expansion in urban areas	2.9	14.2	7.6	13.0
Net migration	18.7	19.6	21.7	21.0

Source: Mitra and Murayama (2009).

Dubey et al. (2006) find that migration is dominated by pull factors: those in upper castes with higher levels of education are more likely to migrate. The authors also find that migrating from rural to urban areas makes households twice as better off on average. This is in line with field work conducted by Sato (2011) in Tamil Nadu, which found that children, especially males, moved to urban areas to pursue higher education and obtain a job afterward. They may also get married and remain in the city, and later bring their aging parents to the city to care for them. Females are most likely to migrate for the purposes of marriage (Haan 2011).

Migration of disadvantaged groups also occurs, although it is lower than that of advantaged groups, and is aided by the presence of scheduled castes and scheduled tribes in urban areas (Mitra and Murayama 2009). The informal sector provides employment for scheduled castes and tribes moving to urban areas. Both lower and higher castes may send remittances back to their family in order to enhance family income.

MIGRATION IN JAPAN

Japan's agricultural population remained virtually unchanged from the Meiji Restoration until 1930, whereafter rural to urban migration occurred in large numbers (Taeuber 1951). In 1920, Japan's urban areas accounted for 36 percent of the population, and 20 years later in 1940, urban areas accounted for 83 percent of the population. The growth of urban populations was due mainly to rural-to-urban migration.

Much of the manufacturing activity before 1930 and especially before 1920 was performed in both rural and urban areas, as piecework taken up by households or small factories (Taeuber 1951). Migration from rural to urban areas attempted to preserve family life. In Tokyo in 1930, place of work and place of residence were the same for 60 percent of employed males and for 80 percent of employed females. Even as late as 1940, one-third of all employed individuals worked in a family enterprise. The family provided an informal type of social security, since social provisions were not given by the government.

The agricultural population declined due to migration after 1930 (Taeuber 1951). The decision to migrate was a family decision. In industrial provinces, migrants outnumbered residents, particularly in Tokyo and Osaka. Urban living led to difficulties in finding child care and increases in costs of raising children.

In the 1940s and 1950s, internal migration increased the populations of central urban areas such as Tokyo and Osaka (Dzienis 2012). This migration was generally viewed as an ongoing component of the industrialization process. During World War II, more women were brought into the labor force (Taeuber 1951). After the war, population pressures due to repatriation of those living abroad, and natural increase, led the Japanese to look again to the family to ensure survival. The prevalence of family workers continued, especially in commerce and finance. Young men and women also migrated in order to find work, and young women were called home in their early twenties to marry.

Migration in the early 1950s occurred from rural areas closest to large industrial centers into the industrial centers, and the countryside experienced depopulation. This was addressed by administrative measures to improve depopulated areas and encourage some repopulation (Palmer 1988). This resulted in a change in migration patterns in the 1960s as people increasingly moved away from the three large urban areas of Tokyo, Nagoya, and Osaka to non-urban zones, moved between or within big cities, and moved between prefectures (Dzienis 2012). By the late 1970s, the migration between urban and non-urban areas was almost balanced. The Comprehensive National Development Plan (1962) and subsequent plans increased infrastructure and other public investments in other regions, allowing for the spread of industrialization.

BOTTOM LINE

The urbanization, industrialization and development processes that occurred in China, Japan, and India resulted in movement away from rural areas and toward urban areas, giving rise to megacities teeming with large populations. Patterns of urbanization and migration diverged in the three countries, as Japan industrialized over a long period, and also placed some focus on household-based industry at the outset, as well as on family migration. India, through its process of semi-industrialization, has experienced mixed patterns of migration and the creation of urban slums and overpopulation of urban areas. China, through the *hukou* system, was restrained in its urbanization and migration process, but nevertheless these forces played a large role in its industrialization process.

DISCUSSION QUESTIONS

1. Why is it said that China is under-urbanized?
2. Compare and contrast the pattern of urbanization in China, India, and Japan.
3. Name and describe one megacity in China, Japan, and India.
4. Discuss the ways in which the migration theories referred to in this chapter can be applied to China, India, and Japan.
5. What has been the motivation for rural-to-urban migration in China, India, and Japan? How has this influenced the pattern of migration in each of these three countries?
6. What is the *hukou* system of registration and what does it do?
7. What are the differences in migration patterns between the rich and poor in India?
8. What is the driving factor for family migration in Japan to urban areas?
9. What does seasonal migration imply about India's economic model?

NOTE

1. Fact contributed by Abubakar Nuruzzaman, SUNY New Paltz student.

8. Demographics, education, health, and labor

Demographics and the well-being of the population play a critical role in the development and reform process. Aging or very large populations have presented unique challenges to growth and place pressure on social services. The level of human capital among the citizenry must be sufficient to allow individuals to contribute fully to economic life. Changing demographics and human capital lead to shifting labor conditions. In this chapter, we first discuss demographic theory, then we turn to examining the demographics of and status of education, health, and labor in China, India, and Japan.

DEMOGRAPHIC THEORY

The theory of demographic transition has been widely used to explain population changes in developed and developing countries. Before industrialization, the theory states, birth rates and death rates are both high, as living conditions are difficult and living standards are low. As a country industrializes, the birth rates continue to be high, as the population has not shifted psychologically away from birth patterns, but the death rate begins to decline, as living standards rise and access to better health care and education improve somewhat. After a country is industrialized, birth rates decline, as the population feels less of a need to have more children. Infant and child mortality rates decline, and fewer family laborers are needed (contrasted to the case of farming). Both birth rates and death rates are reduced. This is illustrated in Figure 8.1.

This theory was first used to explain the patterns in Western European populations in the 1930s, and has continued to hold explanatory value. There are criticisms of the theory, however, which find exceptions to the generalization even within Western countries. The theory does not explain the baby boom in the United States, for example, nor does it explain the declining birth rate, high death rate phenomenon found in Spain and other Southern European countries. However, the theory provides a useful framework from which to work in understanding how demographics change over time.

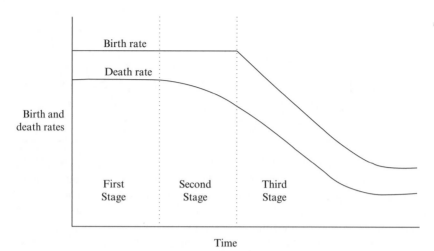

Figure 8.1   The theory of demographic transition

Population demographics and life expectancy have changed in China, Japan, and India since reforms began. We next turn to the case of China's population and human capital status.

CHINA'S DEMOGRAPHICS

Although still the most populous nation in the world, China's average family size has declined since reform began in 1979 with the introduction of the one-child policy. The one-child policy was introduced to stem the rapid growth of China's population, since China was home to a quarter of the world's population living on only 7 percent of the world's arable land (Hesketh et al. 2005). Regulations restricted family size, late marriage and childbearing, while family planning committees at provincial and county levels implemented measures to enforce the regulations. The policy was strictly enforced with urban residents and government employees, while a second child was generally allowed after five years in rural areas, although sometimes only if the first child was a girl. The policy was relaxed in 2013 to allow a second child for couples where both parents are an only child.

According to the theory of demographic transition, described above, a poor nation that has not begun the process of development has high birth rates and high death rates, keeping the population at a low level (Ray 1998). As development occurs, living standards rise and death rates fall, increasing the total population, as birth rates remain high. Over time, birth

Table 8.1   Major demographic indicators for Mainland China

	1953	1964	1982	1990	2000	2010
Population (millions)	594.4	694.6	1008.2	1133.7	1265.8	1334.0
Birth rate (per 1000)	37.0	39.3	22.3	21.1	14.0	12.6
Death rate (per 1000)	14.0	11.6	6.6	6.7	6.5	7.1
Natural increase (per 1000)	23.0	27.8	15.7	14.4	7.6	5.5
Family household size	4.3	4.4	4.4	4.0	3.4	3.1
% aged 65+	4.4	3.6	4.9	5.6	7.0	8.9
% aged 0 to 14	36.0	39.9	33.6	27.7	22.9	16.6
Total fertility rate	5.8	5.8	2.6	2.3	1.7	1.5
Female life expectancy	–	–	69.3	70.5	73.3	76.0
Male life expectancy	–	–	66.3	66.8	69.6	72.0
Infant mortality rate	138.5	84.3	34.7	32.9	28.9	13.8
Sex ratio at birth (female = 100)	104.88	103.86	108.47	111.3	116.86	118.06
Illiteracy rate	–	33.6	22.8	15.9	6.7	4.1
% urban	13.0	18.3	20.9	26.4	36.2	49.7
Per capita GDP (RMB)	–	–	528	1644	7858	25 575

Source: Peng (2011).

rates fall and the population as a whole declines. China is considered to be in the third stage of the demographic transition, particularly with the enforced decline in fertility through the one-child policy. Death rates and birth rates have declined.

China's population is also aging rapidly, with the proportion over 65 rising from 7.0 percent of the population in 2000 to 8.9 percent in 2010 (Peng 2011). Nearly half the population lives in urban areas currently. Demographic statistics can be viewed in Table 8.1. The death rate has declined and life expectancy at birth has almost doubled, as in many nations, due to improvements in health and food technology. Figure 8.2 is a photograph of some of China's population in Shanghai, China.

Literacy rates have increased: the adult literacy rate has risen from 67 percent in 1980 to 93 percent in 2007 (Basu 2009). This level of literacy is better than that of many other middle-income nations, not far behind that of high-income countries.

China's "Missing Girls"

Many Chinese parents prefer to have sons rather than daughters, since sons have a higher wage-earning capacity particularly in farming, they carry on the family name, and they traditionally care for parents in their

Source: Author's photo.

Figure 8.2   Shanghai, illustrating China's population

old age. This preference has been rooted in Chinese history for centuries. The son preference is highest in the eastern Han regions (Ebenstein and Sharygin 2009).

China's deep-seated preference for boys has led to a case of the "missing girls": girl babies and fetuses are aborted or killed in order to allow for the production of boy children. Therefore girls that should have been born to reflect the natural sex ratio are "missing" from the population. Cohorts born between 1980 and 2000 include 22 million more men than women. Recent figures from 2008 indicate that the sex ratio has reached 120 boys for every 100 girls (Ebenstein and Sharygin 2009). Legalization of abortion in 1979 and introduction of ultrasound technology in the 1980s led to a large number of sex-selective abortions. In addition, female under-five child mortality increased until 2000, then slowly declined (Das Gupta et al. 2009). This may be partly due to infanticide, partly due to lower medical care sought for female girls.

The Chinese government has been wary of the effect of the "missing girls" phenomenon. Officials have been concerned that a larger male population, without wives or children, would destabilize society. However, the "missing girls" problem has been compounded by the one-child policy, which has resulted in the widespread exercise of sex-selective abortions. China's National Population and Family Planning Commission carried out a Care for Girls program beginning in 2003 in order to improve the perceptions about girls (Hesketh et al. 2011). A study carried out in 2007 found that this policy was successful in reducing the son preference.

CHINA AND EDUCATION

The education system was reformed in China in the 1980s. In June 1985, the Ministry of Education was replaced with the State Education Commission in order to implement reforms. The Compulsory Education Law of the People's Republic of China (PRC) was adopted in 1986, requiring nine years of compulsory education to be implemented in the cities by 1990 and in the countryside by 2000 (Mackerras et al. 1998).

In China, human capital has increasingly played a role in employment and wages. Human capital can be defined as the stock of skills, education, and training possessed by a population, and in some cases the term is used to include other human qualities such as health. Human capital generally increased over the period of industrialization in all three countries. Whereas under the Maoist regime, seniority used to take precedence over skill or education level in relation to promotions and other employment benefits, in today's competitive marketplace, skilled and educated workers are essential. Returns to schooling increased greatly after 1990, especially in urban areas (Cai et al. 2008). Heckman and Li (2004) find that the effect of college attendance on a randomly selected person in urban areas results in an 11 percent annual increase in earnings in urban areas.

Human capital has also improved total factor productivity over the reform period and has driven regional income disparities (Fleisher et al. 2010). China began to increase expenditures on college education in 1999, and the enrollment of college students increased 43 percent by 2003. The proportion of high school graduates was, in 2003, 43 percent of the adult population in the coastal region, 53 percent in the northeast, and 38 percent in the far west and interior regions.

Although "brain drain," in the context of losing highly educated workers to economies abroad, is a problem in many developing countries, both China and India appear to be net winners in the situation, gaining more talent than they lose (Beine et al. 2008).

CHINA AND HEALTH

China made great strides in improving health care under Mao, as urban populations were covered by their work units, and rural populations were cared for by "barefoot doctors" who, with minimal training, were able to control infectious diseases and improve the overall health of the people. After reform and opening up occurred in 1979, many people lost access to public health care and were forced to pay large out-of-pocket fees for health care, particularly in rural areas. Medical institutions became profit seeking as they lost government support, and preferred not to treat those who could not pay (Zhang et al. 2011). By 1998, 44 percent of urban residents and 87 percent of rural residents did not have health care.

The Urban Employees' Basic Medical Insurance system was begun in 1998 in urban areas to replace work-unit coverage (Eggleston 2012). This system covered about one-third of the urban population by 2006. To increase urban health care coverage, the government started the Urban Residents' Basic Medical Insurance Program, which provides voluntary coverage for urban residents who do not belong to the employee insurance program.

The central government provided some financial support for the New Rural Cooperative Medical Scheme with participation from local governments and households (Eggleston 2012). The program was implemented as a voluntary scheme. Wealthier regions generally offer better health care coverage, as they have more funds for this program. Between 2006 and 2009, insurance coverage grew to cover 90 percent of China's citizens (Zhang et al. 2011).

China still has a long way to go in offering a modern health care system. Doctors are underpaid, there is inequity in the distribution of health care, and local hospitals are often of low quality and are therefore underused. Reforms attempt to address these gaps by improving the quality of health care coverage and restructuring the provider infrastructure to encourage residents to seek care locally for minor ailments before moving on to larger public hospitals. Public hospitals continue to dominate, although private hospitals number more than 12 000 (Roland Berger 2014).

CHINA'S LABOR FORCE

China's labor force has become increasingly skilled, resulting in rising wages over the period 1978–2007 (Yang et al. 2010). Before reform began, urban workers in particular were assured employment, housing, and some income, but all of this changed after Deng Xiaoping came to power. A long reform period encompassed privatization of many state-owned enterprises, a surge in manufacturing, and regional development. The private sector enjoyed higher wages than the state-owned sector in the 1990s, but state-owned enterprise wages had caught up as of 2003. Talent followed the money as returns to education increased.

Informal employment also grew during the mid-1990s, through 2005 (Park and Cai 2009). Ten percent of workers classified themselves as self-employed, while 36 percent were unaccounted for. This phenomenon has been dubbed the case of the "missing" workers, many of whom were migrant workers with few social protections. Some workers were also to all intents and purposes unemployed, even though they were not counted in official statistics. Liu (2012) notes that laid-off workers were not counted among the unemployed, but in fact were looking for work and without a job. The official unemployment rate also failed to account for rural residents.

Labor conditions in the manufacturing sector have often been pointed to as deplorable, but these "sweat shops" have improved over time. Poor safety conditions, low pay, long hours, overwork, excessively hot or cold conditions, and other negative features have long plagued the Chinese manufacturing sector. Labor strikes and workers' suicides, coupled with new labor regulations, have improved conditions in Chinese factories to some extent. The Labor Contract Law, which came into effect on January 1, 2008, aimed to improve employment contract procedures and improve social insurance coverage for employees. This law has generally been viewed as effective in increasing contract and insurance coverage (Freeman and Li 2013). Wages have risen and in some locations working conditions have improved.

Currently, the labor force is in transition along with the economy, as China attempts to shift toward a service-based economy from a manufacturing-based economy. An increasing number of college graduates has created an excess supply of well-educated workers, while shortages of low-skilled, low-wage workers have presented a problem. These labor supply and demand mismatches indicate increasing labor frictions, which have translated to reduced job matching efficiency. Indeed, Liu (2013) shows that job matching efficiency declined between 1996 and 2008, and this can most likely be extended to current circumstances.

INDIA'S DEMOGRAPHICS

India's life expectancy has increased dramatically since 1947, when a person was expected to live around 33 years. Improvements in health have led to decline in mortality rates. In particular, the spraying of DDT to reduce the incidence of malaria has led to a sharp decline in deaths since the 1960s (Visaria 2008). The current life expectancy is 67 years for females and 64 years for males (Kapila 2008b). The country has therefore experienced a sharp decline in death rates, and some slowing in birth rates.

India attempted, in the 1950s, to reduce growth of the population through the promotion of modern contraception (Kapila 2008b). Sterilization programs and setting of demographic targets were attempted, with some success. Demographic goals continue to promote health and population control, and annual population growth continues to decline.

India is currently in the third phase of demographic transition, although the size of the population continues to be a concern. Urbanization has greatly impacted the demographic transition, helping to reduce mortality and fertility by providing access to health and family planning services (Dyson 2008).

Literacy in India, particularly among females, is associated with lower fertility and higher rates of child survival (Kapur and Murthi 2009). However, literacy is low – a legacy of colonial rule – at 65 percent of the population in 2001, particularly in Orissa, Madhya Pradesh, Andhra Pradesh, Uttar Pradesh, Arunachal Pradesh, Rajasthan, and Bihar (Kapila 2008b). The female literacy rate and school enrollment rate are lower than those of males, while rural literacy is lower than that of urban areas. Overall adult literacy is comparable to that of sub-Saharan Africa (Kingdon 2007).

The education system currently lacks sufficient funds to bring about quality education. School infrastructure, teacher quality, textbooks, and appropriate curricula are all lacking. School attendance and literacy rates are shown in Table 8.2.

Drop-out rates are high. One third of primary school children drop

Table 8.2   India, school attendance and literacy rates, 2008–12

Category	Rate (%)
Youth (15–24 years) literacy rate, male	88.4
Youth (15–24 years) literacy rate, female	74.4
Primary school participation, net attendance ratio, male	85.2
Primary school participation, net attendance ratio, female	81.4
Secondary school participation, net attendance ratio, male	58.5
Secondary school participation, net attendance ratio, female	48.7

Source: UNICEF (2014).

out of school, while 50 percent of lower secondary school children drop out (Kapur and Murthi 2009). Drop-out rates are especially high from Scheduled Castes and Scheduled Tribes.

India's "Missing Girls"

India's sex ratio, skewed against females, has risen since the 1980s, increasing once again in the early 1990s and early 2000s, corresponding to increases in sex-selective abortions (Kulkarni 2007). Between 1981 and 2005, as sex-detection technology became more widely available, more than 10 million sex-selective abortions were carried out.

As in China, India has experienced the same phenomenon of "missing girls," as girl fetuses and infants are aborted or killed due to a preference for boy children. Although it became illegal to determine the sex of a fetus in 1996 through the Pre-Conception and Pre-Natal Diagnostics Techniques Act of 1994, the law is not widely enforced.

Uneven sex ratios are highest in the north and west, in states such as Punjab, Delhi, and Gujarat, and closer to normal in the south and east, in states such as Kerala and Andhra Pradesh (Hesketh et al. 2011). However, sex-selective abortion is more common for second and third births with one or two preceding girls, respectively.

INDIA AND EDUCATION

Compulsory education in India is required for children under 14 years of age (Panagariya 2008). India's educational system is divided into four stages: primary, upper primary, secondary, and higher secondary. Higher education is made up of central universities, state universities, deemed universities, and agricultural, medical, and open universities. Some other institutions established by the state and nation are also included (National University of Educational Planning and Administration 2008).

Currently, private schools perform far better than government-run schools. Teacher absenteeism is a serious problem, particularly in rural areas. In 2005, 78 percent of primary schools had three or fewer teachers for all grade levels (Blum and Diwan 2007). Most of these schools are located in rural areas, and often consist of one-room structures in which multiple grades are taught together. Most children do not achieve class-appropriate learning levels.

The aim of implementing compulsory education by 1960 was not achieved, and India continued to struggle with this goal through the 2000s. The Sarva Shiksha Abhiyan program was launched in 2001 to achieve universal primary education by 2007 and elementary education by 2010 (National University of Educational Planning and Administration 2008). Still, despite the fact that enrollment has reached 96 percent since 2009, drop-out rates are high: 29 percent of Indian children drop out of school before completing five years of primary school, and 43 percent of children drop out before finishing upper primary school (Sahni 2015).

Human capital has become increasingly important due to India's economic acceleration based on the information technology (IT) services industry. The number of engineering graduates increased from 50 per million individuals in 1985 to 405 per million in 2003 (Arora and Bagde 2010). Differences across states in terms of numbers of engineers have determined where the software industry has grown. States that allowed the creation of private engineering colleges produced more engineers and therefore were better able to participate in software industry growth. The number of engineering colleges increased from 246 in 1987 to more than 1100 in 2003.

India's software industry, for the most part, hires individuals with undergraduate engineering degrees, even where they are not needed (Arora and Bagde 2010). This is because those with engineering degrees understand computers and know how to program, reducing training time. Workers who were able to travel to client sites internationally, including in the US, were hired initially to get operations under way. Younger workers were also hired to work for companies that, at the time, were relatively unknown and may have required that workers complete repetitive tasks, particularly for the year 2000 (Y2K) issue.

Returns to schooling increased to the secondary level and declined thereafter between 1983 and 1994 (Duraisamy 2002). Heterogeneity within returns to schooling shows that gender and rural–urban differences exist. This also reflects heterogeneity in the quality of schools themselves, which varies across and within states. Differences are such that returns to schooling are much higher for women than for men at the secondary level, and residence in rural areas lowers returns to schooling. Agrawal (2011) uses data from the India Human Development Survey for 2005, finding that hourly wages increase with the level of education, and confirming that gender and rural–urban wage differentials exist.

INDIA AND HEALTH

India's population faces health issues that reflect high incidences of poverty and inadequate access to health care. Individuals die from preventable diseases, and health indicators overall fall behind those of most large middle-income countries. Infants are vulnerable to preventable problems such as pre-term birth complications, lower-respiratory diseases, and diarrheal diseases (Joumard and Kumar 2015). Poor nutrition compounds the vulnerability of mothers and children. Chronic diseases are also prevalent, accounting for 50 percent of all deaths. Such diseases include cardiovascular diseases, diabetes, respiratory conditions, and cancer.

India's government spends a relatively low amount on health; the private sector spends about three times as much (Panagariya 2008). The public sector contains a network of subcenters, primary health centers, and community health centers, as well as government-run hospitals. Community health centers cater to a population of 80000–120000 individuals, primary health centers serve 20000–30000 individuals, and subcenters assist 3000–5000 individuals (Pallikadavath et al. 2013). The private sector includes small clinics and nursing homes.

The public health system faces problems with extensive bureaucracy, lack of accountability, and insufficient funding. Poor individuals often do not have access to sufficient health care, and human resources at health facilities are often seriously lacking. Poor regions in particular suffer from insufficient human capital in health facilities. Many Indian citizens are required to pay out of pocket for health care services, and health expenditures cause many low- and middle-income families to go into debt (Reddy et al. 2011).

As noted above, India continues to face extremely high infant, child, and maternal mortality rates, and high numbers of premature deaths due to chronic diseases (Reddy et al. 2011). Mental illness is often inadequately treated. Public expenditure is insufficient to counteract these problems, and often biased toward urban areas. The National Health Policy proposed in 1983, and the second National Health Policy in 2002, recommend big improvements in the health care system (Balarajan et al. 2011). The National Health Bill of 2009 recognizes the right to health care. However, the implementation of these policies falls far short of providing for the health needs of the people.

INDIA'S LABOR FORCE

India's workforce continues to be dominated by agriculture, even as the share of agriculture in gross domestic product (GDP) is declining. This means that India's high growth rate has not translated into a large expansion of employment. The small shift away from agricultural employment that has occurred has been into self-employment in services (A. Mitra 2008).

Fewer than 10 percent of India's workforce are employed in the organized, or formal sector (Lee et al. 2014). Many workers are therefore employed in the informal sector. In addition, a declining number of individuals have been employed in the public sector since 1991. Private sector employment has increased, but not sufficiently to make up for the decline in public sector employment. Labor unions have become somewhat more powerful. All of this together indicates a deterioration in Indian labor markets.

Women have low levels of participation in the Indian labor force, with stagnating labor force participation rates between 1987 and 2009 (Klasen and Pieters 2013). This can be explained by both supply and demand factors, including rising household income, husband's education level, and insufficient job creation. Participation rates are high for illiterate women, lower for women with low and intermediate education, and very high for post-secondary graduates.

JAPAN'S DEMOGRAPHICS

Japan's demographic circumstances during the Meiji period are unclear. While records show that birth rates and death rates rose between 1875–79 and 1915–19, it is generally believed that underreporting of infant deaths and births declined over time, possibly countering the upward trend in both birth rates and death rates (Mosk 1977). As the death rate declined, the birth rate declined through 1957, signaling that the demographic transition had been completed.

Although population enumerations had taken place since 1721, they failed to account for all citizens, and the first modern population census was taken in 1920 (Ohbuchi 1976). This helped to clarify demographic circumstances from this point forward.

Population growth in Japan was lower relative to China and India during the first and second stages of the demographic transition. This is because population control was an essential policy target of pre-Meiji Japan; high-status families, including samurai, could pass their wealth on to a single heir to maintain their status in villages (Nakamura 1981). Low-income families restricted family size based on the prevailing village view of appropriate family size. The rural population was held virtually constant between 1721 and 1846. Literacy was also emphasized in pre-Meiji Japan, both for village leaders to communicate written directives, and for farmers to better understand crop cultivation.

In Meiji Japan and during the early period of modernization, mortality declined and fertility changed gradually (Taeuber 1950). The rice riots that occurred throughout Japan in 1918 highlighted some of the pressures that population can place on scarce resources (Ohbuchi 1976); rice prices rose for consumption while farmers continued to receive relatively low levels of payment for the crop. Arguments in favor of population control began to surface. Shortly after, whether as a result of arguments for population control or not, by 1925 the marriage age was steadily rising. By the 1930s, fertility fell at a faster rate than deaths.

Life expectancy for males by 1930 was 45 years (Steiner 1944). At the same time, the rural population remained relatively constant between 1872 and 1930, as the proportion of the population living in rural areas declined over time (Taeuber 1950). Urbanization became a phenomenon and its spread served to control fertility, as those in urban areas tended to have lower fertility rates than those in rural areas. In 1920, one in 12 people lived in cities of 100 000 or more, while in 1940, one in five lived in cities of this size.

Starting after World War II, there was a brief baby boom for three years, but this ended immediately after 1949 (Ohbuchi 1976). Population problems, including food shortages, followed the baby boom and repatriation after the war. Japan's family structure began to change, with a shift from the stem family (living with grandparents, parents, and children) to the nuclear family (living with parents and children only) (Morioka 1974). This may have been caused in part by the industrialization process, in which families had to be more mobile and therefore moved away from their ancestral homes, or by a declining need for the extended-family presence as "insurance" against external financial shocks.

By the 1980s, Japan was a developed nation, but unbalanced in terms of density. Clear urban areas received the preference of companies and individuals. The Third Comprehensive National Development Plan, introduced in 1977, sought to expand society outward by building and enlarging towns and villages to support a redistribution of population. Still, the density of urban areas continued to persist and has been referred to as a "high-density society."

JAPAN AND EDUCATION

The Meiji government pushed forward the School System Rule (*gakusei*) of 1872, which laid out the design of a modern educational system (Godo and Hayami 2002). The Primary School Order (*shogakko rei*) of 1886 made education compulsory and laid out the structures of primary schools and higher primary schools. These laws set the framework for pre-World War II education. Universities were available to a select population. Girls and women were prevented from obtaining higher university education at this time.

The Japanese education system was restructured along the lines of the US educational system during the Allied Occupation of Japan after World War II (Godo and Hayami 2002). The new system was written into the School Fundamental Law (*gakko kihon ho*) of 1947, which added three years of junior high school and three years of senior high school to primary education.

Although before World War II universities were institutions serving a small elite group of students, they played a large role in Japan's technological progress. Before the Meiji Restoration, higher-level skills were obtained through learning by doing (Nakamura 1981). Kobayashi (1980) divides Japan's period of development into four periods corresponding to development of the university. The first period, 1868 to 1886, in which Westernization occurred, saw the establishment of universities to study the technology of the West. Foreign scholars were hired to teach in universities until after the turn of the century, when the university was then Japanized; that is, Western knowledge was transmitted to students in Japanese and incorporated into Japanese knowledge. The idea of academic freedom was introduced from the West. The second period, 1886 to 1914, in which Japan's industrial revolution took place, saw the creation of the Imperial University Ordinance, which created the Imperial University system and specified that university education must serve the interests of the state. The third period was 1914 to 1945, in which industrial development occurred and higher education flourished. Research institutions were established both within and outside the universities. The fourth period, 1945 through 1980, was a period of post-war industrial progress. All higher education institutions were transformed under a unified system of higher education into four-year undergraduate colleges, with or without graduate schools.

By the 1970s, Japanese employment had developed, in some cases, into lifetime relationships between employer and employee. The employee received skill training from the employer, which added to the human capital base particularly when employees were educated (Hashimoto 1979).

JAPAN'S LABOR FORCE

Japan began its industrialization process in the Meiji period with three types of workers: male workers in heavy industry, female workers in the textile (light) industry, and male workers in the mining industry (Hazama 1976). Female workers in the textile industry comprised the largest percentage of these workers. In fact, female workers comprised 62 percent of blue-collar workers in 1909 (this eventually declined to 33.8 percent in 1940) (Cole and Tominaga 1976). Female textile workers were often recruited from rural areas by recruiting agents (Brinton 1993).

The private factory labor force were paid low wages and worked very long hours, usually ten to 12 hours excluding overtime (Hazama 1976). Factory workers earned less than artisans and day laborers. Heavy industry workers experienced high volatility in employment; although they were skilled, economic conditions were insufficient to employ a constant body of workers. Skilled workers were mainly male and took time and money to train, and were in relatively high demand (Brinton 1993). Traineeships could take up to six years, particularly in industries with many advanced technologies.

Female workers were mainly young, unmarried, and employed in extremely poor working conditions, in dusty factories with unclean dormitories. Like the female factory workers, miners' lives were tightly controlled and they lived on the work site. Middlemen contracted some of the miners and violence was often used to force men to work.

During the interwar period, the level of mechanization increased, as did demand for skilled workers (Hazama 1976). Large factories implemented labor management practices used in the West in order to increase labor productivity, just as Japanese labor unions were calling for a reduced work day. Wages increased, working hours were reduced, and the class of factory workers was on the whole upgraded. Seniority played into the wage system, as workers were given raises at regular intervals for retention purposes (Brinton 1993). The workers who most benefited from improved working conditions were also those who were in highest demand during this period: those employed in heavy industry.

After World War II, labor unions became increasingly vocal (Hazama 1976). Labor conditions continued to improve, particularly in larger enterprises that received pressure from the unions. Job security increased among large enterprises as labor unions demanded explicit guarantees of permanent employment. The seniority-based promotion system, *nenkō joretsu*, spread as the economy expanded (Brinton 1993). The proportion of female white-collar workers rose to 25.2 percent in 1960 (Cole and Tominaga 1976).

With demographic changes in the 1970s, the incremental salary increases became more difficult for employers to provide. In order to continue to pay these increases, employers laid off older male workers, part-time workers, and women workers (Brinton 1993). Young male graduates faced a tighter job market than in the high-growth period of the 1950s and 1960s.

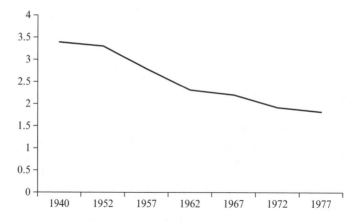

Sources: Fertility Survey carried out by the Institute of Population Problems. IPP
(Institute of Population Problems): Future Population Estimates for Japan, According Sex
and Age, made in 1976, Institute of Population Problems, 1976. IPP (Institute of Population
Problems): Dainanaji Shussanryoku Chosa Kekka Gaikyo (The Report of the 7th Fertility
Survey). Institute of Population Problems, 1978.

Figure 8.3   Average number of live births per married couple, Japan

JAPAN'S AGING POPULATION

Japan began to face a demographic problem in the 1980s, when the
number of aging citizens began to outpace the number of young people
(Figure 8.3). The number of dependents per working-age person declined
until 1970, but rose steadily thereafter due to an increase in the elderly
population. Indeed, this became a real problem, and over time put pressure
on the pension system.

JAPAN AND HEALTH

Japan's health care system was modernized starting in the Meiji period.
A program to eradicate infectious diseases and improve sanitation began
at this time (Tanaka 1978). Medical care improved in the private sector
through World War II. The Health Insurance Scheme was implemented in
1922 to cover industrial employees, and participation was not mandatory.
The National Health Insurance Scheme was enacted in 1938 for farmers
and self-employed individuals. Health insurance became compulsory after
World War II. In both of these programs, participation was relatively low.

The National Health Insurance Law required local authorities to form a National Health Insurance Association, insuring households based on the resources of the head of household (Tanaka 1978). Local governments attempted to address the problem of insufficient medical human resources after World War II, and the national government turned military hospitals into public hospitals. The target was to eventually establish universal health insurance.

This was achieved when Japan established a universal health insurance system in 1961 (Kobayashi 2009). The National Health Insurance system did not include an employer contribution (as opposed to the Health Insurance system, which did), therefore transferring the burden of payment to national and local governments. Access to physicians and medical facilities presented a problem, particularly in rural areas.

Health insurance reforms in 1973 included a ceiling on patient cost-sharing to reduce out-of-pocket expenditures (Fukawa 2002). Reforms in the 1980s focused on cost containment, since health expenditures had increased dramatically since 1961. A health insurance deductible was introduced in 1984. In addition, certain treatments, particularly high-tech treatments, were excluded from coverage.

BOTTOM LINE

While all three nations have striven to improve health and education among their populations, some programs have been more successful than others. India continues to lag behind in both health and education, while Japan has achieved high levels of education and health, and China is in the process of catching up.

DISCUSSION QUESTIONS

1. How is the theory of demographic transition reflected in the demographics of China, Japan, and India?
2. How has human capital evolved in China, India, and Japan? Which country would you consider most successful in terms of improving human capital in these countries?
3. Contrast the status of health care in China, India, and Japan.
4. What is the case of the "missing girls" and what impact has this had on society?

9.   The impact of development on the environment

In this chapter, we examine the impact of development on the environment. All three countries are in the process of, or have gone through a period of, rapid development which has had adverse impacts on the environment. The industrialization process in particular negatively affected ecosystems in China and Japan. Since India has not yet been through a full industrialization process, the nation has not experienced the severity of environmental problems stemming from human production processes; however, even so, India faces its own environmental challenges. We discuss those challenges in this chapter, starting with a general framework on environmental economic theory.

ENVIRONMENTAL ECONOMIC THEORY

In this modern context the issue of development and environmental impact has been fiercely debated: does progress result in an increasingly polluted planet or does it allow people the means to make less of a negative effect? One contemporary position in the development argument that has stood out due to its large amount of supporters and detractors has been the theory of the environmental Kuznets curve (EKC), which was coined by Grossman and Krueger (1995) in their work on economic development and pollution rates.

The EKC theory describes the progressive relationship between economic development and environmental pollution. Essential to this approach is the idea that the environmental impact of a country is determined based upon what level of income it has attained (Grossman and Krueger 1995). The theory states that countries undergo three general stages of the development process in relation to their environmental repercussions.

The base level, or the first stage, is the period prior to industrialization of an economy. At this point there is little to no pollution because production is done on a smaller scale. The economy is comprised of cottage-based industries run out of households, rather than the more modern model of mass production accomplished through technological advances.

The second stage is characterized as the environmentally negative upswing in economic industrialization. When economic development is initially undergone there is a dramatically negative effect on the environment. This is because the early technologies used in development are more rudimentary, as well as the majority of focus being on the end product and not the means by which it is attained. More simply put, production in the early stages of development uses dirtier and more wasteful techniques because there is limited technology with which to make finished products. Poor nations cannot afford alternative options that are cleaner and more efficient because the technology is too advanced and/or the inputs are too hard to obtain in sufficient quantities.

The seminal point of Grossman and Krueger's position occurs in stage three, when there is a turning point at which economic development shifts from exerting a negative impact on the environment to a positive one. While this occurs at different points for different countries, in general it occurs at about the middle-income range for a country, which is an income of about $8000 per person in 1985 US dollars. After this point, the theory finds that pollution decreases due to better practices in production. From a growth standpoint alone, for the most part it is in an industry's interest to produce as efficiently as possible. This would include updated technologies that use fewer inputs and result in less waste, with the benefit that production costs are decreased, resources are under less strain, and there are less environmental costs. The development process as outlined by the EKC theory has drawn a significant volume of additional study seeking to prove or disprove the findings in other circumstances.

Grossman and Krueger specifically looked at both developing and developed countries and measured the effect of development in terms of air and water pollution levels. Their findings show that pollution levels with regard to development take on an inverted U-shaped curve, with pollution starting at a low level, followed by an increase and subsequent decrease.

Others have tried to apply the same tests to other countries to determine whether the theory holds for their paths of development. In the case of Japan, the area around the city of Yokkaichi, one of Japan's first "modern" cities and the source of environmental hazards during development, was found to have experienced an inverted U-curve between industrialization and sulfur dioxide (SO_2) emissions, with the turning point actually occurring at a lower level income point than the original study had revealed (Asahi and Yakita 2012). In China a study found a development and pollution relationship that took on an inverted N-shaped curve (Fan and Zheng 2013), which follows the EKC model at its core. Additionally, India has been found in some studies to also follow a development path that bears the inverted U-shaped curve (Managi and Jena 2007). Yet, for as many as there are in favor of the EKC view of development there are just as many who view that the model is inaccurate or is not broad enough in determining the environmental impact of development.

For those who are opposed, there have been criticisms of both the workings of the theory, and of what the theory excludes. Some have found that the EKC method of testing is contradictory if certain factors are altered. If there are additional countries, years, controlling variables, and fixed rather than random effects, the results do not yield the characteristic U-shape (Harbaugh et al. 2002). This detraction of the model demonstrates that the underlying theory of the EKC is weak, or that it only occurs under specifically prescribed circumstances which are then not applicable on any grand scale. Others have discovered that even if the basic assumptions of the model are correct, it does not allow for other effects.

For more advanced economies other pollutants such as "new toxics" continue to increase regardless of country income level (Dasgupta et al. 2013). Just as technology might be developed to be less polluting, as in the case of production powered by solar and wind energy, it can also bring about new pollutants, as witnessed with nuclear technology and radioactive waste.

Alternative EKC criticism also comes from many environmentalists who condemn the consequences of development that cannot be reversed. For example, the Chinese river dolphin, the Baiji, which lived only in the fresh water of the Yangtze River, was pushed to the point where in 2006 it was declared to be functionally extinct due to human development. This marked an end to a species that had been in existence for more than 20 million years. On an even larger scale, there is the growing realization that all the waste from industrialization, such as fossil fuel emissions, will have a snowball effect in the form of global warming that cannot be undone without a significant reappraisal of how development occurs and continues.

JAPAN, CHINA, AND INDIA

This section looks at how the Asian countries of Japan, China, and India have developed, and the resulting impact on the environment. As the first of the three to develop, Japan provides the most background information in terms of documented progression over time. Japan developed over the course of the last century, earlier than many of its counterparts outside of Europe and North America. Over its progression, Japan faced the problems of learning-while-doing and competing with foreign imperialists. Since Japan is at a later stage of development, it can serve as a basis of comparison for China and India.

China's and India's development paths were undertaken over a much briefer period, and in many ways they are still ongoing. Their major problems have arisen from the desire to reach a level of advancement at a fast pace, while also improving the lives of more than 1 billion persons in each country. These factors of rate and magnitude of development result in unique environmental problems.

For each of the three countries, we look at the development of industrialization and the resulting impact on environmental issues. We first turn to the case of Japan.

Japan

Industrialization took hold in Japan in the 1870s under the leadership of the Meiji government, which took over from the Tokugawa Shogunate in 1868. Modernizing the economy was led by the government in collaboration with business elites, to focus on building up-to-date infrastructure and strengthening key industries.

One such industry that received particular attention was the mining sector, and the extraction of copper ore. Copper has been used for more than 10 000 years because of its desirable qualities in tool making. Once modernization began, the metal was again prized for its usefulness in construction and telecommunications. In the late nineteenth century copper was sought worldwide for import from those countries that had consistent sources of it. Japan was able to benefit economically from its copper reserves through exporting.

The Ashio copper mine had been in use since the 1600s. By the time of the Meiji Restoration, however, the mine had been brought to a point where copper production did not keep up with the costs of operation. At this point, in 1877, Japanese industrialist Furukawa Ichibe, in combination with other business leaders, bought the mine. The new owners brought about expansion of the mine via deeper shafts. Additionally, an extensive tram railway system network to transport materials and a supplementary drainage system were implemented to increase efficiency. Eight years after buying the Ashio mine, the amount of copper mined had increased by 90 times. Six years after that, in 1891, the mine was producing more than double that amount, generating about 40 percent of the nation's total copper production (Notehelfer 1975). Table 9.1 shows the percentage of national copper output produced by the Ashio copper mine.

Beginning in the early 1880s, pollution in the local rivers of the mine, the Watarase and the Tone, turned the waters to a "bluish-white," killing off fish and poisoning those that ate them. The mine had required a large amount of wood for its expansion, so much of the surrounding forests had

Table 9.1   Ashio copper mine output

Year	% of national output
1877	3.3
1882	14.2
1887	39.8
1892	38.3
1897	40.2

Sources: Shozo (1925), Notehelfer (1975).

been clear cut. This allowed the region around the mine to become very prone to flooding. By the late 1880s, and in particular by the 1890s, flooding occurred in Tochigi prefecture. The flood waters were contaminated with sulfuric acid, ammonia, aluminum oxide, magnesium, and iron, which killed most vegetation that it came in contact with, and afflicted people in the immediate area with sores (Notehelfer 1975).

The local Diet member of the disaster area was Tanaka Shozo. He called upon the national government to respond to the incident by ceasing polluting activities, preventing future pollution, and compensating those that were negatively affected by pollution. The momentum he initiated contributed to establishing Japan's first major environmental legislation, the Factory Law of 1911. The law called for large factories to first have government approval before construction, and for inspectors to check for pollution. But the government did little to enforce the regulation in order to truly curb environmental degradation (Imura 2005).

The case of the Ashio mine illustrates two major features of Japan's development progression and its resulting environmental impact. The first is that the length of time within which modernization took place was very short. The Meiji government got off to a quick start and directed its efforts into transitioning the economy from one that was primarily agricultural to one that was industrial. The second is that the small area of Japan's easily accessible terrain puts economic development and all of its pollutants in close proximity to large population centers. Japan has just less than 1/26th of the total land of China, and of the 377915 square miles, 70 percent is rough terrain, with roughly 70 percent of the population being settled in the area between Tokyo and the northern part of Kyushu Island (Imura 2005).

The Ashio copper mine was one of the first government-initiated enterprises that was sold in the early years to a leading industrialist with close ties to many famous political leaders. The introduction of modern mining practices more than doubled production in a few years and increased it exponentially in the decades that followed. With little thought given to how such accelerated progress would create excess waste from production and the alteration of the landscape, there was bound to be an adverse environmental impact on those living in the immediate area. The national government played a very limited role in addressing these concerns. Until the 1970s, when the fullest recompense was offered to Ashio victims, as well as to other pollution victims, the national government tended to pass on responsibility to the local government. When the government did respond to requests for environmental intervention, it offered little in terms of punitive measures and requirements to prevent a recurrence of pollution.

The fifth clause of the Charter Oath issued by the Meiji regime after defeating the Tokugawa Shogunate stated that "knowledge shall be sought throughout the world in order to promote the welfare of the empire." The government held to this principle closely, and imported the best available technologies. Yet it should be pointed out that even the best technology of the time would be rudimentary compared to modern standards. So, while the Japanese government skirted around its duty to respond to pollution measures, technology restricted the extent to which the overall process could be improved.

The Meiji era and subsequent Taisho era of Japan that lasted until 1926 made it clear that environmental policies must be utilized if the country was to survive and even thrive. Other than the Factory Law of 1911, there had been only small governmental measures taken in order to promote environmental issues. The 1897 Forest Law, the Hunting Law of 1895 and its amendment in 1918, and the 1919 Law for Protection of Historical Sites, Scenic Beauty and Natural Monuments, were the first environmental laws of modern-day Japan (Ministry of Environment 2013). These laws all sought to preserve certain environmental aspects, but lacked the direction or weight required to bring environmental standards to new industries.

The Taisho era, known as the Taisho Democracy, would be the last before Japan was ruled by the military-focused Showa regime. Yet, the Taisho regime was in power during the course of World War I, and took great advantage of the war-focused economies of the United States and Western Europe in greatly increasing the amount of exports of industrialized goods. This window of opportunity allowed Japanese industries to expand and develop in order to close the gap that had existed with their foreign competitors. During the period from 1900 to 1920, Japanese heavy and chemical industries more than doubled their total production (Teranishi 2005).

Japan's industrialization policies after World War II made the problem of pollution apparent (Harashima 2000). Environmental concerns were at first viewed as local problems to be corrected by local governments, but soon this view changed. Illnesses caused by the presence of heavy metals in water prompted the national government to pass laws to regulate water pollution, starting in 1958. An example was Minamata disease, symptoms of which included paralysis and derangement, caused by contamination of fish by organic mercury coming from industrial pollution of the Chisso Corporation and, later, of the Kanose factory of Showa Denko Limited (Fisher and Sargent 1975). Another disease, Itai-Itai disease, was caused by cadmium discharge from the Kamioka mine of Mitsui Mining & Smelting. An outbreak of lung disease and bronchitis caused by air pollution resulted in the passage of a law in 1962 restricting industrial smoke. And later, petrol refining and its associated sulfur dioxide fumes in Yokkaichi caused a severe form of asthma called *Yokkaichi zensoku.*

Civil society was increasingly opposed to polluting development projects. American condemnation of Japanese industry, coupled with opposition of civil society to polluting industry, prompted Japan's passage in 1967 of the Basic Law for Environmental Pollution Control, which was to restrict all types of pollution (Harashima 2000). In addition, controls on car emissions helped to reduce smog.

Water pollution was also a huge issue, with rivers filled with polluted runoff from factories (Fisher and Sargent 1975). This threatened the Japanese inshore fishing industry. The Water Quality Conservation Law was enacted in 1958 to systematize water pollution control (Hayashi 1980). The Law allowed the Director General of the Economic Planning Agency to identify public water with significant amounts of pollution. Limits were set as guidelines, with no penalties for violation. The Factory Effluents Control Law supplemented this law by requiring that notification be given before a plant was built that would emit effluents, so that improvements could be ordered for the plant. In 1970, the Water Pollution Control Law replaced both of these laws in order to better abate pollution and to penalize violators. Further measures were enacted under the Basic Law for Environmental Pollution Control of 1967, to create guidelines and assign responsibility for pollution control (Hayashi 1980).

The Environment Agency was created to enforce these laws, and to promote environmental protection by coordinating government agencies to be responsible for various aspects of protection (Hayashi 1980). Environmental policy making was enhanced in the late 1980s and 1990s to include long-term environmental objectives.

China

China is currently known for its strenuous utilization of natural resources, and its environmental pollution. China's impact on the environment has contributed greatly to global warming. Pollution in China is considered to be a contemporary concern, specifically in the post-Mao era. This is largely true in terms of the sheer overall scale of industrialization that took place in China following the Mao era. Yet, the factors that often describe China, such as its large population and state-led political and economic regime, also had an impact on the environment during the early stage of Communist China.

Once the Communists had won the civil war against Chiang Kai-Shek and the Nationalists, peacetime and industrialization began in 1950. Since that point it has been observed that China has undergone two stages of industrialization. The first stage, which runs until the transition after Mao, was industrialization through capital-led growth. The Chinese took advantage of the country's large stock of human capital and developed physical capital to build the modern economy. The second stage of industrialization was characterized by productivity-led growth after 1978 (Zhu 2012). While the modernization during Mao's years featured less total pollution, in actuality pollution was brought to many areas and was widely spread through small smelters.

During Mao's tenure, certain state policies had drastic consequences on the people and environment. One particular misguided policy was the "War on Pests." Ostensibly, the goal was to irradiate common pests such as mice or even sparrows, while also unifying the people into a larger collective effort. Unfortunately, combined with the disastrous Great Leap Forward, which collectivized farming, the "War" led to a grave situation of crop loss and severe famine. Mice, sparrows, and other pests have a crucial role in the ecosystem keeping other species in check. Without some of the pests, there was an inevitable spike in the number of crop-killing insects.

During much of this period, China was unaware of its environmental footprint. From 1949 until the early 1970s, China under Mao Zedong insisted that environmental pollution originated in capitalist countries (Harashima 2000). Severe water pollution in Dalian Bay and the Guanting Reservoir prompted China's participation in the 1972 Stockholm Conference on the Human Environment. Environmental protection was included in the Chinese constitution of 1978.

China, like many other countries, went through stages of trial and error during its industrialization process. Around the early 1970s a series of events, domestically and abroad, led to the first real concern by the Chinese government for environmental issues. In 1972, poisoned fish from the Guanting Reservoir were found in Beijing markets. In the same year, the coastal city of Dalian also had a pollution incident: the city's beaches turned black, and local fish and shellfish died in large numbers.

In retrospect it is not surprising that the port city of Dalian suffered one of the first modern pollution incidents in China. The city sits on the coast of the Liaodong peninsula, which is itself situated east of the Bohai Sea and west of the Yellow Sea. It serves as the shipping hub to north-east China and the Beijing–Tianjin corridor due to its strategic positioning. Most likely as a result of the resulting pollution from the heightened commercial activity of the area, there were the occurrences of red tides, which killed large portions of the aquatic life in the surrounding Dalian Bay (Muldavin 2000). Red tides refer to the occurrence of a mass concentration of a particular type of algae, in such numbers that deplete the surrounding water of most of its oxygen, thereby suffocating any other life. A more recent study of red tides found that runoff from the Yangtze River had pollutants including high levels of inorganic nitrogen, phosphates, oil hydrocarbons, organic matter, and heavy metals. These substances alter the composition of an aquatic ecosystem, causing eutrophication, or an excess of nutrients in the water system, which causes red tides among other algae blooms (Li and Daler 2004).

The Guanting Reservoir incident was felt closer to home for the Chinese political elites in Beijing. Located off the Yongding River just outside Beijing, the reservoir was in an area of increased industrialization. Fish obtained from the polluted body of water were poisonous to humans. Once these fish had come to market in Beijing, a public outcry broke out that received the attention of the government. Then Premier of China, Zhou Enlai, and the State Council, formed an investigation and treatment committee to address the incident. This was significant in historical environmental terms as the Chinese government's first top-level acknowledgment of widespread pollution (Muldavin 2000).

These two pollution incidents imposed the consequences of development upon China. After 1950, when the Communists had full control of the country, it was apparent that to maintain power, it would be necessary to grow China's economy. Industrialization in its early stages has adverse impacts on the environment, but when done with great speed, its consequences can accumulate rapidly. China rightly took advantage of the large stock of human capital available and developed most of its initial industries around densely populated urban centers. These centers are also usually located in strategic coastal or river delta areas for easy access to trade and foreign resources. It may come as no surprise that pollution incidents garnered early attention around highly populated coastal areas.

The state acknowledgment of the incident was the first step toward addressing pollution as an issue of national concern, but it was still directed toward one particular instance of pollution. In order to move to a more environmentally friendly position, the Chinese government would need an environmental protection body that was permanent and able to address the many occurrences of pollution.

The international community came together for the 1972 United Nations Conference on Human Environment in Stockholm, after which China committed to opening its first government offices committed to environmental protection (Economy 2004). It should be noted, though, that this first step towards environmental accountability left plenty of room for improvement (Muldavin 2000). While the office was on its way to becoming permanent, it still had to contend with questions over its being able to carry out its objective, due to the dilution of its mandate in the face of myriad contending voices in favor of rapid industrialization.

As initially mentioned, China began giving serious consideration to the issue of rising environmental problems from rapid industrialization only in the post-Mao era. Significantly, in 1979, the government passed the Environmental Protection Law for Trial Implementation (Stalley 2010). Environmental regulation, like the early stages of modern industrialization, seems to have been explored cautiously, another instance of "crossing the river by feeling for stones." The slow introduction of environmental regulation arose due to the desire to maintain the economic momentum that industrialization was bringing. It was not until 1989 that the "Trial Implementation" status of the Environmental Protection Law was removed and the Environmental Protection Law (EPL) stood as the pre-eminent national environmental law. Additional statutes were adopted thereafter, dealing with pollution control and natural resource conservation (Ferris and Zhang 2005).

Environmental law set about general policies and targets that were to be executed on the local level. The existence of many local pieces of legislation, however, has made understanding Chinese environmental laws in all their diversity very difficult (Ferris and Zhang 2005). In addition, local officials may report results to those specifications without regard to actual circumstances, in an effort to comply with national directives. Lack of transparency compounds the problem of proper implementation of regulations.

China's environmental institutions have attempted to address pollution. The State Environmental Protection Administration (SEPA) was a part of the State Council, but was allowed to vote only on environmental issues (Stalley 2010). This would be an obvious restriction on environmental representation: when industrial issues arose that would have an environmental impact, they could not be addressed by SEPA. Once SEPA was upgraded to the Ministry of Environmental Protection (MEP) the staff was increased and five regional offices were opened.

On the national level, environmental government offices have transitioned over the years. Locally, they are run by Environmental Protection Bureaus (EPBs). The EPBs operate on the provincial, prefectural, and county levels. While the EPBs represent the local presence, and accountability not provided for by the national government, there are still problems due to the local influences around them (Stalley 2010). They often must answer to local governments which have different objectives in mind. In most instances economic progress wins out over environmental consequences. In addition, China's environmental policies have increased in number, but are not enforced uniformly across provinces. Van Rooij and Lo (2011) find that enforcement is carried out more strictly in coastal regions as opposed to inland. Enforcement issues are created by the relationship between the local government and the environmental enforcement authorities.

China implemented a "polluter pays" fee system and additional central and local environmental regulations in the 1980s (Harashima 2000). This is insufficient, however, to cover the extensive damages caused by pollution. "Polluter pays" fees are too low to force firms to adopt environmentally friendly policies. SEPA found that pollution in 2005 alone cost more than US$200 billion, or 10 percent of gross domestic product (GDP) (Liu and Diamond 2008). The number of environmental accidents increased between 1997 and 2000, and fell between 2000 and 2003 (Wang et al. 2008). Water pollution accidents, however, increased over this period.

Rapid economic growth and industrial agglomeration in coastal areas have resulted in environmental degradation in these regions. The ecological footprint in Beijing, for example, was 4.99 global hectares per capita, while the footprint in China as a whole was 1.78 global hectares per capita (Hubacek et al. 2009). China's overall energy output increased continuously until 1996, dropped to a lower value during the Asian financial crisis, and increased once again starting in 2000 (Tian et al. 2007). The drop-off in production can be attributed to a decline in coal use, much of which is used for industry and thermal energy.

Environmental issues include desertification, water pollution, and air pollution. Desertification approaches one-third of China's land territory. Air pollution is so severe that total suspended particulates in the majority of Chinese cities amount to twice the standard set by the World Health Organization, while sulfur dioxide (SO_2) emissions also remain exceedingly high (Diao et al. 2009).

SO_2 and nitrogen oxides (NO_x) emissions in China cause acid rain, and nitrogen compounds cause eutrophication (overfertilization) (Vennemo et al. 2009). The World Bank estimates that as much as 13 percent of all deaths in urban areas can be attributable to air pollution, which also causes respiratory and cardiovascular diseases. Carbon dioxide (CO_2)

emissions from export production have increased as a percentage of all CO_2 emissions, underscoring the need for reduction of coal usage (Weber et al. 2008). China is, after all, the world's largest producer and consumer of coal.

Water is the most critical resource, and is often polluted or wasted. Sixty percent of all rivers in China are Class IV or worse according to China's surface water quality standard, which means that humans must avoid direct contact with the water in these areas (Vennemo et al. 2009). Polluted water is used to irrigate crops in many instances; half of the rice yield, for example, is polluted with mercury, cadmium, and lead. Rural industries consume a large amount of water and are responsible for a great deal of pollution (Wang et al. 2008). Rural enterprises generally have out-dated technology and equipment that require large water resources.

Groundwater is also becoming rapidly depleted. Water pollution is a serious problem, making potable water increasingly scarce. Industrial waste and a lack of water treatment facilities have created enormous issues, particularly in areas that are experiencing water shortages (Naughton 2007). Water shortages in the north are intense and water dammed during the dry periods traps pollutants, spreading them downstream after the rains begin to fall.

On a positive note, China has been investing heavily in green energy technology to reduce its reliance on coal and other fossil fuels (Remais and Zhang 2011). China's renewable energy is at the same level as that of the United States, but it is increasing its installed capacity, and will soon use more renewable energy than the United States. China was also the first developing country to adopt national fuel efficiency standards for vehicles.

The National Development and Reform Commission (NDRC) intro-duced the Mid- and Long-Term Development Plan for Renewable Energy in 2007, setting renewable energy targets for fulfillment by 2020 (Lo 2013). However, there are insufficient monitoring and compliance requirements, and the targets have not been met. The NDRC revised this plan in 2012 to create targets for individual companies. Incentives for grid companies to purchase renewable energy were increased, and the National Energy Administration was made responsible for ensuring compliance with the new plan.

The feed-in tariff policy was also put into place to provide renewable electricity generators with a price above market value (Lo 2013). Feed-in tariffs have been somewhat successful in the wind energy industry but less so in the solar photovoltaic industry. Photovoltaic power subsidies were implemented in 2009 to encourage the use of this type of renewable energy. The Solar Roof program provides a subsidy for building rooftop photovoltaic systems, while the Golden Sun Demonstration project supports a wider range of photovoltaic projects, including rural electrification projects and large-scale photovoltaic power projects.

India

In India, population pressures have given way to environmental degradation (Ray and Ray 2011). This has included habitat destruction and loss of biodiversity, which have led to air pollution, global warming, climate change, water pollution, and loss of natural resources. India has 18 percent of the world's population and 2.4 percent of the world's total area. Ecological stresses have forced many families to migrate to urban areas.

A study by ITT Delhi and the Central Pollution Control Board found that pollution levels in ten major industrial hubs were exceedingly high. These areas were: Ankleshwar and Vapi (Gujarat), Ghaziabad and Singrauli (Uttar Pradesh), Korba (Chhattisgarh), Chandrapur (Maharashtra), Ludhiana (Punjab), Vellore (Tamil Nadu), Bhiwadi (Rajasthan), and Angul Talcher (Orissa) (Singh and Kohli 2012). Much of the air pollution is caused by the burning of coal, producing large amounts of sulfur oxides (SO_x) and NO_x (Garg et al. 2009). High levels of SO_2 can cause respiratory illness and genetic mutations. SO_2 emissions can be controlled by using fuel with lower sulfur content, while NO_x emissions can be controlled by using low-NO_x burners; however, both of these controls face challenges to implementation in Indian industry.

Air monitoring stations have been set up around India in order to combat pollution underreporting. Some of the data collected in particulates is shown in Table 9.2, arranged by most polluted cities.

Levels of outdoor air pollution are consistently above the World Health Organization (WHO) air quality guideline levels across most cities in India (Balakrishnan et al. 2011). While part of it is driven by firms, as mentioned above, part is also driven by burning of solid fuels in the home.

India has several policies to protect against environmental degradation. These were implemented starting in the 1970s, when India included a clause in its constitution protecting public health, forests, and wildlife (Managi and Jena 2007). The Air Prevention and Control of Pollution Act of 1981 and the Environmental Protection Act of 1986 also sought to protect the environment. Both Central and State Pollution Control Boards were responsible for enforcing environmental legislation.

The Department of Environment was created in 1980 to collect information and coordinate activities between various levels of governments, although it was criticized by environmental groups for lacking power. The

Table 9.2   Annual particulates suspended in air, average, 2010

State	City	Annual average particulates
Bihar	Patna	720
Jharkhand	West Singhbhum	661
Maharashtra	Chandrapur	643
Delhi	Delhi	576
Uttar Pradesh	Ghaziabad	565
Rajasthan	Jaipur	547
Chattisgarh	Raipur	539
Uttar Pradesh	Agra	523
Rajasthan	Alwar	520
Uttar Pradesh	Allahabad	518
Maharashtra	Navi Mumbai	497
Uttar Pradesh	Kanpur	493
Uttar Pradesh	Meerut	486
Madhya Pradesh	Gwalior	474
Rajasthan	Jodhpur	453

Source: Central Pollution Control Board (2015).

Ministry of Environment and Forests was created in 1985 to continue the functions of the Department of Environment, but also to provide promotional work about the environment. In December 1993, the Ministry of Environment and Forests put into place an Environmental Action Plan to include environmental considerations into developmental policies. Pollution control, however, fell short of its aims.

Indian firms are not required to disclose pollution information; disclosing such information about CO_2 and other emissions is voluntary (Jaggi et al. 2011). Lack of information about emissions and discharges from factories, from either external or internal sources, makes it difficult to implement better regulations. In addition, pollution is based on the polluter-pays principle, with the same price for each unit of pollution generated, rather than with costs equal to the actual marginal cost of abatement (Devi and Moses 2011).

The worst-polluting industries include the cement industry, the iron industry, the steel industry, and the aluminium industry (Pandey 2005). Part of the problems is the patchwork of regulation to control pollution. In the chemical industry, for example, overlapping jurisdictions and outdated risk management mechanisms have led to insufficient control of toxic chemicals (Sharma et al. 2014).

BOTTOM LINE

All three countries have experienced serious problems with pollution since embarking on the reform process. The most developed country, Japan, has been successful in implementing proper laws to curb pollution. India and China continue to struggle, as economic growth has generally been prioritized over pollution reduction.

DISCUSSION QUESTIONS

1. How has environmental destruction been a "side-effect" of industrialization in China, India, and Japan?
2. What types of measures have been taken to improve the environmental record in China, India, and Japan?
3. What are some examples of how pollution became evident in China, India, and Japan? What was the response?
4. How have institutions worked to resolve the pollution problem in China, India, and Japan?
5. Have the patterns of development in the three countries proved the environmental Kuznets curve?
6. What is the reason for high-polluting activities in these countries?
7. Why has China's Environmental Protection Bureau been ineffective?
8. What is the progression of environmental policies in China?

10. Trade in China, India, and Japan

TRADE THEORY

Trade theory goes back to Adam Smith in 1776 and to David Ricardo in 1826. These theories developed the concept of free trade and stressed the advantages of trade. While Smith laid the foundations of the theory, Ricardo developed the theory of comparative advantage (as discussed in Chapter 2) that we continue to use today.

Mills and Marshall both contributed to trade theory. However, the theory put forward by Eli Heckscher and Bertil Ohlin became a dominant theory in the 1930s. This theory was based on the idea of opportunity cost, or utility of foregone consumption. Heckscher–Ohlin theory states that countries will import products whose factors of production are scarce and export products whose factors of production are abundant. This theory viewed free trade as Pareto optimal, or optimizing of production, consumption, and exchange for two trading nations at equilibrium (Sen 2010). Heckscher–Ohlin theory placed resource endowments of nations as the determining factor of international trade. Consumer preferences determine commodity and factor prices. Then, with identical consumer preferences between two trading nations, factor endowments determine how price competitive traded goods are.

Corollaries to the Heckscher–Ohlin theory include the Stolper–Samuelson theorem and the factor price equalization theorem. The Lerner–Pearce diagram can be used to show the workings of the factor price equalization theorem and the Stolper–Samuelson theorem. Figure 10.1 shows two unit value isoquants for machinery and apparel, which show various combinations of capital and labor that can be used to produce $1's worth of output. The line connecting the points $1/r$ and $1/w$ is the only efficient isocost line that can be used for both products. Its equation is $\$1 = wL + rK$.

Given full employment, the set of capital-to-labor factor supply ratios for production of both goods is the region of potential capital-to-labor ratios in apparel and machinery. This region is called the "cone of diversification" (Leamer 1995). From this the factor price equalization theorem can be derived. This states that countries that produce the same product

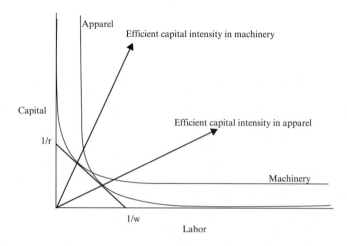

Source: Leamer (1995).

Figure 10.1   Lerner–Pearce diagram

with the same technologies, facing the same product prices, must have the same factor prices.

The Stolper–Samuelson theorem, which can also be derived from the Lerner–Pearce theorem, finds that international trade lowers the real wage of scarce factors of production embodied in produced goods (Stolper and Samuelson 1941). The theory is set forth in a general equilibrium framework based on the Heckscher–Ohlin model, and assumes that goods within a particular industry are perfect substitutes, no matter where they are produced, and that the cost of production depends on the wages paid to fixed factors of production. This theory implies that wages for skilled workers will rise in countries with many high-skilled workers and that wages for unskilled workers will fall in countries with many high-skilled workers.

Leamer (1995) finds that the diagram can be used to show other findings: first, that high wages come from product upgrading from labor-intensive to capital-intensive products, trading capital-intensive products for labor-intensive products; and second, that high wages come from high demand for non-traded goods that can be labor intensive, as long as a country produces capital-intensive products for export. Leamer also finds that talented workers receive a wage premium only in capital-abundant countries.

"New trade theory" later removed the many assumptions of traditional trade theory and allowed for other characteristics of production such as economies of scale (Sen 2010). New trade theory also allowed for identical countries to trade with one another. These countries trade to achieve increasing returns to scale, maintain imperfect competition, or expand markets for differentiated goods.

New trade theory was developed by economists such as Deardorff (1984) and Helpman and Krugman (1985) to explain why the share of trade has increased and become more concentrated among industrialized countries, mainly in intra-industry trade. Helpman and Krugman emphasize distribution of income among industrialized nations as an explanation for the expanded share of trade, while Deardorff notes the strong expansion of intra-industry trade.

TRADING CHARACTERISTICS OF CHINA, INDIA, AND JAPAN

China, India, and Japan are in the top 20 trading nations, in terms of exports plus imports. This can be viewed in Figure 10.2. Increases in service and merchandise exports in China, India, and Japan can be viewed in Figure 10.3.

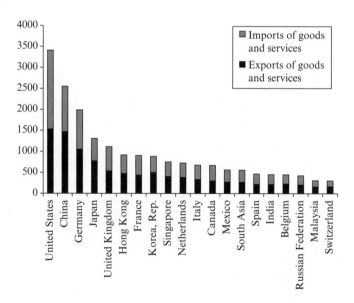

Source: World Development Indicators Database, World Bank.

Figure 10.2   Top 20 trading nations, 2010 (constant billion US dollars)

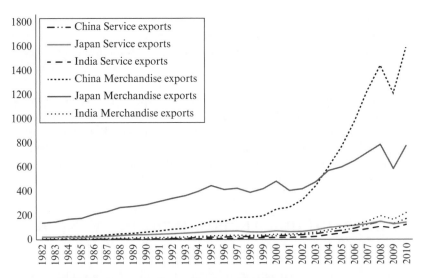

Source: World Development Indicators Database, World Bank.

Figure 10.3   Service and merchandise exports, 1982–2010 (current billion US dollars)

JAPAN'S TRADING HISTORY

Japan's lack of domestic resources has resulted in a dependency on imports. In particular, Japan is dependent on raw cotton, raw wool, bauxite, copra, phosphate ore, nickel, and crude rubber (Ozaki 1967). Despite this, Japan has performed exceedingly well, relying to a great extent on its export regime for growth.

Japan began the reform period with little trading experience. From the period of the "unequal treaties" through the beginning of the Meiji Restoration, the Japanese found they had little expertise in trading with the outside world. They employed Chinese experts as interpreters and go-betweens to assist them in trade (Yamamura 1976). Japanese traders also had insufficient capital to fund their operations, and were unable to keep stocks of goods. Much of the trading activity occurred through *shōkan bōeki*, trade via often exploitative Western-owned merchant houses in port cities. Later, as the Meiji government became more experienced, Japan participated in international expositions in Vienna in 1873 and in Philadelphia in 1876, providing subsidies to shipping firms and trading companies.

The Japanese yen was adopted as the central currency at the outset of reform during the Meiji Restoration. The Meiji government also set up trade boards in the treaty ports in April 1869, but this effort quickly failed in 1871 as domains' lords and their trading facilities were eliminated (Tamaki 1995). National banks rose, and many traders were also national bank owners. Masayoshi Matsukata, who was appointed Minister of Finance in 1881, had early on recognized the importance of financing Japanese goods for export to collect specie that could be used to issue convertible notes for trade. The foreign exchange fund was thus deposited with the Yokohama Specie Bank. Exchange transactions were closely monitored and trade balances improved.

Japan began its large-scale reform process by expanding exports. Japan was first forced to open in 1854 by Commodore Perry, and to combat potential domination by foreign powers, Japan tied its industrialization process to trade. Silk dominated Japan's exports from the Meiji Restoration to 1930. Silk exports rose from 656 000 kilograms per year in the 1868–72 period, soaring to 34 275 000 kilograms in 1929 (Li 1982). Government-sponsored model factories for silk arose after the Meiji Restoration, improving Japan's export competitiveness in the silk industry (Li 1982). The silk trade became an important source of exchange earnings, financing 40 percent of foreign machinery and raw material imports between 1870 and 1930.

Emphasis on growing the shipbuilding industry and increasing the number of shipping routes traversed by Japanese companies helped to expand trade (Yamamura 1976). The Mitsubishi Shipbuilding Company came out with a ship made of steel and containing a boiler in 1887; these so-called "black ships" were strong enough to conduct trade and to fight in wars.

In its treaty with foreign powers in 1866, Japan's import and export duties were limited to as low as 5 percent on most commodities (Yamazawa 1975). This restriction was part of the "unequal treaties" that limited Japan's tariff revenues. Most raw materials were not exempted from these duties. Japan regained tariff autonomy in 1899, and tariffs climbed until 1930, with the exception of before and after World War I. Special tariffs were implemented as emergency measures. Tariffs were implemented not only as a means of protection, but also as a means of raising government revenues. Raw materials were exempted from duty one by one, beginning with ginned cotton in 1896, increasing Japan's dependence on imports of raw materials.

Trading companies were used in Japan to manage risks associated with fluctuation of exchange rates, create economies of scale, and to efficiently use capital and act as credit providers where necessary (Yamamura 1976). The Meiji government first experimented with using government trading companies to manage trade, but soon switched the regime to direct trading between private trading companies and the outside world (Francks 1992). These private general trading companies exerted influence for decades to come. Export promotion was an important policy in this early period due to trade deficits with the outside world. The current account deficit persisted, as only imports increased.

Japan adopted the gold standard in October 1897, which was the standard used in Western nations, and Japan's banking system became more internationalized (Tamaki 1995). However, at the turn of the century, Japan's engagement in the Russo-Japanese War induced the nation to incur trade deficits as a result of increasing imports of heavy industrial and chemical products. This reduced the specie reserve. The situation reversed with a sharp increase in exports between 1914 and 1919 as a result of World War I. Along with Western nations, Japan exited the gold standard in 1917.

World War I had an enormous impact on Japanese trade. As a result of the war, Europe dramatically slowed production and export of textiles and other manufactured goods to the rest of the world. Japan became the center of industrial production, rapidly increasing its exports to the rest of the world. Shipbuilding in particular expanded. Other industries that performed well during this export boom included machinery, steel, chemicals, and textiles.

Export promotion became an increasingly important policy after World War I (Yamazawa 1975). This policy was pursued in the 1920s and 1930s, and established a quality control system for traditional Japanese exports such as silk and cotton textiles, as well as encouraging exports to markets in Latin America, the Middle East, and Australia. Markets were also presented by governments for Japan's increasing exports of heavy manufactures, including metals, chemicals, and machinery.

Japan's export regime suffered after World War I as export demand declined, and specie exports were prohibited (Tamaki 1995). Trade deficits mounted. The 1920s presented serious financial challenges to the government. The Tokyo–Yokohama earthquake of 1923 resulted in large loss of human life and high costs of reconstruction. Japan used its foreign reserves to provide relief after the earthquake, but this caused yen depreciation. Foreign borrowers of yen, particularly through trade channels, found it difficult to repay loans, causing a financial panic in 1927 (Alexander 2007). A brief lifting of the specie embargo resulted in the worst outflow in Japanese history, and exchange controls were imposed in June 1932.

Japan returned to the gold standard in 1930, causing a large appreciation of the yen and a fall-off in export activity. When Finance Minister Korekiyo Takahashi took Japan off the gold standard once again in 1931, the yen quickly depreciated, and trading conditions improved for Japan.

Japan pegged its currency to the British pound. Exports rebounded and firms engaged in cut-throat trading practices, undercutting European manufacturers. Japan geared up for war in the late 1930s, and national resources were mobilized.

Overall, manufactured goods exports grew more rapidly than imports and gross output between 1890 and 1940 (Yamazawa 1975). Cotton textiles, matches, and other labor-intensive articles were substituted for imports and later exported. Full import substitution of chemicals and machinery was achieved by World War II.

Japan was heavily dependent on the United States for oil imports, and due to Japan's aggression in Asia, the US placed an embargo on oil exports to Japan and later on all trade with Japan in 1941. This led to Japanese retaliation on the US with an attack on Pearl Harbor, launching Japan into World War II. Trade with the United States and much of Europe diminished as Japan was viewed as an enemy nation.

Japanese trade suffered after World War II, as major trading companies were eliminated and replaced with small trading companies. Much of the trade that resumed immediately after the war took place with the United States, and was on terms unfavorable to the Japanese (Yamamura 1976). Exports and imports fell from 5 percent each in 1937 to 1.8 percent of exports and 2.5 percent of imports in 1951 (Cohen 1952). Silk lost its footing as an export with the introduction of nylon (Yoshihara 1994). Cotton textiles lost their footing in the export market as newly industrialized countries set up trade barriers. Light industrial goods took the place of silk as major exports.

After World War II, the American Occupation consolidated Japan's fractured exchange rate regime and changed the structure of trade administration (Alexander 2007). The yen was priced relatively low to encourage exports and to ensure the viability of the yen to the British sterling, which was to be devalued. An American Supreme Commander for the Allied Powers (SCAP) organization purchased products from a Japanese government agency, and then exported goods at a dollar price. The dollars generated from sales of Japanese goods were used to purchase imported goods for Japanese domestic use, which were sold by the Japanese government agency for yen. The trade deficit was covered by American aid.

Japanese exports to Asia declined after the war since Japan lost control over parts of Asia (Hunsberger 1957). Exports to developing countries included mainly capital-intensive products, while exports to developed countries like the United States included mainly labor-intensive products (Ozaki and Osaki 1963). Tariffs remained in place over this period, and non-tariff barriers on general imports were used after 1937 (Yamazawa 1975).

Exports picked up speed again during the Korean War in the early 1950s. Export expansion continued until the oil crisis in 1973 (Yoshihara 1994). Heavy industrial products, including electronic products, became increasingly important exports particularly in the 1960s. The share of heavy industrial products in total exports reached 76 percent in 1970 (Yoshihara 1994). Imports grew once again with the growth in foreign exchange after World War II. After World War II, primary products occupied an increasingly large share of imports. Table 10.1 includes the export and import quantity indexes as well as the terms of trade for Japan over the reform period.

Table 10.1 *Export and import quantity index, terms of trade for Japan, 1873–1991 (1960: 100)*

	Export quantity index	Import quantity index	Terms of trade
1873–77	1.4	1.6	111.3
1878–82	2.0	2.4	129.2
1883–87	2.8	2.6	137.9
1888–92	4.5	4.9	131.3
1893–97	5.7	7.9	135.4
1898–1902	8.4	11.8	134.8
1903–1907	11.6	16.4	144.9
1908–12	15.5	17.7	125.2
1913–17	26.1	21.5	110.0
1918–22	26.8	31.2	112.2
1923–27	32.2	43.4	121.3
1928–32	44.4	45.2	104.2
1933–37	73.5	53.0	76.1
1948–52	19.2	22.8	82.7
1953–57	50.2	56.9	88.4
1958–62	99.0	101.1	97.7
1963–67	219.3	193.6	96.4
1968–72	471.4	367.4	98.6
1973–77	801.4	521.7	70.0
1978–82	1130.0	584.3	52.0
1983–87	1563.9	668.4	53.8
1988–91	1823.8	990.9	70.6

Source: Francks (1992), interpretation of Economic Planning Agency, Nikon no Keizai Tokei (Japanese Economic Statistics) Volume 1 and Office of the Prime Minister, Japan Statistical Yearbook.

CHINA'S TRADING HISTORY

Until China's reform period, the country was relatively closed off to the rest of the world in trade. The goal, under Mao, was to be economically self-sufficient. Trade was limited to a relationship with the Soviet bloc. Opening up to the outside world after reform began with gradual opening through Special Economic Zones, the first four of which were located in Guangdong and Fujian provinces, due to their proximity to Hong Kong (Naughton 2007). These areas allowed in imports without a duty for export processing. The south-east and eastern coastal regions remain most important to the export regime. In the 1980s, the export regime was further liberalized to allow for more trade activity in the economy. Fourteen coastal cities were opened up in 1984, while Pudong in Shanghai was opened up in 1990 (Fung et al. 2002).

In addition, at the outset of reform, while foreign trade was still a centralized process, the number of companies permitted to trade increased greatly (Naughton 2007). Some manufacturing firms were also allowed to directly import and export goods. Tariffs were implemented in the 1980s to protect the domestic economy as trade was liberalized.

China's currency continued to be relatively controlled for some time after reform began in 1979. First, China set up currency swap centers in 1988 to trade the renminbi (RMB) at a market rate. The official and market rates were different. These rates were aligned in 1994, and the RMB was first made convertible under the current account in 1996. China's currency was purely fixed to the US dollar between 1994 and 2005, but began to float within a band after that period. China's government is currently attempting to increase the RMB's sensitivity to market forces by somewhat further liberalizing the exchange rate and increasing RMB convertibility.

Special Economic Zones have played an important role in China's export regime. Given benefits to establishing subsidiaries in China, multinationals increased foreign direct investment (FDI) in Special Economic Zones. China became the largest recipient of FDI from 1993 (Long et al. 2015). Multinationals continued to locate in China not only for its relatively inexpensive labor, but also for its proximity to the Asian processing trade.

As a result, China developed a dualist trade regime: one for export processing, and another for ordinary trade (Naughton 2007). Export processing refers to the process by which raw materials and other inputs are imported from abroad and incorporated into finished products that are re-exported, allowing China to make the most of its comparative advantage in labor (Bai 2011). Many inputs into production come from other Asian nations which specialize in manufacturing specific goods. The export processing regime became the basis for a large expansion in trade through the 1990s, based first on increases in volume, and later, in the 2000s, on improvements in efficiency.

As China's trade regime grew, the leadership looked to obtain higher international status by participating in the World Trade Organization. China applied to rejoin the General Agreement on Tariffs and Trade (GATT), the predecessor of the World Trade Organization (WTO), in 1986, but after the Tiananmen Square massacre in 1989 the process became more difficult, as attitudes toward the Communist nation changed. China had also greatly increased exports and was viewed as a serious competitor. China committed to allowing all types of firms to obtain trading rights and to lower tariffs in an attempt to join the WTO.

China was finally admitted to the WTO in December 2001. After this, China's trade boomed, and it became the so-called "factory of the world." Accession to the WTO became a means to an end: Premier Zhu Rongji believed that WTO membership would speed up reform in both industrial and service sectors (Chow 2001). China committed to substantially reducing tariffs to less than 10 percent by 2005, introducing a tariff rate quota system almost wholly eliminating tariffs for agricultural commodities, eliminating quotas and licenses on imports, reducing the role of the state in controlling agricultural imports, and opening important service sectors up to trade (Lardy 2001).

China's accession to the World Trade Organization has not rendered the country blameless. China has been the target of more anti-dumping investigations than any other country in the world. Developing countries are at the top of the list of nations filing complaints (Zeng 2011). What is more, China is often blamed for maintaining an undervalued currency, so that it can have a trade surplus with the US, the European Union (EU), and Japan. China's trade surplus with the US and Europe grew significantly between 1997 and 2002 (Rumbaugh and Blancher 2004). China's currency regime is referred to as a "managed float," with the renminbi tied to a basket of major foreign currencies (Morrison 2011). In order to maintain the float, the government has maintained capital controls and has made major purchases of dollars and dollar assets. Despite this, some Western policy makers argue that China maintains an undervalued currency relative to other currencies so that it can continue to export abroad at low costs. Chinese officials counter that the policy is meant to offer stability.

Over time, China's manufacturing sector changed the focus of production from low-technology, labor-intensive goods to higher-technology and capital-intensive goods. China's top exports in 2005 included exports of machines, telecommunication and electronic equipment, clothing, footwear, furniture, and toys (Qureshi and Wan 2008). Top exports currently include exports of machines, electronic equipment, furniture, medical

BOX 10.1   SHENZHEN SPECIAL ECONOMIC ZONE

Shenzhen was China's first Special Economic Zone. Shenzhen was to become a "window" to the outside world. The small township was converted into a massive city with modern infrastructure. The city is situated across the border from Hong Kong and has provided both Mainland Chinese and overseas Chinese with many investment and trade opportunities (Li 1996).

Source: Photograph in public domain, attributed to Dr NanTu.

supplies, clothing, and plastics. China has created production networks with East Asian nations to take advantage of specialization and wage differentials between countries. These countries work together to trade in machinery parts and components in order to lower costs, leading to the creation of economies of scale (Haddad 2007). China has been able to export high-value-added goods by importing and assembling high-value-added components. Because of this, intra-regional trade has expanded more rapidly than extraregional trade.

China is currently experiencing an economic restructuring, with more policy emphasis on producing goods for domestic consumption rather than for export. The nation is also attempting to build up its services sector and high-technology manufacturing sector. This may translate over time into increased exports of these types of goods and services.

INDIA'S TRADING HISTORY

India's trade has increased dramatically in the past 20 years. India had very high barriers to trade, with average tariffs surpassing 200 percent, and presence of quantitative restrictions on imports (Yadav 2012). The balance-of-payments crisis in 1991 forced the government to become less inward looking. In that year, India liberalized many tariff and non-tariff barriers to importing, and eliminated many licenses as barriers to exporting. It is estimated that India's trade openness has tripled since the late 1980s.

Import quantity restrictions were further reduced on 1400 goods in

2000 and 2001. Tariffs were also gradually reduced; the weighted average of tariffs declined from 24 percent in 2001 to 7 percent in 2009 (Banga and Das 2012). Reforms were particularly focused on the manufacturing sector (Sen et al. 2010). Exports in the manufacturing sector were dominated by intermediate products and consumer durables between 1988 and 2009 (Banga and Das 2012).

Some barriers to trade remain. As Alessandrini et al. (2011) remark, India's trade reform was neither "comprehensive nor unbiased." The government monitors imports of around 300 sensitive products and uses state trading companies in agriculture (Henry 2008). India remains one of the most protected markets for agricultural products in the developing world, maintaining tariffs of 40.8 percent on these goods (Polaski et al. 2008).

Currently, China is one of India's largest trading partners. India has a trade deficit to China, which has become ever larger since 2007–08. India imports electronics, coal, chemicals, machinery, and pharmaceuticals from China, and exports ores, iron, organic chemicals, and cotton to China, revealing a strong difference in export value added between the two nations. Therefore India and China have not been major competitors in terms of exports because they produce different types of goods at this stage. India's major competitors in exports to developed nations include Turkey, Sri Lanka, Morocco, and Pakistan. Between 1990 and 2006, India experienced a decline in exports to industrial countries, dropping from 55 percent in 1990 to 44 percent in 2006, and an increase in exports to developing countries (Qureshi and Wan 2008).

Real imports grew at 13.3 percent per year, dominated by intermediate goods and raw materials since 1990, with capital goods imports increasing somewhat through 2009 (Banga and Das 2012). Imports are dominated by manufactured products, including chemicals, machinery and equipment, and materials such as leather (Yadav 2012). Agricultural imports exceeded exports in the early 1980s but declined thereafter. Trade in agriculture, however, continues to be regulated in order to protect domestic production.

Petroleum products comprise a large percentage of manufacturing exports, rising from 2 percent in 1996–97 to 19 percent in 2007–08 (Goldar 2009). The share of merchandise in exports has also risen. At the same time, the shares of cotton yarn, fabrics, and garments have fallen. The increase in exports increased employment in the food products, beverages, and tobacco products group; the wood, paper, and printing group; the chemicals, refinery, rubber, and plastic products group; and the metal products and machinery group. What is more, India has also experienced an increase in the relative demand for and return to skilled labor.

India has built up several Special Economic Zones to encourage foreign direct investment in manufacturing, but these remain unpopular. One reason behind this is that the Special Economic Zones have used the land of residents who are insufficiently compensated. Some Special Economic Zones were based on export processing zones set up between 1960 and 2000, which were operated by the central government until the 1990s and whose effectiveness was muffled by the License Raj. Special economic zones today, however, continue to lag in efficiency, especially since export incentives have been given to exporters outside of the zones.

Service exports have grown a large amount since 1990–91, particularly in the software (information technology) category. This occurred in general as a result of technological change and cheaper costs of communication and, specific to India, due to the existence of an educated, English-speaking labor force that is less costly in terms of wages. As Alessandrini et al. (2011) find, a reduction in tariffs increased specialization in India's high-technology industries. The information technology services category includes information technology, business process outsourcing, and engineering design and product development (Hyvonen and Wang 2012). Other major items in the services category include travel and transportation. Travel exports have increased due to a rise in foreign residents visiting India, and transportation exports have increased due to rising demand for freight services, passenger transport, and postal and courier services.

India's trade progress has not been consistent. The Asian financial crisis of 1997 negatively impacted India's exports, reversing them by 2.33 percent. The consequent devaluation of competitor Asian nations' currencies reduced India's export competitiveness. The downturn in the United States in 2001–02 also adversely impacted India's exports. The 2008 global crisis severely impacted Indian exports, moving from a growth rate of 20 percent between 2002 and 2008 to −20 percent between 2008 and 2009 (Mukherjee and Mukherjee 2012); it has in recent years rebounded.

India was a founding member of the GATT in 1947 and of the WTO in 1995. India was a cautious participant in the GATT until reforms began in 1991. While India did liberalize in 1991, it was concerned about being vulnerable to international nations as part of the WTO later on (Ray and Saha 2009). India became a key negotiating partner after the Doha round in 2001, emerging successfully on several issues. As a developing nation, India is allowed more time under WTO regulations to implement agreements and commitments (Henry 2008).

Until 2000, India was isolated from regional trading blocs, refraining from joining the Asia-Pacific Economic Community (Henry 2008). Currently, India is more active in trading blocs, joining Indian regional trade agreements (RTAs) as part of a multilateral strategy. India also

Table 10.2   Indicators of economic openness in India

	1990–91	2005–06
Exports/GDP	5.8	13.1
Imports/GDP	8.8	19.6
Current receipts/GDP	8.0	24.5
Foreign investment/GDP	0.0	2.5
Debt service ratio	35.3	10.2

Source: Reserve Bank of India (2006).

found strategic partners in Brazil and South Africa. India has entered into RTAs with West Asian states, including Gulf Cooperation Council states and Iran, from which the nation imports oil. India has maintained its relationship with Iran despite pressure from Western nations to reduce its oil imports due to Iran's nuclear crisis, maintaining "inclusive trade diplomacy" (Nath 2014). Table 10.2 provides indicators of economic openness in India in 1990–91 and 2005–06.

The impact of trade reforms has had varying impacts by state, depending on the rigidity of local labor regulations in each state (Sen et al. 2010). Trade openness also resulted in a large increase of the informal sector, such that currently, only 20 percent of employed workers in the manufacturing sector are in the formal sector. Formal sector workers are usually part of labor unions and are able to obtain higher wages and better working conditions than those in the informal sector. Trade liberalization also appears to have reduced workers' bargaining power. Opening up to trade has reduced labor's share in revenue in particular for larger, less labor-intensive firms (Ahsan and Mitra 2014).

India has increased its FDI, which accounted for $6.2 billion in 2001–02, and rose to $23 billion in 2006–07 (Henry 2008). India faces difficulties in attracting FDI due to its lack of infrastructure, particularly in transport and electricity.

As in other nations, India's exchange rate has impacted trade. Real exchange rate depreciation is positively related to the trade balance in the long run (Dhasmana 2012). Non-information technology (IT) service sector firms in particular are impacted by fluctuations in the exchange rate, especially exchange rate appreciations (Cheung and Sengupta 2013). Exchange rate volatility, however, has adversely impacted trade (Srinivasan and Kalaivani 2012), as volatility increases uncertainty.

ASIA AND EXPORT-ORIENTED GROWTH

Japan initiated the Asian model of export-led growth, which was followed by similar patterns in Singapore, Hong Kong, Taiwan, and South Korea in the 1960s. China's opening up represented a continuation of export-led growth. This was followed by growth in Malaysia, Thailand, Indonesia, and Vietnam. Exports provided a pathway for developing countries to catch up to industrialized nations, given a set of external global conditions. These included an open international environment, the presence of a large external market, and sufficiency of raw materials (Song 2012).

While some of these nations focused on import substitution strategies before implementing export promotion strategies, economists have focused on export strategies as primary drivers of growth. Positive net exports generate external demand for goods. As poor nations, East Asian countries contained insufficient domestic demand at the outset of reform. In addition, there is evidence that exporting firms tend to be more efficient and may have better access to technology and know-how from importing countries (Hernandez and Razmi 2011).

The paradigm of export-led growth is under attack these days, post-global crisis. The reason for this is that export-led growth requires global imbalances through which some countries run chronic trade deficits to finance trade surpluses in other nations (Hernandez and Razmi 2011). The United States and Europe experienced a decline in demand for exports, leading to volatility in external demand. Asian nations that attempt to grow through increasing exports have been and are shifting exports to alternative markets, such as the intra-regional market (Song 2012). Exporting Asian countries have also shifted to other countries of the global South.

BOTTOM LINE

It has taken some time for Japan, China, and India to become the trading nations they are today. China and India still seek to restructure to some extent. India may boost its manufacturing exports, while China may boost its services exports. These nations are part of an Asian export-led growth paradigm that continues to change as world conditions also change.

DISCUSSION QUESTIONS

1. Compare and contrast the trading history in China, India, and Japan.

2. Summarize the different trade theories presented in this chapter. How do these theories explain trade in China, India, and Japan?
3. What is the difference between the Heckscher–Ohlin trade theories and the "new trade theory," and how is this relevant to the reform trajectories of these three nations?
4. Why has export-oriented growth been important for Asian nations?
5. Of what importance was the World Trade Organization to the trade regimes of these countries?

11. Economic future of China, India, and Japan

Given past levels of success, one might presume that growth and development will continue without very high barriers to progress. Expectations are certainly great that advancement will continue. Japan is a case that we can study since its "future," or post-reform period, has already been under way for two decades. China and India are facing limitations that may or may not prove insurmountable, depending on both external global circumstances and internal policies. In this chapter, we discuss the case of Japan, as well as potential economic futures of China and India.

JAPAN

Japan's economic development after the reform period ended in the 1970s and 1980s took a turn for the worse. The real estate and stock markets were booming in the 1980s, and economic growth was increasingly fueled by financial gains. Loose monetary policy, favorable real estate tax incentives, and financial deregulation all contributed to excessive speculation, creating incentives for individuals to pour money into capital, and particularly real estate, markets (Fukao 2004).

A real estate and stock market crash in 1990, coupled with a decline in technological innovation in the real economy, resulted in economic malaise that continues to linger. The decline in asset prices after 1989 left institutions holding debts that they could not repay.

In the late 1980s, Japan also moved many production processes overseas due to an appreciation of the yen which made Japanese exports less competitive, increasing wages, and rising land prices (Karan 2005). The financial crash in the 1990s resulted in decreased foreign direct investment coming from Japan, as enterprises scaled back their production.

At the outset of the bursting of the asset price bubble, banks attempted to wait for recovery, and problem loans mounted. Banks' credit ratings declined, and Japanese bank funding costs relative to those in European and American banks rose (Fukao 2004). The Japanese government attempted to shore up *jusen*, the suffering non-bank housing loan companies, with capital injections, but this move was highly unpopular. An amendment to the Deposit Insurance Law in 1996 temporarily suspended limits on deposit production (Fujii and Kawai 2010). The failure of several important securities companies in 1997 produced an increase in financial instability, and mistrust of Japanese financial institutions rose.

In response, the government made 30 trillion yen in funds available to the Deposit Insurance Corporation of Japan for strengthening bank balance sheets and the deposit system (Fujii and Kawai 2010). Public funds were also injected into banks in March 1998 to increase their capital adequacy. However, this proved insufficient to recapitalize the banking system, and another round of capital injections were carried out in March 1999. An asset management company, the Industrial Revitalization Corporation of Japan, was set up by the government in April 2003 in order to purchase higher-quality troubled loans from bank books. The banking system began to recover thereafter through 2005.

The result of the financial crash was a long period of decline in gross domestic product (GDP) growth, decline in purchase of luxury goods, and increase in poverty and inequality, including a rise in homelessness. GDP growth declined due to decreasing productivity and also due to a relatively declining population; "zombie" firms kept in business with support from bank loans in the 1990s put a drag on productivity, along with excessive regulations requiring approval for market entry and the satisfaction of very high standards (Dekle 2012). Homeless individuals, mainly men in their late forties and fifties who faced unemployment after the collapse of the market in the 1990s and the resulting decline in demand for casual labor, live in Shinjuku Park near the Tokyo Government Metropolitan Office complex, Kawasaki's Fujima Park, and other areas (Karan 2005).

Physical and human capital remained for the most part intact through the 1990s, which means that the slowdown was most likely attributed to diminishing productivity (Posen 1998). According to some analysts, total factor productivity declined as the economy became less productive. Jorgensen and Motohashi (2005), for example, find that while total factor productivity in the information technology (IT) sector increased, total factor productivity in the non-IT sector lagged far behind that of the United States. Some economists have attributed the "lost decade" to ineffective fiscal policy, financial deregulation, and excessive financial competition (Saxonhouse and Stern 2004). Increased financial competition led to a loss of regulatory rents for inefficient commercial banks, which built up bad loans. The economy remained in a slump since neither government spending nor tax cuts were sufficient to increase growth. The decline in GDP growth and increase in unemployment after the 1980s is visible in Figure 11.1.

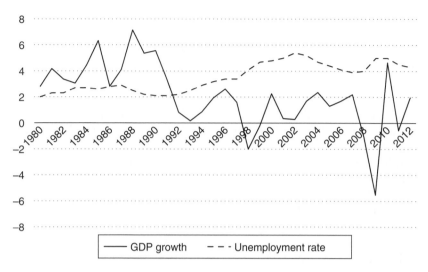

Source: World Development Indicators Database, World Bank.

Figure 11.1 GDP growth and unemployment, 1980–2012

As unemployment rose somewhat after 1990, GDP growth took a plunge, moving into negative territory during the Asian financial crisis in 1998 and during the global Great Recession in 2009. Japan was caught in the middle of the Asian financial crisis, and was already in an economic slump as two large financial institutions failed in November 1997 (Ito 1999). The failure of these institutions was a negative shock, especially since the government had earlier declared that none of the international banks would fail, yet one did. This represented the largest bank failure in postwar Japanese history. The financial system became increasingly fragile as stock prices declined and banks constrained lending. Depreciation of the Japanese yen picked up speed at the end of 1997 and Japan found itself vulnerable in terms of the strength of its financial system and primary and tertiary sectors (Yamazawa 1998). The presence of non-performing loans and stagnant growth in Japan did not prompt the recovery of the Asian economies through external demand. However, Japan was able to provide funds to ailing Asian economies, initially proposing an Asian fund through which to channel funds, and later capitulating to Western demands that the International Monetary Fund (IMF) be the main conduit through which to rescue the Asian nations (Katada 2001).

Although Japan assisted in the bailout of Asian nations, Japan itself had been vulnerable to the crisis due to its weak financial system and deteriorating currency. The crisis worsened matters for Japan, which entered a recession in 1998. Monetary policy had become ineffective, as nominal interest rates approached the zero bound. Liquidity contracted even further, compounding sluggish growth.

The Great Recession also strongly impacted Japan. Although Japan's financial system had been strengthened since the Asian financial crisis, Japan's trade and industrial structures had become more globalized, resulting in the collapse of industrial production after the crisis hit (Kawai and Takagi 2009). Japan was impacted by the negative terms-of-trade shock that hit the country in 2008, as well as the sudden increase in energy and other commodity prices. The Japanese stock market also declined through the fall of 2008, and new loans contracted. Manufacturing production collapsed in November 2008 as exports were sharply impacted. This is because Japan's exports are highly income-elastic goods which responded rapidly to global conditions. Again, Japan hit a near-zero interest rate as monetary policy became ineffective. Japan recovered from the crisis by implementing several fiscal stimulus packages to improve employment, provide investment, and extend government subsidies, among other measures.

Japan's struggle with maintaining growth over the years resulted in a volatility in its political economy. Japanese Prime Ministers focused on a variety of policies, including reduction of working hours (Kiichi Miyazawa, 1991–93), fiscal consolidation (Ryutaro Hashimoto, 1996–98), deregulation and privatization (Junichiro Koizumi, 2001–06), and fiscal stimulus (Shinzo Abe, 2012–present, second term). Koizumi was the most in favor of financial reform, requiring banks to disclose and reduce non-performing loans and privatizing banks that extended loans for political reasons (Dekle 2012). The Koizumi administration also increased labor market flexibility, allowing workers to be employed without protection in a larger number of firms, and created special economic zones, in which some strict regulations for the services sector were waived.

The policies at times conflicted with one another, particularly in terms of fiscal spending versus fiscal constraint, and there was much debate over the source of the economic weakness: Was the problem structural? Was there supply-side or demand-side weakness? Was the recession necessary or preventable? It was unclear whether the problem was inherent to the Japanese model of growth, or whether it was a result of macroeconomic weakness. Some analysts viewed structural weakness as unlikely, since an asset price bubble collapse would likely not impede the fundamental ability of the economy to function without some additional reason (Posen 1998).

Japan's economy ended its long period of dominance due to this lingering economic weakness, and countries such as China and India which were just starting to industrialize rose to the fore. Japan's example of a rise to imminence, followed by a languishing performance, made economic analysts uneasy, as this indicated that so much success could end up being unsustainable after all. During the Great Recession, some feared that the US and Europe may end up like Japan, marooned in a similar "Lost Decade." We now turn to an examination of China, which faces clear challenges as well.

CHINA

China has arguably fully industrialized, having become the so-called "factory of the world." The economy is now attempting to move in a different direction, from an export-led, investment-intensive model of growth to a consumption-led model of growth.

The agriculture industry has declined since it lost policy focus in the 1980s, while the services sector has filled the gap in GDP production. After China's manufacturing boom in the 1990s and 2000s, the economy entered a slowdown in external demand for exports in 2008, when the Great Recession took hold. This forced the nation to turn from a manufacturing-focused model of growth to inward sources of growth. The first and most immediate source of growth was fiscal stimulus. A large stimulus package, worth $589 billion, was implemented at the end of 2008, creating many new construction jobs and stimulating consumption, followed by smaller stimulus packages thereafter. This government spending helped to keep the economy going, but it would not last.

At the same time, a real estate boom was fuelled by non-bank financing and expansion of local government financing vehicles, which were entities that represented local governments, and allowed to borrow to build up properties and infrastructure. The fixed asset investment expansion was permitted by the central government since there were diminishing external sources of growth. The leadership appeared to be waiting until the implementation of reforms that would push forward other sectors, through the Twelfth Five-Year Plan, and riskier origins of growth were therefore allowed to arise.

The Twelfth Plan stated with respect to manufacturing productivity that it would "optimize structure, improve varieties and quality, enhance industry supporting capability, eliminate backward production capacity, develop the advanced equipment manufacturing industry, optimize the raw material industries, transform and improve the consumer goods industry, and promote the enlargement and enhancement of manufacturing industries" (Delegation of the European Union in China 2011). Under the plan, industries of focus were to be the shipbuilding, automobile, smelting and building materials, petrochemical, light textile, packaging, energy, and electronic information industries. Reorganization of the automobile, iron and steel, cement, machine building, electrolytic aluminum, rare earth, electronic information, and pharmaceutical industries would occur. Industries to be developed included the energy conservation, new-generation IT, biological, high-end equipment manufacturing, new energy, new material, and new-energy automobile industries. As the World Bank (2012b) points out, capital spending has been subject to decreasing returns. The industries that therefore can achieve higher returns include industries that can gain from technological and efficiency improvements.

What is the government's view of how China should develop its services sector? The Eleventh and Twelfth Plan have addressed China's services sector. While the Eleventh Plan was not wholly successful in reaching its service sector goal but did expand the sector overall, the Twelfth Plan sought to increase China's service sector by 4 percent of GDP (Casey and Koleski 2011). In addition, China signed an agreement in 2007 with the Association of Southeast Asian Nations to allow wholly foreign-owned corporations to operate in particular sectors, including the software and data processing, real estate, translation, environmental, and freight transport agency services sectors (Zhang and Evenett 2010).

China laid out in the Twelfth Plan goals to increase services in production, high technology, logistics, business services, tourism, and domestic services. The Twelfth Plan also sought to improve public services, including employment and health services, and to improve infrastructure, social, and agricultural conditions in rural areas.

Annual growth in services, as well as foreign direct investment in services, have been increasing. By 2020, it is expected that China's service sector contribution to GDP will exceed 50 percent. Currently, however, China is a net importer of services, particularly of transportation, insurance services, and license fees (Zhang and Evenett 2010). In time, this trend is expected to reverse, as China upgrades its services sector from low-value-added services such as petty retail to higher-value-added services such as financial or business services.

In May 2014, China entered a period of falling real estate asset prices and liquidity shortages, despite its clear agenda to liberalize its financial sector, increase urbanization, and grow its services and technology-intensive manufacturing sectors. China was struggling to maintain its high growth rate. The Chinese leadership stated that the economy was entering a period of slower growth, dubbed the "New Normal." The "New Normal" rate of growth will take the place of China's high growth rates that have been experienced since the outset of reform and opening up, and represents the growth rate of a more mature economy.

A reform agenda laid out in 2013 by the State Council in the Third Plenum Communique aimed to reform the financial sector, state-owned enterprises, fiscal policy, environmental regulation, and rural land use rights. This agenda has been implemented to varying degrees, although changes are slow in coming and major changes have not yet arisen. One reason that implementing reforms is challenging is because the economy is slowing down, and China's leadership has attempted to place a floor on the slowdown by implementing monetary and fiscal stimulus measures. Another reason that reforms appear to be implemented at a slow pace is because there are many small reforms that are being implemented simultaneously that do not make for a "big bang" reform effect. This is in line with China's gradual pace of reform.

INDIA

Like many countries, India was adversely impacted by the Great Recession that hit in 2008. India was exposed through a reversal of capital inflows, corporate and banking sector borrowings, and trade channels. Global investors sold their holdings in Indian companies to ease liquidity conditions in their home markets. The rupee depreciated by 23 percent in 11 months, increasing dollar liquidity and reducing India's foreign exchange reserve (Arora et al. 2010). However, Indian banks were not directly exposed to toxic assets sold in the United States and Europe, and much of India's growth has been driven by domestic demand, somewhat reducing the impact of the crisis on India.

Still, India did not emerge from the crisis unscathed. India's fiscal stimulus policies in response to the crisis focused on tax cuts and subsidies, without an increase in capital outlays (Mohan and Kapur 2015). An attempt to improve public investment infrastructure tapered off after 2010, leading to a decline in growth in manufacturing and infrastructure-oriented sectors. Global conditions remained weak in 2012, with ongoing volatility in financial markets and low levels of external demand. This resulted in an investment and growth decline in India.

India's growth has therefore stagnated, slowing to 4.4 percent in 2013, the lowest level of growth in a decade (Ezell and Atkinson 2014). India was plagued by a large current account deficit and high unemployment and inflation rates, but the macroeconomic situation has been gradually improving. It has been pointed out that India's economy also possesses many positive attributes, such as a high rate of savings, an increasingly skilled workforce, and a strong private sector. Indeed, Patnaik and Pundit (2014) find that India's growth can pick up again given the right policy measures to improve the allocation of resources in factor markets and stimulate the economy.

India is attempting to build up its manufacturing sector, having put in place the National Manufacturing Plan to create 100 million new manufacturing jobs within the decade. The plan focuses on creating jobs within India's domestic manufacturing sector to increase manufacturing's contribution to GDP.

India's government, led by the Bharatiya Janata Party (BJP) and headed by Prime Minister Narendra Modi, was elected in May 2014. This government is committed to free market ideals, focusing on reducing bureaucracy and liberalizing trade and foreign investment. The Modi government has undertaken many new reforms, including improving market forces in the gas, coal, and mining, and land sectors, raising taxes on energy products, promoting inclusive finance, and piloting labor reforms in Rajasthan (Ministry of Finance 2014).

In addition, India's "Vision 2022," laid out in its annual budget, seeks to ensure employment, economic opportunity, housing, electricity, water, sanitation, connectivity, medical facility, and schools for all its people by 2022, the 75th year after independence (World Bank 2015). To promote these goals, India seeks to generate stable growth, promote macroeconomic stability, and extend social benefits.

BOTTOM LINE

Japan, India, and China are currently struggling to revive economic growth. The three economies are in different stages, with Japan's economy highly developed yet somewhat stagnant, China's economy attempting to move up the value chain and convert from a manufacturing-based economy to a service-based economy, and India's economy attempting to continue high levels of growth while placing policy focus on its manufacturing sector. The three economies all represent clear historical successes, having pulled their populations up to higher standards of living and reduced poverty during the reform processes. These nations have achieved much since the beginning of their reform periods, and many lessons can be gleaned from their growth trajectories. While the future growth of these nations is not known, they are all better off for their own unique experiences with growth success.

DISCUSSION QUESTIONS

1. Does Japan's post-reform experience show that Japan's reform trajectory was somehow flawed? Explain.
2. What are some factors that contributed to Japan's post-reform slowdown?
3. What are some factors that contributed to China's current economic slowdown?
4. What are some challenges that India's economy currently faces?
5. How did the Great Recession impact Japan, India, and China?
6. How was Japan impacted by the Asian financial crisis?

References

Acemoglu, Daron, Philippe Aghion, and Fabrizio Zilibotti. 2006. Growth, Development, and Appropriate Versus Inappropriate Institutions. Japan–Europe Cooperation Fund Working Paper. http://www.ebrd.org/downloads/research/economics/japan/jrp1.pdf.

Acemoglu, Daron, James A. Robinson, and Simon Johnson. 2001. The Colonial Origins of Comparative Development: An Empirical Investigation. *American Economic Review* 91: 1369–1401.

Acemoglu, Daron, James A. Robinson, and Simon Johnson. 2002. Reversal of Fortune: Geography and Institutions in the Making of the Modern World Income Distribution. *Quarterly Journal of Economics* 118: 1231–1294.

Acharya, Shankar. 2002. India: Crisis, Reforms and Growth in the Nineties. Center for Research on Economic Development, Stanford University, Working Paper No. 139.

Agrawal, Tushar. 2011. Returns to Education in India: Some Recent Evidence. Indira Gandhi Institute of Development Research, Mumbai Working Paper, September, http://oii.igidr.ac.in:8080/jspui/bitstream/2275/144/1/WP-2011-017.pdf.

Ahluwahlia, Montek S. 2002. Economic Reforms in India since 1991: Has Gradualism Worked? *Journal of Economic Perspectives* 16(3): 67–88.

Ahsan, Reshad N. and Devashish Mitra. 2014. Trade Liberalization and Labor's Slice of the Pie: Evidence from Indian Firms. *Journal of Development Economics* 108: 1–16.

Aiyar, Swaminathan S. Anklesaria. 2011. The Elephant That Became a Tiger: 20 Years of Economic Reform in India. CATO Institute Development Policy Analysis 13.

Akamatsu, Kaname. 1962. A Historical Pattern of Economic Growth in Developing Countries. *Journal of Developing Economies* 1(1): 3–25.

Alagh, Yoginder K. 1992. Growth Performance of the Indian Economy, 1950–1989: Problems of Employment and Poverty. *Developing Economies* (June): 97–116.

Albin, Thaarcis. 2008. Women in India: Visibility of the Invisibility. In *Women in the Indian Economy*, ed. V.S. Ganesamurthy. New Delhi: New Century Publications.

Alessandrini, Michele, Bassam Fattouh, Benno Ferrarini, and Pasquale Scaramozzino. 2011. Tariff Liberalization and Trade Specialization: Lessons from India. *Journal of Comparative Economics* 39: 499–513.

Alexander, Arthur. 2007. *The Arc of Japan's Economic Development.* New York: Routledge.

Anand, Rahul, Volodymyr Tulin, and Naresh Kumar. 2014. India: Defining and Explaining Inclusive Growth and Poverty Reduction. World Bank Working Paper WP/14/63.

Andrienko, Yuri and Sergei Guriev. 2004. Determinants of Interregional Mobility in Russia. Evidence from Panel Data. *Economics of Transition* 12(1): 1–27.

Appadurai, Arjun. 2004. The Capacity to Aspire. In *Culture and Public Action*, eds V. Rao and M. Walton. Stanford, CA: Stanford University Press.

Appleton, Simon, John D. Knight, Lina Song, and Qingjie Xia. 2002. Labor Retrenchment in China: Determinants and Consequences. *China Economic Review* 13(2–3), 252–275.

Arora, Ashish and Surenda K. Bagde. 2010. Human Capital and the Indian Software Industry. NBER Working Paper No. 16167.

Arora, Dayanand, Francis Xavier Rathinam, and Mohammed Shuheb Khan. 2010. India's Experience during Current Global Crisis: A Capital Account Perspective. Policy Research Institute, Ministry of Finance, Japan. *Public Policy Review* 6(5): 807–836.

Asahi, Sachiyo and Akira Yakita. 2012. SO_x Emissions Reduction Policy and Economic Development: A Case of Yokkaichi. *Modern Economy* 3(1): 23–31.

Athreye, Suma and Sandeep Kapur. 2006. Industrial Concentration in a Liberalising Economy: A Study of Indian Manufacturing. *Journal of Development Studies* 42(6): 981–999.

Bai, Ming. 2011. The Future of "Made in China." *China Today* (December). http://www.chinatoday.com.cn/english/report/2011-12/30/content_436342_2.htm.

Bajpai, Nirumpam. 1996. Economic Crisis, Structural Reforms and the Prospects of Growth in India. Harvard Institute for International Development Working Paper 530.

Balakrishnan, Kalpana, R.S. Dhaliwal, and Bela Shah. 2011. Guest Editorial. *Environmental Health Perspectives* 119(1): A12–A13.

Balarajan, Y., S. Selvaraj, and S.V. Subramanian. 2011. Health Care and Equity in India. *Lancet* 377: 505–515.

Banerjee, Abhijit V., Shawn Cole, and Esther Duflo. 2004. Banking Reform in India. In *India Policy Forum*, Vol. 1, eds A. Panagariya, B. Bosworth and S. Berry. Washington, DC: Brookings Institution.

Banerjee, Abhijit and Andrew F. Newman. 1993. Occupational Choice and the Process of Development. *Journal of Political Economy* 101, 274–298.

Banerjee, Arindam. 2011. Risk Management in Banking Sector: An Overview. *Management Accountant* (August): 679–682.

Banga, Rashmi and Abhijit Das. 2012. Role of Trade Policies in Growth of Indian Manufacturing Sector. In *Twenty Years of India's Liberalization*, eds Rashmi Banga and Abhijit Das. New York: UNCTAD Center for WTO Studies.

Bao, Zonghao. 2011. Challenges for the Sustainability for China's Urbanization. *Chinascope* (July–August): 35–37.

Bardhan, Pranab. 2005. Theory or Empirics in Development Economics. *Economic and Political Weekly* (October 1): 4333–4335.

Bassino, Jean-Pascal. 2007. Market Integration and Famines in Early Modern Japan, 1717–1857. http://federation.ens.fr/ydepot/semin/texte0708/BAS2007MAR.pdf.

Basu, Sudip Ranjan. 2009. Comparing China and India: Is the Dividend of Economic Reforms Polarized? *European Journal of Comparative Economics* 6(1): 57–99.

Baulch, B. and J. Hoddinott (eds). 2000. Special Issue on Economic Mobility and Poverty Dynamics in Developing Countries. *Journal of Development Studies* 36: 1–180.

BBC. 2015. Life in a Slum. http://news.bbc.co.uk/2/shared/spl/hi/world/06/dharavi_slum/html/dharavi_slum_intro.stm. Accessed July 4.

BBC History. 2014. Mao Zedong. http://www.bbc.co.uk/history/historic_figures/mao_zedong.shtml. Accessed February 16.

Beijing Review. 2008. Thirty Years of Rural Improvement. *Beijing Review* (December 25).

Beine, Michel, Fréderic Docquier, and Hillel Rapoport. 2008. Brain Drain and Human Capital Formation in Developing Countries: Winners and Losers. *Economic Journal* 118: 631–652.

Benjamin, Dwayne, Loren Brandt, and John Giles. 2005. The Evolution of Income Inequality in Rural China. *Economic Development and Cultural Change* 53(4): 769–824.

Bennett, John W. and Solomon B. Levine. 1977. Industrialization and Urbanization in Japan: The Emergence of Public Discontent. *Habitat* 2(1–2): 205–218.

Besley, Timothy and Robin Burgess. 2000. Land Reform, Poverty Reduction, and Growth: Evidence from India. *Quarterly Journal of Economics* 115(2): 389–430.

Bhagat, R.B. 2011. Emerging Pattern of Urbanization in India. *Economic and Political Weekly* 46(34): 10–12.

Bhattacharya, Dipankar. 1999. Political Economy of Reforms in India. *Economic and Political Weekly* 34(23): 1408–1410.

Blum, Nicole and Rashmi Diwan. 2007. Small, Multigrade Schools and Increasing Access to Primary Education in India: National Context and NGO Initiatives. The Consortium for Educational Access, Transitions and Equity (CREATE) White Paper.

Borjas, George J. 1989. Economic Theory and International Migration. Special Silver Anniversary Issue: International Migration an Assessment for the 90's. *International Migration Review* 23(3): 457–485.

Borjas, George J., Stephen G. Bronars, and Stephen J. Trejo. 1990. Self-Selection and Internal Migration in the United States. National Longitudinal Surveys, US Department of Labor and Bureau of Labor Statistics, Discussion Paper.

Bosworth, Barry, Susan M. Collins, and Arvind Virmani. 2007. Sources of Growth in the Indian Economy. In *India Policy Forum* Vol. 3, eds S. Bery, B. Bosworth, and A. Panagariya. Washington, DC: Brookings Institution.

Brinton, Mary C. 1993. *Women and the Economic Miracle*. Berkeley, CA: University of California Press.

Brown, Alexander D. 2005. Meiji Japan a Unique Technological Experience? *Student Economic Review* 19: 71–83.

Cai, Fang, Albert Park, and Yaohui Zhao. 2008. The Chinese Labor Market in the Reform Era. In *China's Great Economic Transformation*, eds L. Brandt and T.G. Rawski. Cambridge: Cambridge University Press.

Casey, Joseph and Katherine Koleski. 2011. Backgrounder: China's 12th Five-Year Plan. US–China Economic and Security Review Commission Backgrounder.

Central Pollution Control Board. 2015. National Ambient Air Quality Status and Trends in India – 2010 Data. http://cpcb.nic.in/. Accessed July 4, 2015.

Centre for Economic and Social Studies. 2007. Andhra Pradesh Human Development Report 2007. Prepared for Government of Andhra Pradesh.

Cerra, Valerie and Sweta Chaman Saxena. 2000. What Caused the 1991 Currency Crisis in India? IMF Working Paper 157.

Cha, Myung Soo. 2003. Did Takahashi Korekiyo Rescue Japan from the Great Depression? *Journal of Economic History* 63(1): 127–144.

Chai, Joseph C.H. and Kartik C. Roy. 2006. *Economic Reform in China and India: Development Experience in a Comparative Perspective*. Cheltenham, UK and Northampton, MA, USA: Edward Elgar Publishing.

Chan, Kam-Wing. 2010. Fundamentals of China's Urbanization Policy. *China Review* 10(1): 63–94.

Chen, Jie. 2007. Rapid Urbanization in China: A Real Challenge to Soil Protection and Food Security. *Catena* 69: 1–15.

Chen, Shaohua and Martin Ravallion. 2008. China is Poorer than we Thought, But No Less Successful in the Fight against Poverty. World Bank Policy Research Paper 4621.

Cheng, Tiejun and Mark Selden. 1994. The Origins and Social Consequences of China's Hukou System. *China Quarterly* 139: 644–668.

Cheung, Yin-Wong and Rajeswari Sengupta. 2013. Impact of Exchange Rate Movements on Exports: An Analysis of Indian Non-Financial Sector Firms. BOFIT Discussion Paper 10.

China.org.cn. 2013a. The 6th Five-Year Plan (1981–1985). http://www.china.org.cn/english/MATERIAL/157619.htm.

China.org.cn. 2013b. The 8th Five Year Plan (1991–1995). http://www.china.org.cn/english/MATERIAL/157625.htm.

China.org.cn. 2013c. Premier Zhu Rongji's Explanation of 10th Five-Year Plan Drafting. http://www.china.org.cn/e-15/15-3-g/15-3-g-1.htm.

Chinn, Mingxing, Weidong Liu, and Xiaoli Tao. 2013. Evolution and Assessment on China's Urbanization 1960–2010: Under-urbanization or Over-urbanization? *Habitat International* 38: 25–33.

Chong, Alberto and Mark Gradstein. 2007. Inequality and Institutions. *Review of Economics and Statistics* 89(3): 454–465.

Chopra, Ajai, Charles Collins, Richard Hemming, Karen Elizabeth Parker, Woosik Chu and Oliver Fratzscher. 1995. India: Economic Reform and Growth. IMF Occasional Paper No. 134.

Chow, Gregory. 2001. The Impact of Joining WTO on China's Economic, Legal and Political Institutions. Speech delivered at the International Conference on Greater China and the WTO, March 22–24, organized by the City University of Hong Kong.

Chow, Gregory C. 2004. Economic Reform and Growth in China. *Annals of Economics and Finance* 5: 127–152.

Chow, Gregory. 2007. *China's Economic Transformation*. Malden, MA: Blackwell Publishing.

Chūbachi, Masayoshi and Koji Taira. 1976. Poverty in Modern Japan: Perception and Realities. In *Japanese Industrialization and its Social Consequences*, eds H.T. Patrick and L. Meissner. Berkeley, CA: University of California Press.

Cohen, Jerome. 1952. Japan's Foreign Trade Problems. *Far Eastern Survey* 21(16): 167–170.

Cole, Robert E. and Ken'ichi Tominaga. 1976. Japan's Changing Occupational Structure. In *Japanese Industrialization and its Social Consequences*, eds H.T. Patrick and L. Meissner. Berkeley, CA: University of California Press.

Das, Gurcharan. 2002. *India Unbound*. New York: Anchor Books.

Das, Gurcharan. 2006. The India Model. *Foreign Affairs* (July–August). http://www.foreignaffairs.com/articles/61728/gurcharan-das/the-india-model.

Das Gupta, Monica, Woojin Chung, and Shuzhuo Li. 2009. Evidence for an Incipient Decline in Numbers of Missing Girls in China and India. *Population and Development Review* 35(2): 401–416.

Dasgupta, Partha and Debraj Ray. 1986. Inequality as a Determinant of Malnutrition and Unemployment: Theory. *Economic Journal* 96: 1011–1034.

Dasgupta, Susmita, Asvani K. Gosain, Sandhya Rao, Subhendu Roy, and Maria Sarraf. 2013. A Megacity in a Changing Climate: The Case of Kolkata. *Climatic Change* 116: 747–766.

Dash, Shreemanta Kumar. 2006. Violence against Women: Evidence from Rural Andhra Pradesh, India. *Journal of Indian Academy of Forensic Medicine* 28(4): 184–186.

Deardorff, Alan V. 1984. Testing Trade Theories and Predicting Trade Flows. In *Handbook of International Economics*, Vol. 1, eds R.W. Jones and P. Kenen. Amsterdam: North-Holland.

Deaton, Angus and Jean Drèze. 2002. Poverty and Inequality in India: A Reexamination. *Economic and Political Weekly* (September 7): 3729–3748.

Deininger, Klaus, Songqing Jin and Hari K. Nagarajan. 2009. Land Reforms, Poverty Reduction, and Economic Growth: Evidence from India. *Journal of Development Studies* 45(4): 496–521.

Dekle, Robert. 2012. The Japanese Economy. *Milken Institute Review* (Second Quarter): 6–15.

Delegation of the European Union in China. 2011. China's Twelfth Five Year Plan (2011–2015) – the Full English Version. http://cbi.typepad.com/files/full-translation-5-yr-plan-2011-2015.doc.

Delhi Development Authority. 2009. Master Plan for Delhi – 2021.

Deng, F. Frederic and Youqin Huang. 2004. Uneven Land Reform and Urban Sprawl in China: The Case of Beijing. *Progress in Planning* 61: 211–236.

Desai, Meghnad. 2003. India and China: An Essay in Comparative Political Economy. Paper for IMF Conference on India/China, Delhi, November.

Deshingkar, Priya and Daniel Start. 2003. Seasonal Migration for Livelihoods in India: Coping, Accumulation and Exclusion. Overseas Development Institute Working Paper 220.

Devi, V. Renuka and Anita Pratibha Revathi Moses. 2011. Economics of Pollution Control. *Indian Journal of Science and Technology* 4(3): 343–347.

Dhasmana, Anubha. 2012. India's Real Exchange Rate and Trade Balance: Fresh Empirical Evidence. Indian Institute of Management, Bangalore, Working Paper 373.

Dholakia, Bakul H. 1991. India's Economic Crisis: Nature and Remedies. *Vikalpa* 16(3): 47–53.

Diao, X., S.X. Zeng, C.M. Tam, and V. Tam. 2009. EKC Analysis for Studying Economic Growth and Environmental Quality: A Case Study in China. *Journal of Cleaner Production* 17(5): 541–548.

Ding, Chengri and Xingshuo Zhao. 2011. Urbanization in Japan, South Korea, and China: Policy and Reality. In *The Oxford Handbook of Urban Economics and Planning*, eds Nancy Brooks, Kieran Donaghy, and Gerrit-Jan Knaap. New York: Oxford University Press.

Dossani, Rafiq and Martin Kenney. 2009. Service Provision for the Global Economy: The Evolving Indian Experience. *Review of Policy Research* 26(1–2): 77–104.

Dubey, Amaresh, Richard Palmer-Jones and Kunal Sen. 2006. Surplus Labour, Social Structure and Rural to Urban Migration: Evidence from Indian Data. *European Journal of Development Research* 18: 86–104.

Duchâtel, Mathieu and François Godement. 2009. China's Politics under Hu. *Journal of Current Chinese Affairs* 38(3): 3–11.

Duckett, Jane. 2003. China's Social Security Reforms and the Comparative Politics of Market Transition. *Journal of Communist Studies and Transition Politics* 19(1): 80–101.

Duraisamy, P. 2002. Changes in Returns to Education in India, 1983–94: By Gender, Age-Cohort and Location. *Economics of Education Review* 21(6): 609–622.

Dutta, Dilip. 2011. Recent Economic Developments in the Indian Economy. *Ecodate* 25(3): 6–8.

Duus, Peter. 1998. *Modern Japan*. New York: Houghton Mifflin Company.

Dyson, Tim. 2008. India's Demographic Transition and its Consequences for Development. In *Indian Economy since Independence*, 19th edn, ed. Uma Kapila. New Delhi: Academic Foundation.

Dzienis, Anna Maria. 2012. Japanese Internal Migration as a Growth Factor. *Research Papers of the Wroclaw University of Economics / Prace* 257: 157–184.

Ebenstein, Avraham Y. and Ethan Jennings Sharygin. 2009. The Consequences of the "Missing Girls" of China. *World Bank Economic Review* 23(3): 399–425.

The Economist. 2008. China Seeks Stimulation. *The Economist* (November 10).

The Economist. 2010. A Bumpier but Freer Road. *The Economist* 397(8702): 75–77.

Economist Intelligence Unit. 2012. Supersized Cities: China's 13 Megalopolises. Report from Economist Intelligence Unit.

Economy, Elizabeth. 2004. *The River Runs Black: The Environmental Challenge to China's Future*. Ithaca, NY: Cornell University Press.

Eggleston, Karen. 2012. An Overview of China's Health System. Stanford University Asia Health Policy Program Working Paper #28.

Encyclopædia Britannica. 2014. Meiji. February 16. http://www.britannica.com/EBchecked/topic/373294/Meiji.

Ericson, Steven J. 2000. The Industrial Revolution in the Twentieth Century, with a Focus on Japan and the East Asian Followers. Special Issue: The Industrial Revolution. *OAH Magazine of History* 15(1): 24–29.

Ezell, Stephen and Robert Atkinson. 2014. The Indian Economy at a Crossroads. Information Technology and Innovation Foundation. http://www2.itif.org/2014-indian-economy-at-crossroads.pdf.

Fan, C. Cindy. 1997. Uneven Development and Beyond: Regional Development in Post-Mao China. *International Journal of Urban and Regional Research* 21(4): 620–639.

Fan, Chuanqi and Xiaojun Zheng. 2013. An Empirical Study of the Environmental Kuznets Curve in Sichuan Province, China. *Environment and Pollution* 2(3): 107–115.

Fan, Shenggen, Peter Hazell, and Sukhadeo Thorat. 1999. Linkages between Government Spending, Growth and Poverty. IFPRI Research Report 110.

Fan, Shenggen, Linxiu Zhang, and Xiaobo Zhang. 2002. Growth, Inequality and Poverty in Rural China. International Food Policy Research Institute Research Report 125.

Ferris, Jr, Richard J. and Hongjun Zhang. 2005. Environmental Law in the PRC. In *China's Environment and the Challenge of Sustainable Development*, ed. Kristen Day. London: ME Sharpe.

Fischer, Stanley. 1996. Stanley Fischer: Lessons from East Asia and the Pacific Rim. *Brookings Papers on Economic Activity* 2: 345–350.

Fisher, Charles A. and John Sargent. 1975. Japan's Ecological Crisis. *Geographical Journal* 141(2): 165–176.

Fleisher, Belton, Haizheng Li, and Min Qiang Zhao. 2010. Human Capital, Economic Growth and Regional Inequality in China. *Journal of Development Economics* 92(2): 215–231.

Foster, Andrew D. and Mark R. Rosenzweig. 2004. Agricultural Productivity Growth, Rural Economic Diversity, and Economic Reforms: India, 1970–2000. *Economic Development and Cultural Change* 52(3): 509–542.

Francks, Penelope. 1992. *Japanese Economic Development: Theory and Practice*. New York: Routledge.

Francks, Penelope. 2009. *The Japanese Consumer*. Cambridge: Cambridge University Press.

Freeman, Richard and Xiaoying Li. 2013. Has China's New Labor Contract Worker? Voxeu.org, December 22.

Fujii, Mariko and Masahiro Kawai. 2010. Lessons from Japan's Banking Crisis, 1991–2005. ADBI Working Paper 222.

Fukao, Mitsuhiro. 2004. Japan's Lost Decade and its Financial System. In *Japan's Lost Decade: Origins, Consequences and Prospects for Recovery*, eds G. Saxonhouse and R. Stern. Hoboken, NJ: Wiley-Blackwell.

Fukasaku, Yukiko and Sachiko Ishizaka. 2005. Science and Technology Policy in Japan. In *Science and Technology Policy*, ed. Rigas Arvanitis. Marseilles: Institut de Recherche pour le Developpement (IRD).

Fukawa, Tetsuo. 2002. *Public Health Insurance in Japan*. Washington, DC: World Bank.

Fung, K.C., Hitomi Iizaka, and Sarah Tong. 2002. Foreign Trade of China. Paper prepared for international conference on China's Economy in the 21st Century, June 24–25, Hong Kong.

Galab, S., S. Vijay Kumar, P. Prudvikhar Reddy, Renu Singh, and Uma Vennam. 2011. The Impact of Growth on Childhood Poverty in Andhra Pradesh. Young Lives Round 3 Survey Report. Oxford: Young Lives.

Galor, Oded. 1996. Convergence? Inferences for Theoretical Models. *Economic Journal* 106: 1056–1069.

Galor, Oded and Joseph Zeira. 1993. Income Distribution and Macroeconomics. *Review of Economic Studies* 60: 35–52.

Ganesamurthy, V.S. 2008. *Women in the Indian Economy*. New Delhi: New Century Publications.

Gao, Shangquan. 1999. *Two Decades of Reform in China*. Singapore: World Scientific.

Garg, Sanjeev, Vanita Garg, and Y.S. Brar. 2009. SOX/NOX Impact and its Removal in Coal Based Thermal Power Plants. *Proceedings of International Conference on Energy and Environment*, March 19–21.

Garnaut, Ross. 2004. The Origins of Successful Economic Reform in China. Paper presented at the Tenth Anniversary of the China Center for Economic Research, Peking University, Beijing, September 16–17.

Garnaut, Ross, Ligang Song, and Yang Yao. 2006. Impact and Significance of State Owned Enterprise Restructuring in China. *China Journal* 55: 35–63.

Garon, Sheldon. 2002. Japanese Policies Towards Poverty and Public Assistance: A Historical Perspective. World Bank Institute Working Paper.

Ghose, Aurobindo. 1990. Growth Strategy: Past, Present and Future. In *The Indian Economy and its Performance Since Independence*, eds

R.A. Choudhury, Shama Gamkhar, and Aurobindo Ghose. Delhi: Oxford University Press.

Ghosh, Sajal and Kakali Kanjilal. 2014. Long-Term Equilibrium Relationship between Urbanization, Energy Consumption and Economic Activity: Empirical Evidence from India. *Energy* 66: 324–331.

Gibson, J. 2001. Measuring Chronic Poverty Without a Panel. *Journal of Development Economics* 65: 243–266.

Godo, Yoshihisa and Yujiro Hayami. 2002. Catching Up in Education in the Economic Catch-up of Japan with the United States, 1890–1990. *Economic Development and Cultural Change* 58(4): 961–978.

Goldar, Bishwanath. 2009. Impact of Trade on Employment Generation in Manufacturing in India. Institute of Economic Growth, University of Delhi, Working Paper Series No. E/297/2009.

Golub, Stephen S. and Chang-Tai Hsieh. 2000. Classical Ricardian Theory of Comparative Advantage Revisited. *Review of International Economics* 8(2): 221–234.

Gov.cn. 2006a. The 7th Five Year Plan (1986–1990). http://www.gov.cn/english/2006-04/05/content_245695.htm.

Gov.cn. 2006b. Ten Features in China's 11th Five-Year Plan. http://english.gov.cn/2006-03/08/content_246945.htm.

Grinsell, Scott. 2010. Caste and the Problem of Social Reform in Indian Equality Law. *Yale Journal of International Law* 35: 199–236.

Grossman, Gene and Alan Krueger. 1995. Economic Growth and the Environment. *Quarterly Journal of Economics* 110: 353–377.

Guha, Ramachandra. 2007. *India After Gandhi: The History of the World's Largest Democracy.* New York: HarperCollins Publishers.

Haan, Arjan de. 2011. Inclusive Growth? Labour Migration and Poverty in India. International Institute of Social Studies Working Paper 513.

Haddad, Mona. 2007. Trade Integration in East Asia: The Role of China and Production Networks. Policy Research Working Paper Series 4160.

Hamada, Koichi. 1996. Japan 1968: A Reflection Point during the Era of the Economic Miracle. Yale University Economic Growth Center Discussion Paper 764.

Harashima, Yohei. 2000. Effects of Economic Growth on Environmental Policies in Northeast Asia. *Environment* 42(6): 28–41.

Harayama, Yuko. 2001. Japanese Technology Policy: History and a New Perspective. RIETI Discussion Paper Series 01-E-001.

Harbaugh, William T., Arik Levinson, and David Molloy Wilson. 2002. Reexamining the Empirical Evidence for an Environmental Kuznets Curve. *Review of Economics and Statistics* 84(3): 541–551.

Harris, Chauncy D. 1982. The Urban and Industrial Transformation of Japan. *Geographical Review* 72(1): 50–89.

Hashimoto, Masanori. 1979. Bonus Payments, On-the-Job Training, and Lifetime Employment in Japan. *Journal of Political Economy* 87(5) Part 1: 1086–1104.

Hayashi, Toru. 1980. Water Pollution Control in Japan. *Journal (Water Pollution Control Federation)* 52(5): 850–861.

Hazama, Hiroshi. 1976. Historical Changes in the Life Style of Industrial Workers. In *Japanese Industrialization and its Social Consequences*, eds H.T. Patrick and L. Meissner. Berkeley, CA: University of California Press.

Heckman, James J. and Xuesong Li. 2004. Selection Bias, Comparative Advantage and Heterogeneous Returns to Education: Evidence from China in 2000. *Pacific Economic Review* 9(3): 155–171.

Heilig, Gerhard K., Ming Zhang, Hualou Long, Xiubin Li, and Xiuqin Wu. 2005. Poverty Alleviation in China: A Lesson for the Developing World? Presented in part at International Conference on the West Development and Sustainable Development, August 2–4, Urumqi, China.

Helpman, Elhanan and Paul Krugman. 1985. *Market Structure and International Trade*. Cambridge, MA: MIT Press.

Henderson, Vernon. 2002. Urbanization in Developing Countries. *World Bank Research Observer* 17(1): 89–112.

Henry, Laurence. 2008. India's International Trade Policy. Centre Asie Ifri, Asie Visions 9.

Herd, Richard, Paul Conway, Sam Hill, Vincent Koen, and Thomas Chalaux. 2011. Can India Achieve Double-Digit Growth? OECD Economics Department Working Papers, No. 883, OECD Publishing.

Hernandez, Gonzalo and Arslan Razmi. 2011. Can Asia Sustain an Export-Led Growth Strategy in the Aftermath of the Global Crisis? An Empirical Exploration. University of Massachusetts Amherst Working Paper 2011-29.

Hesketh, Therese, Lu Li, and Wei Xing Zhu. 2005. The Effect of China's One-Child Family Policy after 25 Years. *New England Journal of Medicine* 353(11): 1171–1176.

Hesketh, Therese, Lu Li, and Wei Xing Zhu. 2011. The Consequences of Son Preference and Sex-Selective Abortion in China and Other Asian Countries. *Canadian Medical Association Journal* 183(12): 1374–1377.

Hirschman, Albert. 1958. *The Strategy of Economic Development*. New Haven, CT: Yale University Press.

History Channel. 2014. Tokugawa Period and Meiji Restoration. http://www.history.com/topics/meiji-restoration. Accessed January 24, 2014.

Hoff, Karla and Joseph E. Stiglitz. 2001. Modern Economic Theory and

Development. In *Frontiers of Economic Development*, eds G. Meier and J. Stiglitz. New York: Oxford University Press.

Honda, Gail. 1997. Differential Structure, Differential Health: Industrialization in Japan, 1868–1940. In *Health and Welfare during Industrialization*, eds Richard H. Steckel and Roderick Floud. Chicago, IL: University of Chicago Press.

Huang, Zhangkai and Kun Wang. 2011. Ultimate Privatization and Change in Firm Performance: Evidence from China. *China Economic Review* 22: 121–132.

Hubacek, Klaus, Dabo Guan, John Barrett, and Thomas Wiedmann. 2009. Environmental Implications of Urbanization and Lifestyle Change in China: Ecological and Water Footprints. *Journal of Cleaner Production* 17(14): 1241–1248.

Hulme, D. and Shepherd, A. 2003. Conceptualizing Chronic Poverty. *World Development* 31: 403–423.

Hunsberger, Warren S. 1957. Japanese Exports and the American Market. *Far Eastern Survey* 26(9): 129–140.

Hyvonen, Markus and Hao Wang. 2012. India's Services Exports. Reserve Bank of Australia Bulletin, December.

Imura, Hidefumi. 2005. Japan's Environmental Policy: Past and Future. In *Environmental Policy in Japan*, eds H. Imura and M. Schreurs. Cheltenham, UK and Northampton, MA, USA: Edward Elgar Publishing.

Ito, Takatoshi. 1999. Japan and the Asian Financial Crisis: The Role of Financial Supervision in Restoring Growth. Institute of Economic Research Hitotsubashi University Working Paper Series Vol. 99-10.

Iyer, Lakshmi. 2003. The Long-term Impact of Colonial Rule: Evidence from India. Paper prepared for Northeast Universities Development Consortium Conference, October 17–19, Yale University.

Jaggi, Bikki, Martin Freedman, and Charles Martin. 2011. Global Warming, Kyoto Protocol, and the Need for Corporate Pollution Disclosures in India: A Case Study. *International Journal of Business, Humanities and Technology* 1(3): 60–67.

Jalan, J. and M. Ravallion. 1998. Transient Poverty in Postreform Rural China. *Journal of Comparative Economics* 26: 338–357.

Jalan, Jyotsna and Martin Ravallion. 2002. Geographic Poverty Traps? A Micro Model of Consumption Growth in Rural China. *Journal of Applied Econometrics* 17: 329–346.

Jha, Prem Shankar. 2002. *The Perilous Road to the Market*. London: Pluto Press.

Jorgensen, Dale W. and Kazu Motohashi. 2005. Information Technology and the Japanese Economy. NBER Working Paper 11801.

Joumard, Isabelle and Ankit Kumar. 2015. Improving Health Outcomes and Health Care in India. OECD Economics Department Working Papers, No. 1184.

Justino, Patricia. 2003. Social Security in Developing Countries: Myth or Necessity? Evidence from India. PRUS Working Paper No. 23.

Kanbur, Ravi and Xiaobo Zhang. 1999. Which Regional Inequality? The Evolution of Rural–Urban and Inland–Coastal Inequality in China from 1983 to 1995. *Journal of Comparative Economics* 27: 686–701.

Kapila, Uma. 2008a. Planning and the Market. In *Indian Economy since Independence*, ed. Uma Kapila. New Delhi: Academic Foundation.

Kapila, Uma. 2008b. Demographic Constraint: Population Change and Economic Development. In *Indian Economy since Independence*, ed. Uma Kapila. New Delhi: Academic Foundation.

Kapur, Sandeep and Mamtha Murthi. 2009. Literacy in India. Birbeck University of London Working Paper 907.

Karan, Pradyumna. 2005. *Japan in the 21st Century: Environment, Economy and Society*. Lexington, KY: University of Kentucky Press.

Katada, Saori N. 2001. *Banking on Stability: Japan and the Cross-Pacific Dynamics of International Financial Crisis Management*. Ann Arbor, MI: University of Michigan Press.

Kawabe, Nobuo. 1989. The Development of Distribution Systems in Japan before World War II. *Business and Economic History* 18: 33–44.

Kawai, Masahiro and Shinki Takagi. 2009. Why was Japan Hit So Hard by the Global Financial Crisis? ADBI Working Paper 153. Tokyo: Asian Development Bank Institute.

Kennedy, Scott. 2011. The Myth of the Beijing Consensus. In *In Search of China's Development Model: Beyond the Beijing Consensus*, eds S. Philip Hsu, Yu-Shan Wu, and Suisheng Zhao. New York: Routledge.

Kingdon, Geeta Gandhi. 2007. The Progress of School Education in India. Global Poverty Research Group Working Paper GPRG-WPS-071.

Kiyota, Kozo and Shujiro Urata. 2005. The Role of Multinational Firms in International Trade: The Case of Japan. RIETE Discussion Paper Series 05-E-012.

Klasen, Stephan and Janneke Pieters. 2013. What Explains the Stagnation of Female Labor Force Participation in Urban India? IZA Discussion Paper 7597.

Knight, John and Ramani Gunatilaka. 2010. Great Expectations? The Subjective Well-being of Rural–Urban Migrants in China. *World Development* 38(1): 113–124.

Knight, John and Lina Song. 1993. The Spatial Contribution to Income Inequality in Rural China. *Cambridge Journal of Economics* 17: 195–213.

Knight, John and Lina Song. 2003. Increasing Urban Wage Inequality in China. *Economics of Transition* 11(4): 597–619.

Kobayashi, Tetsuya. 1980. The University and the Technical Revolution in Japan: A Model for Developing Countries? *Higher Education* 9: 681–692.

Kobayashi, Yasuki. 2009. Five Decades of Universal Health Insurance Coverage in Japan: Lessons and Future Challenges. *Japanese Medical Association Journal* 52(4): 263–268.

Kochhar, Kalpana, Utsav Kumar, Raghuram Rajan, and Arvind Subramanian. 2006. India's Patterns of Development: What Happened, What Follows. NBER Working Paper No. 12023.

Kohli, Atul. 2006. Politics of Economic Growth in India, 1980–2005. Part II: The 1990s and Beyond. *Economic and Political Weekly* (April 8): 1361–1370.

Kojima, Kiyoshi. 1978. *Direct Foreign Investment. A Japanese Model of Multinational Business Operations*. London: Croom Helm.

Krishna, Anirudh. 2006. Pathways Out of and Into Poverty in 36 Villages of Andhra Pradesh, India. *World Development* 34(2): 271–288.

Kulkarni, P.M. 2007. Estimation of Missing Girls at Birth and Juvenile Ages in India. Paper prepared for United Nations Population Fund, India. http://countryoffice.unfpa.org/india/drive/MissingGirlsatBirthpaper-Au gust2007Kulkarni.pdf.

Kumar, T. Krisha, Sushanta Mallick, and Jayarama Holla. 2009. Estimating Consumption Deprivation in India Using Survey Data: A State-Level Rural–Urban Analysis Before and During Reform Period. *Journal of Development Studies* 45(4): 441–470.

Kundu, Amitabh. 2011. Trends and Processes of Urbanization in India. International Institute for Environment and Development (IIED) paper.

Kundu, Nitai. 2003. The Case of Kolkata, India. UN Urban Slums Report. http://www.ucl.ac.uk/dpu-projects/Global_Report/pdfs/Kolka ta_bw.pdf.

Kunn, Anthony. 2006. Eking Out an Existence in China's Remote Badlands. *NPR* (May 15).

Kuwayama, Patricia Hagan. 1982. Success Story. *Wilson Quarterly* 6(1): 133–144.

Kuznets, Paul. 1994. Asian Industrialization: Is There a Paradigm? *Journal of Asian Economics* 5(4): 491–497.

Lai, Hongyi. 2006. *Reform and the Non-State Economy in China*. New York: Palgrave Macmillan.

Lardy, Nicholas. 2001. Issues in China's WTO Accession. http://www. brookings.edu/testimony/2001/0509foreignpolicy_lardy.aspx

Laxminarayan, H. 1990. Performance of Indian Agriculture. In *The Indian

Economy and its Performance Since Independence, eds R.A. Choudhury, Shama Gamkhar and Aurobindo Ghose. Delhi: Oxford University Press.

Leamer, Edward E. 1995. The Heckscher–Ohlin Model in Theory and Practice. Princeton Studies in International Finance Number 77.

Leckie, Stuart. 2009. A Review of the National Social Security Fund in China. Pensions, Benefits, and Social Security Colloquium, Tokyo, Japan, October 4–6.

Lewis, W. Arthur. 1954. Economic Development with Unlimited Supplies of Labour. *Manchester School* 22(2): 139–191.

Li, Daoji and Dag Daler. 2004. Ocean Pollution from Land-Based Sources: East China Sea, China. *Journal of the Human Environment* 33(1): 107–113.

Li, Hao. 1996. Development of the Shenzhen Special Economic Zone. Northeast Asia Economic Forum Annual Meeting Publication. http://www.neaef.org/public/neaef/files/documents/publications_pdf/annual_meeting/6th-1996/6.1.Li_6an_1996.pdf.

Li, Hongbin and Scott Rozelle. 2000. Saving or Stripping Rural Industry: An Analysis of Privatization and Efficiency in China. *Agricultural Economics* 2: 241–252.

Li, Lillian M. 1982. Silks by Sea: Trade, Technology, and Enterprise in China and Japan. *Business History Review* 56(2): 192–217.

Li, Ying, Tingting Guo, and Jing Zhou. 2011. Study on the Development of Rural Urbanization in Beijing. *Procedia Environmental Sciences* 11: 893–898.

Lin, Justin Yifu. 2011. *New Structural Economics*. Washington, DC: World Bank.

Liu, Jianguo and Jared Diamond. 2008. Revolutionizing China's Environmental Protection. *ASEAN Environment News* (January 4).

Liu, Qian. 2012. Unemployment and Labor Force Participation in Urban China. *China Economic Review* 23(1): 18–33.

Liu, Yang. 2013. Labor Market Matching and Unemployment in Urban China. *China Economic Review* 24: 108–128.

Lo, Kevin. 2013. A Critical Review of China's Rapidly Developing Renewable Energy and Energy Efficiency Policies. *Renewable and Sustainable Energy Reviews* 29: 508–516.

Long, Cheryl, Jin Yang, and Jing Zhang. 2015. Institutional Impact of Foreign Direct Investment in China. *World Development* 66: 31–48.

Long, Hualou, Jian Zou, Jessica Pykett, and Yurui Li. 2011. Analysis of Rural Transformation Development in China since the Turn of the New Millennium. *Applied Geography* 31: 1094–1105.

Lou, Peimin. 2006. Urbanization: When Farmers Lose Their Land. *China Economist* (May): 70–82.

Lu, Zheng and Xiang Deng. 2011. China's Western Development Strategy: Policies, Effects and Prospects. MPRA Paper No. 35201.

Mackerras, Colin, Pradeep Taneja and Graham Young. 1998. *China Since 1978*. South Melbourne: Addison Wesley Longman.

Maddison, Angus. 1971. The Economic and Social Impact of Colonial Rule in India. In *Class Structure and Economic Growth: India and Pakistan since the Moghuls*. New York: W.W. Norton.

Maeda, Masana. 1971. Kogyo Iken. Reprinted in *Seikatsu Koten Sosho*, Vol. 1, eds Y. Ando and H. Yamamoto. Tokyo: Koseikan.

Mahajan, Vijay and Suman Laskar. 2010. Transition and Innovation in Rural Finance in India – A Call for Action in this Golden Decade. http://ssrn.com/abstract=2419137 or http://dx.doi.org/10.2139/ssrn.2419137.

Managi, Shunsuke and Pradyot Ranjan Jena. 2007. Environmental Productivity and Kuznets Curve in India. *Ecological Economics* 65(2): 432–440.

Masoodi, Ashwaq and Rachel Ratan. 2014. Andhra Pradesh is the Worst State in India for Women. *Live Mint (Wall Street Journal)*, July 1.

McCleery, Robert K. and Fernando De Paolis. 2008. The Washington Consensus: A Post-Mortem. *Journal of Asian Economics* 19: 438–446.

Meng, Xin. 2004. Economic Restructuring and Income Inequality in Urban China. *Review of Income and Wealth* 50(3): 357–379.

Meng, Xin, Robert Gregory, and Guanhua Wan. 2007. Urban Poverty in China and its Contributing Factors, 1986–2000. *Review of Income and Wealth* 53(1): 167–189.

Menton, Linda K., Noren W. Lush, Eileen H. Tamura, and Chance L. Gusukuma. 2003. *The Rise of Modern Japan*. Honolulu, HI: University of Hawaii Press.

Minami, Ryoshin. 1977. Mechanical Power in the Industrialization of Japan. *Journal of Economic History* 37(4): 935–958.

Minami, Ryoshin. 2008. Income Distribution of Japan: Historical Perspective and its Implications. *Japan Labor Review* 5(4): 5–20.

Ministry of Environment. 2013. Ministry of Environment Japan Website. https://www.env.go.jp/en/. Accessed January 4, 2013.

Ministry of Finance. 2014. Economic Survey 2014–2015. http://indiabudget.nic.in/es2014-15/echapvol1-01.pdf.

Ministry of Internal Affairs and Communications. 2012. Population of Tokyo (Estimates). Population Census. Statistics Division, Bureau of General Affairs.

Ministry of Women and Child Development, Government of India. 2009. Gendering Human Development Indices. Summary Report. http://wcd.nic.in/publication/GDIGEReport/Part2.pdf.

Mishra, Uma Sankar, Kalyan Kumar Sahoo, and Satyakama Mishra.

2010. Service Quality Assessment in Banking Industry of India: A Comparative Study between Public and Private Sectors. *European Journal of Social Sciences* 16(4): 663–679.

Mitra, Arup. 2008. The Indian Labor Market: An Overview. ILO Asia-Pacific Working Paper Series.

Mitra, Arup and Mayumi Murayama. 2009. Rural to Urban Migration: A District-Level Analysis for India. *International Journal of Migration, Health and Social Care* 5(2): 35–52.

Mitra, Sharmishtha. 2008. Studying the Impact of Policy Reforms on Industrial Development in India Using Self-Organizing Maps. *Applied Artificial Intelligence* 22: 870–895.

Mizuuchi, Toshio. 2002. The Historical Transformation of Poverty, Discrimination, and Urban Policy in Japanese City: The Case of Osaka. In *Keizai Shakai no Chirigaku* (Geography of Economy and Society), ed. Fujio Mizuoka. Tokyo: Yuhikaku.

Mohan, Rakesh and Muneesh Kapur. 2015. Pressing the Indian Growth Accelerator: Policy Imperatives. IMF Working Paper 15/53.

Mooij, Jos. 2007. Hype, Skill and Class: The Politics of Reform in Andhra Pradesh, India. *Commonwealth and Comparative Politics* 45(1): 34–56.

Moreno-Monroy, Ana I., Janneke Pieters, and Abdul A. Erumban. 2012. Subcontracting and the Size and Composition of the Informal Sector: Evidence from Indian Manufacturing. IZA Discussion Paper 6785.

Moriguchi, Chiaki and Emmanuel Saez. 2008. The Evolution of Income Concentration in Japan, 1886–2005: Evidence from Income Tax Statistics. *Review of Economics and Statistics* 90(4): 713–734.

Morioka, Kiyomi. 1974. Industrialization, Family Ideologies, and Demographic Factors in Family Change in Contemporary Japan. *International Journal of Sociology of the Family* 4(2): 148–160.

Morrison, Wayne. 2011. China–US Trade Issues. Congressional Research Service Report for Congress 7-5700.

Mosk, Carl. 1977. Demographic Transition in Japan. *Journal of Economic History* 37(3): 655–674.

Moulder, Frances V. 1977. *Japan, China and the Modern World Economy: Toward a Reinterpretation of East Asian Development ca. 1600 to ca. 1918*. Cambridge: Cambridge University Press.

Mukherjee, Shameek and Shahana Mukherjee. 2012. Overview of India's Export Performance: Trends and Drivers. Indian Institute of Management Bangalore Working Paper 363.

Muldavin, Joshua. 2000. The Paradoxes of Environmental Policy and Resource Management in Reform-Era China. *Economic Geography* 76(3): 244–271.

Mundell, Robert A. 1957. International Trade and Factor Mobility. *American Economic Review* 47(3): 321–335.

Myrdal, Gunnar. 1974. What is Development? *Journal of Economic Issues* 8(4): 729–736.

Nagamine, Haruo. 1986. The Land Readjustment Techniques of Japan. *Habitat* 10(1–2): 51–58.

Nakamura, J.I. 1981. Human Capital Accumulation in Premodern Rural Japan. *Journal of Economic History* 41(2): 263–281.

Narayan, Deepa, Binayak Sen, and Katy Hull. 2009. Moving Out of Poverty in India: An Overview. In *Moving Out of Poverty: The Promise of Empowerment and Democracy in India*, ed. D. Narayan. Washington, DC: World Bank.

Narayanan, Raviprasad. 2006. The Politics of Reform in China: Deng, Jiang and Hu. *Strategic Analysis* 30(2): 329–353.

Nath, Sanghamitra. 2014. Strategic Partnership for Economic Development: India's New "Inclusive Trade Diplomacy." *Procedia Social and Behavioral Sciences* 157: 236–243.

National People's Congress (NPC). 2013. Shandong: "Localized Urbanization" Demands In-Depth Reforms. December 17. http://www.npc.gov.cn/englishnpc/NPCChina/2013-12/17/content_1817369.htm.

National University of Educational Planning and Administration. 2008. Status of Education in India National Report. http://www.ibe.unesco.org/National_Reports/ICE_2008/india_NR08.pdf.

Naughton, Barry. 2007. *The Chinese Economy*. Cambridge, MA: MIT Press.

NCAER. 1982. ARIS/REDS10 Survey. New Delhi: National Council for Applied Economic Research (NCAER).

NCAER. 1999. ARIS/REDS10 Survey. New Delhi: National Council for Applied Economic Research (NCAER).

Nicholas, Tom and Hiroshi Shimuzu. 2012. Intermediary Functions and the Market for Innovation in Meiji and Taishō Japan. www.people.hbs.edu/tnicholas/Japan_Market.pdf.

Notehelfer, F.G. 1975. Japan's First Pollution Incident. *Journal of Japanese Studies* 1(2): 351–383.

Ohbuchi, Hiroshi. 1976. The Demographic Transition. In *Japan's Lost Decade: Origins, Consequences and Prospects for Recovery*, eds G. Saxonhouse and R. Stern. Hoboken, NJ: Wiley-Blackwell.

Ohkawa, Kazushi and Miyohei Shinohara. 1979. *Patterns of Japanese Economic Development: A Quantitative Appraisal*. New Haven, CT: Yale University Press.

Okata, Junichiro and Akito Murayama. 2010. Tokyo's Urban Growth, Urban Form and Sustainability. In *Megacities: Urban Form, Governance, and Sustainability*, eds A. Sorensen and J. Okata. Dordrecht: Springer.

Öniş, Ziya. 1991. The Logic of the Developmental State. *Comparative Politics* 24(1): 109–126.

Ono, Akira and Tsunehiko Watanabe. 1976. Changes in Income Inequality. In *Japan's Lost Decade: Origins, Consequences and Prospects for Recovery*, eds G. Saxonhouse and R. Stern. Hoboken, NJ: Wiley-Blackwell.

Ozaki, Robert S. 1967. Trade, Growth, and the Balance of Payments of Post-War Japan. *Social and Economic Studies* 16(2): 169–190.

Ozaki, Robert S. and Robert S. Osaki. 1963. A Note on Duality in the Structure of Japanese Exports. *Social and Economic Studies* 12(4): 471–474.

Palley, Thomas I. 2003. Export-Led Growth: Evidence of Developing Country Crowding-out. In *Economic Integration, Regionalism, and Globalization*, eds P. Arestis, M. Baddeley, and J. McCombie. Cheltenham, UK and Northampton, MA, USA: Edward Elgar Publishing.

Pallikadavath, Saseendran, Abhishek Singh, Reuben Ogollah, Tara Dean, and William Stones. 2013. Human Resource Inequalities at the Base of India's Public Health Care System. *Health and Place* 23: 26–32.

Palmer, Edwina. 1988. Planned Relocation of Severely Depopulated Rural Settlements: A Case Study from Japan. *Journal of Rural Studies* 4(1): 21–34.

Palmer-Jones, Richard and Kunal Sen. 2003. What Has Luck Got To Do With It? A Regional Analysis of Poverty and Agricultural Growth in Rural India. *Journal of Development Studies* 40(1): 1–31.

Panagariya, Arvind. 2002. India's Economic Reforms: What Has Been Accomplished? What Remains to Be Done? Asian Development Bank ERD Policy Brief Series No. 2.

Panagariya, Arvind. 2008. *India: The Emerging Giant*. New York: Oxford University Press.

Pandey, Rita. 2005. Estimating Sectoral and Geographical Industrial Pollution Inventories in India: Implications for Using Effluent Charge Versus Regulation. *Journal of Development Studies* 41(1): 33–61.

Park, Albert and Fang Cai. 2009. The Informalization of the Chinese Labor Market. Oxford University Working Paper. http://economics. ouls.ox.ac.uk/15040/1/informalization.pdf.

Park, Albert, Sangui Wang, and Guobao Wu. 2002. Regional Poverty Targeting in China. *Journal of Public Economics* 86(1): 123–153.

Park, Yung-Chul. 1990. Development Lessons from Asia: The Role of Government in South Korea and Taiwan. *American Economic Review*, 80(2), *Papers and Proceedings of the Hundred and Second Annual Meeting of the American Economic Association*: 118–121.

Patnaik, Ila and Madhavi Pundit. 2014. Is India's Long-term Trend Growth Declining? Asian Development Bank Working Paper 424.

PBS Newshour. 2009. Leader Profile: Chinese Patriarch Deng Xiaoping. June 2. http://www.pbs.org/newshour/updates/asia/jan-june09/deng_06-02.html.

Peng, Xizhe. 2011. China's Demographic History and Future Challenges. *Science* 333, 581–587.

Perkins, F.C. 1996. Productivity Performance and Priorities for the Reform of China's State-Owned Enterprises. *Journal of Development Studies* 32(3): 414–445.

Polaski, Sandra, A. Ganesh-Kumar, Scott McDonald, Manoj Panda, and Sherman Robinson. 2008. *India's Trade Policy Choices: Managing Diverse Challenges*. Washington, DC: Carnegie Endowment for International Peace.

Posen, Adam S. 1998. *Restoring Japan's Economic Growth*. Washington, DC: Peterson Institute.

Pritchard, Lant. 1997. Divergence, Big Time. *Journal of Economic Perspectives* 11(3): 3–17.

Pyle, Kenneth B. 1996. *The Making of Modern Japan*. Lexington, MA: D.C. Heath.

Qureshi, Mahvash Saeed and Guanghua Wan. 2008. Trade Expansion of China and India: Threat or Opportunity. UNU WIDER Working Paper 2008/08.

Rai, Mridu. 2009. Interview with Professor Mridu Rai: Caste System in India. Yale University Video, March 31. http://www.youtube.com/watch?v=Q7_zmUghLmw&feature=results_video&playnext=1&list=PL1B7901D8D220D7DE.

Ramachandraiah, C. and V.K. Bawa. 2000. Hyderabad in the Changing Political Economy. *Journal of Contemporary Asia* 30(4): 562–575.

Ramo, Joshua Cooper. 2004. *The Beijing Consensus*. London: Foreign Policy Centre.

Rani, Uma and Jeemol Unni. 2009. Do Economic Reforms Influence Home-Based Work? Evidence from India. *Feminist Economics* 15(3): 191–225.

Ranis, Gustav and John C.H. Fei. 1961. A Theory of Economic Development. *American Economic Review* 51(4): 533–565.

Ravallion, M. 1988. Expected Poverty under Risk-Induced Welfare Variability. *Economic Journal* 98: 1171–1182.

Ray, Amit Shovon and Sabyasachi Saha. 2009. India's Stance at the WTO: Shifting Coordinates, Unaltered Paradigm. Centre for International Trade and Development, School of International Studies, Jawaharlal Nehru University Discussion Paper 09-06.

Ray, Debraj. 1998. *Development Economics*. Princeton, NJ: Princeton University Press.

Ray, Debraj. 2006. Aspirations, Poverty and Economic Change. In *Understanding Poverty*, eds A. Banerjee, R. Benabou and D. Mookherjee. New York: Oxford University Press.

Ray, Debraj. 2008. Development Economics. In *The New Palgrave Dictionary of Economics*, 2nd edn, eds Steven N. Durlauf and Lawrence E. Blume. New York: Palgrave Macmillan.

Ray, Sarbapriya and Ishita Aditya Ray. 2011. Impact of Population Growth on Environmental Degradation: Case of India. *Journal of Economics and Sustainable Development* 2(8): 72–77.

Raychaudhuri, Tapan. 1990. British Rule in India: An Assessment. In *The Cambridge Illustrated History of the British Empire*, ed. P.J. Marshall. Cambridge: Cambridge University Press.

Reddy, K. Srinath, Vikram Patel, Prabhat Jha, Vinod K. Paul, A.K. Shiva Kumar, and Lalit Dandona. 2011. Towards Achievement of Universal Health Care in India by 2020: A Call to Action. *Lancet* 377: 760–768.

Reed, Deborah. 1994. Migration in Brazil: Evidence of Credit Constraints. Department of Economics, Yale University, November.

Remais, Justin V. and Junfeng Zhang. 2011. Environmental Lessons from China: Finding Promising Policies in Unlikely Places. *Environmental Health Perspectives* 119(7): 893–895.

Reserve Bank of India. 2006. Reserve Bank of India Annual Report, 2005–06. New Delhi: Reserve Bank of India.

Rode, Philipp. 2009. Mumbai: The Compact Mega City. In *Urban India: Understanding the Maximum City*, ed. Urban Age. London: Urban Age, London School of Economics.

Rodrik, Dani. 2004. Getting Institutions Right. CESifo DICE Report, 2/2004.

Roland Berger. 2014. Entering China's Private Hospital Segment. Think Act, Roland Berger Strategy Paper.

Rosenbluth, Frances McCall and Michael F. Thies. 2010. *Japan Transformed: Political Change and Economic Restructuring*. Princeton, NJ: Princeton University Press.

Rosenstein-Rodan, Paul. 1943. Problems of Industrialisation of Eastern and South-Eastern Europe. *Economic Journal* 53(210–211): 202–211.

Rosenstein-Rodan, Paul. 1984. Natura Facit Saltum: Analysis of the Disequilibrium Growth Process. In *Pioneers in Development*, eds G. Meier and D. Seers. Washington, DC: World Bank.

Rostow, Walt Whitman. 1960. *The Stages of Economic Growth: A Non-Communist Manifesto*. Cambridge: Cambridge University Press.

Rumbaugh, Thomas and Nicolas Blancher. 2004. China: International Trade and WTO Accession. IMF Working Paper WP/04/36.

Sachs, Jeffrey D. and Wing Thye Woo. 2000. Understanding China's Economic Performance. *Journal of Policy Reform* 4(1): 1–50.

Sahni, Urvashi. 2015. Primary Education in India: Progress and Challenges. Brookings India–US Policy Memo, January.

Sahoo, Pravakar. 2011. Transport Infrastructure in India: Developments, Challenges, and Lessons from Japan. VFR Series 465. http://www.ide. go.jp/English/Publish/Download/Vrf/pdf/465.pdf.

Sargent, Thomas. 1987. *Macroeconomic Theory*. London: Academic Press.

Sarkar, Sandip and Balwant Singh Mehta. 2010. Income Inequality in India: Pre and Post Reform Period. *Economic and Political Weekly* (September 11): 45–55.

Sato, Keiko. 2011. Employment Structure and Rural–Urban Migration in a Tamil Nadu Village: Focusing on Differences by Economic Class. *Southeast Asian Studies* 49(1): 22–51.

Saxonhouse, Gary and Robert Stern. 2004. The Bubble and the Lost Decade. In *Japan's Lost Decade: Origins, Consequences and Prospects for Recovery*, eds G. Saxonhouse and R. Stern. Hoboken, NJ: Wiley-Blackwell.

SECC. 2015. Socio Economic and Caste Census 2011. http://www.secc. gov.in. Accessed June 20, 2015.

Sen, Abhijit and Abhiroop Himanshu. 2004. Poverty and Inequality in India: I. *Economic and Political Weekly* 39(38): 4247–4263.

Sen, Amartya. 1970. *Collective Choice and Social Welfare*. Amsterdam: North-Holland.

Sen, Amartya. 1990. Development as Capability Expansion. In *Human Development and the International Development Strategy for the 1990s*, eds Keith Griffin and John Knight. London: Macmillan.

Sen, Amartya. 1998. Amartya Sen – Biographical. Nobel Prize website, nobelprize.org.

Sen, Gautam. 2001. *Post-Reform China and the International Economy*. London: First Press.

Sen, Kunal, Bibhas Saha, and Dibyendu Maiti. 2010. Trade Openness, Labour Institutions and Flexibilisation: Theory and Evidence from India. University of Manchester Brooks World Poverty Institute Working Paper 123.

Sen, Sunanda. 2010. International Trade Theory and Policy: A Review of the Literature. Levy Economic Institute Working Paper 635.

Sharma, Brij Mohan, Girija K. Bharat, Shresth Tayal, Luca Nizzetto, and Thorjørn Larssen. 2014. The Legal Framework to Manage Chemical Pollution in India and the Lesson from the Persistent Organic Pollutants (POPs). *Science of the Total Environment* 490: 733–747.

Sharma, Chanchal Kumar. 2011. A Discursive Dominance Theory of

Economic Reform Sustainability: The Case of India. *India Review* 10(2): 126–184.

Sharma, Shalendra D. 1999. Democracy, Neoliberalism and Growth with Equity: Lessons from India and Chile. *Contemporary South Asia* 8(3): 347–371.

Shen, Jianfa. 2002. A Study of the Temporary Population in Chinese Cities. *Habitat International* 26: 363–377.

Shen, Lei, Shengkui Cheng, Aaron James Gunson, and Hui Wan. 2005. Urbanization, Sustainability and the Utilization of Energy and Mineral Resources in China. *Cities* 22(4): 287–302.

Shi, Li. 2008. Rural Migrant Workers in China: Scenario, Challenges and Public Policy. ILO Working Paper 89.

Shizume, Masato. 2009. The Japanese Economy during the Interwar Period: Instability in the Financial System and the Impact of the World Depression. Bank of Japan Review 2009-E-2.

Shozo, Tanaka. 1925. *Gijin zenshii*, ed. Kurihara Hikosaburo, 5 vols. Yokahama: Chugai Shinron Sha.

Siciliano, Giuseppina. 2012. Urbanization Strategies, Rural Development, and Land Use Changes in China: A Multiple-Level Integrated Assessment. *Land Use Policy* 29: 165–178.

Siggel, Eckhard. 2010. Poverty Alleviation and Economic Reforms in India. *Progress in Development Studies* 10(3): 247–259.

Singh, Arshdeep and Jaypreet Singh Kohli. 2012. Effect of Pollution on Common Man in India: A Legal Perspective. *Advances in Life Science and Technology* 4: 35–41.

Singh, Nirvikar and T.N. Srinivasan. 2006. Indian Federalism, Economic Reform and Globalization. In *Federalism and Economic Reform: International Perspectives*, eds Jessica S. Wallack and T.N. Srinivasan. New York: Cambridge University Press.

Smitka, Michael. 1998. *Japanese Economic History, 1600–1960*, Volume 3. New York: Routledge.

Sokoloff, Kenneth L. and Stanley L. Engerman. 2000. History Lessons: Institutions, Factor Endowments, and Paths of Development in the New World. *Journal of Economic Perspectives* 14: 217–232.

Solow, Robert M. 1956. A Contribution to the Theory of Economic Growth. *Quarterly Journal of Economics* 70(1): 65–94.

Song, Hong. 2012. New Challenges to the Export Oriented Growth Model. In *Moving Toward a New Development Model for East Asia: The Role of Domestic Policy and Regional Cooperation*, eds Y. Zhang, F. Kimura and S. Oum. Jakarta: ERIA Research Project Report.

Spencer, Daniel L. 1969. The New Technology in Japan. *World Affairs* 132(1): 13–27.

Sridar, Kala S. and Surender Kumar. 2012. India's Urban Environment: Air and Water Pollution and Pollution Abatement. MPRA Paper. http://mpra.ub.uni-muenchen.de/43810/.

Srinivasan, P. and M. Kalaivani. 2012. Exchange Rate Volatility and Export Growth in India: An Empirical Investigation. MPRA Paper 43838.

Stalley, Phillip. 2010. *Foreign Firms, Investment, and Environmental Regulation in the People's Republic of China*. Stanford, CA: Stanford University Press.

Steiner, Jesse F. 1944. Population Trends in Japan. *American Sociological Review* 9(1): 36–40.

Stolper, Wolfgang and Paul A. Samuelson. 1941. Protection and Real Wages. *Review of Economic Studies* 9(1): 58–73.

Sumiya, Mikio. 1976. *Nihon chinrōdō no shiteki kenkyū*. Tokyo: Ochanomizu Shobō.

Tachibanaki, Toshiaki. 2006. Inequality and Poverty in Japan. *Japanese Economic Review* 57(1): 1–28.

Taeuber, Irene B. 1950. Population Increase and Manpower Utilization in Imperial Japan. *Milbank Memorial Fund Quarterly* 28(3): 273–293.

Taeuber, Irene B. 1951. Family, Migration, and Industrialization in Japan. *American Sociological Review* 16(2): 149–157.

Taira, Koji. 1970. Factory Legislation and Management Modernization during Japan's Industrialization, 1886–1916. *Business History Review* 44(1): 84–109.

Tamaki, Norio. 1995. *Japanese Banking: A History, 1859–1959*. Cambridge: Cambridge University Press.

Tanaka, Tsuneo. 1978. Medical Care in Japan, Yesterday, Today, and Tomorrow. *Social Science and Medicine* 12A: 479–483.

Taubenböck, H., M. Wegmann, C. Berger, M. Breunig, A. Roth, and H. Mehl. 2008. Spatiotemporal Analysis of Indian Mega Cities. *International Archives of the Photogrammetry, Remote Sensing and Spatial Information Sciences* 37(B2): 75–82.

Taubenböck, H., M. Wegmann, A. Roth, H. Mehl, and S. Dech. 2009. Urbanization in India – Spatiotemporal Analysis using Remote Sensing Data. *Computers, Environment and Urban Systems* 33: 179–188.

Teranishi, Juro. 2005. *Evolution of the Economic System in Japan*. Cheltenham, UK and Northampton, MA, USA: Edward Elgar Publishing.

Thaper, Romila. 2015. India. Brittanica.com. Accessed June 20, 2015.

Tian, He-Zhong, Ji-Ming Hao, Man-Yin Hu, and Yong-Feng Nie. 2007. Recent Trends of Energy Consumption and Air Pollution in China. *Journal of Energy Engineering* (March): 4–12.

Tobin, Damian. 2011. Inequality in China: Rural Poverty Persists as Urban Wealth Balloons. BBC News, June 29. http://www.bbc.co.uk/news/business-13945072.

UNICEF. 2014. India Statistics. http://www.unicef.org/infobycountry/india_statistics.html. Accessed July 25, 2014.

Urata, Shujiro. 2009. The Indian Economy: Growth, Challenges, and Regional Cooperation. Asia Research Report.

US Central Intelligence Agency (CIA). 2012. India World Factbook. https://www.cia.gov/library/publications/the-world-factbook/geos/in.html.

US Department of State. 2011a. Background Note: Japan. http://www.state.gov/r/pa/ei/bgn/4142.htm. Accessed November 24, 2011.

US Department of State. 2011b. Background Note: China. http://www.state.gov/r/pa/ei/bgn/18902.htm. Accessed December 3, 2011.

US Department of State. 2015. Occupation and Reconstruction of Japan, 1945–1952. Office of the Historian Webpage, at https://history.state.gov/milestones/1945-1952/japan-reconstruction. Accessed June 19, 2015.

US Social Security Administration. 2012. Social Security Programs Throughout the World: Asia and the Pacific, 2010. http://www.ssa.gov/policy/docs/progdesc/ssptw/2010-2011/asia/japan.html. Accessed January 28, 2012.

Utsumi, Yoshio. 1959. *Rodojikan no Rekishi*. Tokyo: Otsuki Shoten.

Vakulabharanam, Vamsi. 2005. Growth and Distress in a South Indian Peasant Economy During the Era of Economic Liberalisation. *Journal of Development Studies* 41(6): 971–997.

Van Rooij, Benjamin and Carlos Wing-Hung Lo. 2011. Fragile Convergence: Understanding Variation in the Enforcement of China's Industrial Pollution Law. *Law and Policy* 32(1): 12–37.

Velkoff, Victoria A. 1998. Women's Education in India. US Department of Commerce Bureau of the Census Policy Note 98-1.

Vennemo, Haakon, Kristin Aunan, Henrik Lindhjem, and Hans Martin Seip. 2009. Environmental Pollution in China: Status and Trends. *Review of Environmental Economics and Policy* 3(2): 209–230.

Vestal, James. 1993. *Industrial Policy and Japanese Economic Development 1945–1990*. New York: Oxford University Press.

Visaria, Pravin. 2008. Demographic Aspects of Development: The Indian Experience. In *Indian Economy since Independence*, ed. Uma Kapila. New Delhi: Academic Foundation.

Wadhva, Charan D. 2004. *India Trying to Liberalise: Economic Reforms Since 1991*. Honolulu, HI: Asia-Pacific Center for Security Studies.

Waley, Paul. 2009. Distinctive Patterns of Industrial Urbanization in Modern Tokyo c. 1880–1930. *Journal of Historical Geography* 35: 405–427.

Wang, Mark, Michael Webber, Brian Finlayson, and Jon Barnett. 2008. Rural Industries and Water Pollution in China. *Journal of Environmental Management* 86: 648–659.

Weber, Christopher L., Glen P. Peters, Dabo Guan, and Klaus Hubacek. 2008. The Contribution of Chinese Exports to Climate Change. *Energy Policy* 36(9), 3572–3577.

Wei, Shang-Jin and Yi Wi. 2001. Globalization and Inequality: Evidence from Within China. NBER Working Paper 8611.

Wheelan, Charles. 2005. Economic Reform in India: Task Force Report. Harris School, University of Chicago. http://harris.uchicago.edu/sites/default/files/IPP%20Economic%20Reform%20in%20India.pdf.

Wignaraja, Ganeshan. 2011. Economic Reforms, Regionalism, and Exports: Comparing China and India. East–West Center Policy Study No. 60.

Womack, Brantly. 1986. Where Mao Went Wrong: Epistemology and Ideology in Mao's Leftist Politics. *Australian Journal of Chinese Affairs* 16: 23–40.

World Bank. 2011. India: Foreign Trade Policy. http://go.worldbank.org/RJEB2JGTC0. Accessed December 3, 2011.

World Bank. 2012a. World Bank Development Indicators Database. Accessed February 2, 2012.

World Bank. 2012b. China 2030: Building a Modern, Harmonious, and Creative High-Income Society. World Bank Report.

World Bank. 2014. China Overview. www.worldbank.org/en/country/china/overview.

World Bank and DRC. 2014. *Urban China: Toward Efficient, Inclusive, and Sustainable Urbanization*. Washington, DC: World Bank Group.

World Bank. 2015. India Development Update. Report No. 95979-IN. Washington, DC: World Bank.

Wu, Hsiu-Ling and Chien-Hsun Chen. 2010. Operational Performance of Commercial Banks in the Chinese Transitional Economy. *Journal of Developing Areas* 44(1): 383–396.

Wu, Jinglian. 2009. China's Economy: 60 Years of Progress. *Caijing* (October 1).

Wu, Peilin and Minghong Tan. 2012. Challenges for Sustainable Urbanization: A Case Study of Water Shortage and Water Environment Changes in Shandong, China. *Procedia Environmental Sciences* 13: 919–927.

Yadav, Purva. 2012. India's Changing Trade Pattern in the Process of Globalization. *Procedia Social and Behavioral Sciences* 37: 157–166.

Yamamura, Kozo. 1976. General Trading Companies in Japan. In *Japanese Industrialization and its Social Consequences*, eds H.T. Patrick and L. Meissner. Berkeley, CA: University of California Press.

Yamazawa, Ippei. 1975. Industrial Growth and Trade Policy in Prewar Japan. *Developing Economies* 13(1): 38–65.

Yamazawa, Ippei. 1998. The Asian Economic Crisis and Japan. *Developing Economies* 36(3): 332–351.

Yang, Dennis Tao, Vivian Chen, and Ryan Monarch. 2010. Rising Wages: Has China Lost Its Global Labor Advantage? IZA Discussion Paper 5008.

Yapa, Lakshman. 1998. The Poverty Discourse and the Poor in Sri Lanka. *Transactions of the Institute of British Geographers* (New Series) 23(1): 95–115.

Yeh, Anthony G.O., Jiang Xu, and Kaizhi Liu. 2011. China's Post-Reform Urbanization: Retrospect, Policies, Trends. International Institute for Environment and Development (IIED) Paper.

Yesudian, C.A.K. 2007. Poverty Alleviation Programs in India: A Social Audit. *Indian Journal of Medical Research* 126(October): 364–373.

Yoshihara, Kunio. 1994. *Japan's Development Trajectory*. New York: Oxford University Press.

Zeng, Ka. 2011. The Political Economy of Developing Country Antidumping Investigations against China. *International Interactions* 37: 190–214.

Zhang, Amei. 1996. Economic Growth and Human Development in China. UNDP HDR Occasional Paper 28.

Zhang, Bin and Colin A. Carter. 1997. Reforms, the Weather, and Productivity Growth in China's Grain Sector. *American Journal of Agricultural Economics* 79(4): 1266–1277.

Zhang, Chuanguo and Yan Lin. 2012. Panel Estimation for Urbanization, Energy Consumption and CO_2 Emissions: A Regional Analysis in China. *Energy Policy* 49: 488–498.

Zhang, Jianhong and Arjen van Witteloostuijn. 2004. Economic Openness and Trade Linkages of China: An Empirical Study of the Determinants of Chinese Trade Intensities from 1993 to 1999. *Review of World Economics / Weltwirtschaftliches Archiv* 140(2): 254–281.

Zhang, Linxiu, Hongmei Yi, and Scott Rozelle. 2010. Good and Bad News from China's New Cooperative Medical Scheme. *IDS Bulletin* 41(4): 95–106.

Zhang, Liping and Simon J. Evenett. 2010. The Growth of China's Services Sector and Associated Trade: Complementarities between Structural Change and Sustainability. International Institute for Sustainable Development Report, July.

Zhang, Xiaoshan. 2011. Farmland Capitalization an Urgent Issue in Institutional Reform. *China Economist* 6(1): 42–57.

Zhang, Xuanchang, Li-Wu Chen, Keith Mueller, Qiao Yu, Jiapeng Lu, and Ge Lin. 2011. Tracking the Effectiveness of Health Care Reform in China: A Case Study of Community Health Centers in a District of Beijing. *Health Policy* 100: 181–188.

Zhao, Pengjun. 2012. Urban–Rural Transition in China's Metropolises: New Trends in Peri-Urbanisation in Beijing. *International Development Planning Review* 34(3): 269–294.

Zhao, Suisheng. 2010. The China Model: Can it Replace the Western Model of Modernization? *Journal of Contemporary China* 19(65): 419–436.

Zheng, Siqi, Rui Wang, Edward L. Glaeser, and Matthew E. Kahn. 2011. The Greenness of China: Household Carbon Dioxide Emissions and Urban Development. *Journal of Economic Geography* 11: 761–792.

Zheng, Yongnian. 2007. Hu Jintao's Road Map to China's Future. University of Nottingham China Policy Institute Briefing Series 28.

Zheng, Yongnian and Minjia Chen. 2009. China's State-Owned Enterprise Reform and Its Discontents. *Problems of Post-Communism* 56(2): 36–42.

Zhu, Linchu and Zhi Qian. 2003. The Case of Shanghai, China. Understanding Slums: Case Studies for the Global Report on Human Settlements 2003. http://www.ucl.ac.uk/dpu-projects/Global_Report/pdfs/Shanghai_bw.pdf.

Zhu, Xiaodong. 2012. Understanding China's Growth: Past, Present and Future. *Journal of Economic Perspectives* 26(4): 103–124.

Index